MAVERICK ONE

by the same author

Pathfinder: A Special Forces Mission Behind Enemy Lines

MAVERICK ONE

PARA. PATHFINDER. RENEGADE.
THE MAKING OF A WARRIOR

One way to live.
A thousand ways to die.

DAVID BLAKELEY

© David Blakeley Ltd and Damien Lewis 2013

The right of David Blakeley Ltd and Damien Lewis to be identified as the author of this work has been asserted in accordance with the Copyright, Designs and Patents Act 1988.

First published in Great Britain in 2013 by Orion Books
An imprint of the Orion Publishing Group Ltd
Orion House, 5 Upper St Martin's Lane,
London, WC2H 9EA
An Hachette Livre Company

3 5 7 9 10 8 6 4 2

A CIP catalogue record for this book
is available from the British Library.

HB ISBN 978 1 4091 4412 0
TPB ISBN 978 1 4091 4413 7

Typeset by Input Data Services Ltd, Bridgwater, Somerset

Printed and bound by CPI Group (UK) Ltd, Croydon, CR0 4YY

The Orion Publishing Group's policy is to use papers that are natural, renewable and recyclable products and made from wood grown in sustainable forests. The logging and manufacturing processes are expected to conform to the environmental regulations of the country of origin.

www.orionbooks.co.uk

For all Pathfinders, past, present and future
And for Matt Bacon, rest in peace.
We will remember them.

'Never give in – never, never, never, never, in nothing great or small, large or petty, never give in except to convictions of honour and good sense. Never yield to force; never yield to the apparently overwhelming might of the enemy.'
Winston Churchill, Speech, 1941

ACKNOWLEDGEMENTS

Very special thanks to three people in particular who saved my life on different occasions behind enemy lines on high-risk missions – Tricky, Reuben Boswell and Andy Jackson. A debt that I cannot repay.

Very special thanks to my mother and father and sisters Anna and Lisa, for all your support over the years and especially when I was away on operations with the military.

I would like to thank Damien Lewis for his hard work and support, publishers Lucinda McNeile and Alan Samson, for their inspiration, vision and guidance from the very earliest stages, and all at Orion who did so much to make this book a success. Thanks also to Annabel Merullo, literary agent, and her assistant Laura Williams, for their support and Digby Halsby and team at Flint PR for their great work.

Thank you to: my steadfast friends Gareth Arnold, David Green, Azim Majid, Dan Jarvis, Liam Cradden, Greg Cox, Oliver Peckham, Richard Allen, Charles Towning, Joshua Rayner, Alex Beer, Remco Vanderlinden, Luke Hardy and Big Phil Campion. Also thank you to Michelle Macerlean, Laura Hill, Francesca Root, Claire Morgan, Frederick Forsyth, Adriel Lack, Julie Lowery, Sabina Skala, Mark Kennedy, Jake Steiner, Laura Pradelska, Josh Varney, Luke Speed, Ben Pugh, Patrick Hambleton, Charlie Birch, Kate Riley and Mike Illes.

Thank you to the incredible soldiers who supported me enormously on military operations around the world – Joe Murray, Douggie Muirhead, Frank Gosling to name just a few; and all the rest of you I cannot name individually here.

'FIRST IN'
Pathfinder Platoon Motto

David Blakeley
February 2013

Find out more about David Blakeley at
www.davidblakeley.co.uk

AUTHOR'S NOTE

———————

I have changed some of the names of the soldiers depicted in this book, and a handful of geographical locations and call signs, for operational and personal security reasons, and to protect the identities of members of the British and Allied elite forces.

My story as told in this book concerns my selection into the Parachute Regiment and The Pathfinders and my tours of Northern Ireland, the Balkans, Sierra Leone, Iraq and Afghanistan as I fought them. This book is written from my own personal memory and recollections of the events portrayed, and from the memories of others I have spoken to from those missions who were able to assist, and from my notes of the tours depicted. I have done my best to portray accurately and realistically the events as they happened. However my memory is no doubt fallible, and any mistakes herein are entirely of my own making. I will be happy to address them in future editions.

CHAPTER ONE

I am one of the first to arrive.

I've heard all the rumours. It's best to get here early and claim a decent billet – ideally one tucked away in a corner, and definitely on a lower bunk. It's only a thin, khaki green sheet of foam that I'm laying claim to here, but this is where I'll lay my battered and tortured body every night for the weeks to come, racked with pain and exhaustion and craving sleep.

If you're a late arrival you'll be left with a place by the door, and that could make all the difference between passing or failing whatever hell lies ahead of us. Every time someone opens the door you'll get a blast of bitter, icy, January weather down your neck. And for sure people will be banging in and out for a piss all night long, as we'll need to drink bucket-loads in an effort to rehydrate.

I throw my Bergen onto my chosen billet – the one that's the furthest from the door – and tuck a rough green Army dog blanket into the bottom of the bunk above. That way, the blanket hangs down like a curtain, providing just a touch of privacy and separation from the doss-pits next to mine.

Enshrouded in my dog blanket curtain it'll be total darkness, almost like a makeshift basha in the jungle. After each of the tortuous days that lie ahead I'll need that sanctuary, and some proper sleep, if I'm to stand any chance of making it through.

There's one other crucial advantage to getting a bottom bunk. You avoid the risk of jumping down from one above on sore and battered legs, and the impact further straining or breaking already torn and shredded limbs.

My makeshift dog blanket shelter done, I settle down to wait for the next arrivals.

I'm six foot four, and the steel and corrugated iron bed feels like it's been built for a dwarf. My head's jammed against the wall, and my feet dangle way over the end. I'll have to sleep curled up like a foetus. But at least with a lower bunk, if I do roll out I don't have so far to fall onto the bare concrete below.

I glance around at the inhospitable, spartan billet. It's an old Nissen hut – a thin, corrugated steel construction not a great deal more substantial than a chicken shed. There are ten bunks ranged like skeletal ribs down either side of the room, their paint chipped and fading, the frames sagging in places. It's enough for forty blokes in all, which makes up a full complement for what's coming.

The thin mattress beneath me is encased in a horrible, wipe-clean, sweaty plastic covering – the kind of thing you wouldn't wish on a young kid who pees the bed. It's there so that those who bleed, or puke or piss themselves through exhaustion don't leave a permanent legacy for the next batch who're mad enough to volunteer for this self-inflicted torment.

Welcome to Sennybridge Camp, I tell myself wryly, the base for all British Special Forces selection – including that of the Special Air Service (SAS), the Special Boat Service (SBS) and the tiny, elite unit that I burn to be a part of: The Pathfinders.

British Special Forces selection is widely regarded as being the toughest in the world. The American military model their own selection on what we do here, at this run-down, grotty, rain-lashed dump of a place. Those who founded Delta Force came here to attempt UKSF selection, so as to ascertain just how hard they could afford to abuse and torture their own soldiers.

In a way I've been lucky in my training, for I've been briefed in detail about what to expect. Jack Quinn, a fellow PARA Regiment bloke, had made it into the SAS, but was returned to unit (RTU'd) due to a bit of lightweight skulduggery. He'd switched the wheels from a hire car they were using on SAS business onto his own vehicle.

Unfortunately, he'd been rumbled and RTU'd – at which point I offered him a deal. If he helped me train for selection and briefed me on what to look out for, I'd buy him a new set of alloy wheels for his motor. Pathfinder (PF) selection is basically the same as that for the SAS, only it's shorter – being five weeks of initial torture, as opposed to six months. Jack Quinn would make an ideal mentor.

Some claim that PF selection covers the same ground as the SAS in less time, which makes it more intense and challenging. Others argue that it's quicker, which lowers the attrition rate. Jack didn't particularly give a shit either way. As far as he was concerned, I needed to be every bit as physically and mentally prepared for PF selection as he had been for that of the SAS.

And it was Jack who'd given me the nod to arrive early so as to claim the best billet.

The next bloke to pitch up takes the other corner bunk furthest from the door, so the one directly above mine. He's a little, wiry lance corporal from 3 PARA. He tells me he's an ultra-marathon runner, and he shows me the 'NO FEAR' tattoo he's got emblazoned on one shoulder. He's got a broad Welsh accent, and it's no surprise to learn that everyone calls him 'Taff'.

I tell him I'm a captain from 1 PARA and that everyone knows me as 'Dave'. Because this is selection, it's all first-name terms here regardless of rank. It's very likely the first time that Taff has ever addressed an officer by name, as opposed to 'sir'. It's that kind of classless ethos that has drawn me to the elite forces.

As a young captain not many years out of Sandhurst, I'd always believed that those who wish to lead have to earn the respect of those they expect to follow. Merit, regardless of rank – in my book, that's how the best military units should operate. The Pathfinders, I know, live and breathe that egalitarian kind of a spirit.

Another bloke pitches up. He's a massive, hulking Arnie Schwarzenegger look-alike. Typically, he's from the Royal Engineers, who only ever seem to come in the one size – monstrous. The Royal Engineers are well-respected, hard and toughened soldiers, and after the PARAs they make up the second biggest cap badge in The Pathfinders.

There's a good deal of rivalry between the PARAs and the Royal Engineers. The Engineers joke that PARAs are 'mince' – thick in the head – and that Engineers have a higher level of intellect, because they have to build stuff and not just shoot it up. The set PARA retort is: 'Mate, just concentrate on building us some shitters.' I don't think too many of us will be saying that to our Arnie double.

He dwarfs Taff, and I've got no doubt he's going to be the biggest bloke on selection. He looks absolutely fearsome, but that's not my main concern. As one of the next biggest blokes what I'm really dreading is getting teamed up with Arnie buddy-buddy fashion, and having to carry his massive frame across the rain-and-sleet-lashed moors.

Arnie chooses the corner bunk opposite mine and Taff's – a fine choice, with ours already taken. Next to arrive is another bloke from 3 PARA. He's got a long and morose face. It reminds me of a horse. Taff and the new arrival seem to know each other, for Taff breaks into a wide grin just as soon as he lays eyes on him.

"Ullo, Mark, mate ... but why the long face?' he quips.

Often, the old jokes are still the best ones.

The new arrival tells Taff to 'f-off', and the ice is well and truly broken.

He's a private, Mark Kidman, and he hails from New Zealand. That country produces some highly regarded soldiers, and I've no doubt Mark is a class act. More to the point, he tells us he was offered a place as an officer in the regular British Army, but refused it. He did so simply because he wanted to try for selection into The Pathfinders – and that deserves a great deal of respect.

Two blokes arrive together and they're more 3 PARA lads. Al I know of old. He's tall, lean, scruffy and wolfish looking, and he doesn't give a toss about his appearance. The only time he looks in the mirror is to shave. If anyone comments on his looks, he gives a set response in a thick Leeds accent: 'Not fucking arsed, fucking am I?'

Al doesn't talk much and he's not the sharpest tool in the box, but he's known as being a superlative operator. He greets me with his typical dour, understated humour.

'Fucking all right then, Dave. We're gonna be fucking going on a fucking tab, then, eh?'

Tab is military speak for a Tactical Advance to Battle – a forced march under crushing pack and weapons. We're going to be doing more than just a few tabs on selection, and Al and I know it.

Jez is the other 3 PARA lad, and he's the real enigma. He's a private, but he's balding and well spoken and he sounds distinctly educated. He looks as if he's in completely the wrong kind of place right now. He'd be well at home in a tweed jacket and tie in the Officers' Mess, and being addressed as 'The Colonel'.

One of the last to arrive is Pete, who hails from the Grenadier Guards. He has no option but to take a bunk right next to the door. He is a chain-smoker and a ranker, and he's been in the Guards for a very long time. He wears nothing but Army-issue kit, and he seems to pride himself on being able to take any shit the Army can throw at him – including getting the bunk from hell.

Pete has got zero civvie mountaineering kit, and even his boots are standard Army issue. They've got cheap, flimsy soles and they look like they've been designed for a stint as a petrol pump attendant. As far as I can see he's the only one in the entire hut wearing Army-issue boots. The rest of us all have civvie footwear – either Altbergs or Scarpas, or in my case Lowes.

My Lowes are made of a tough, leather upper with a Vibram sole, to soak up the pounding impact of the forced marches. They're not Gore-Tex lined, as that would make the feet sweat too much, plus the Gore-Tex keeps the water in when wading through bogs, and there'll be plenty of that to come. It's the last thing you need on selection.

The Grenadier Guards are famed for their smartness, plus their drill. Sure enough, all of Pete's standard-issue kit is polished and pressed to perfection. The lads can't help ripping the piss.

'Hey, Pete! They've got a trouser press in the wash-house, mate.'

'Hurry – soon be time to get on parade.'

'You boys need some fucking drill,' Pete retorts. 'Bloody ill-disciplined PARAs.'

Oddly, one of the last pieces of kit that Pete pulls out of his Bergen is a book – some battered sci-fi thriller.

Al stares at it for a long second. 'What – the – fuck – is – that?' he asks, each word punctuated by a disgusted silence.

'It's a book,' says Pete. 'Sorry. Forgot. You PARAs can't read, can you?'

There's something hard and unshakeable in Pete's look, and he doesn't seem the least bit fazed by the slagging. He and I get talking and it turns out that he's a 'pad'. He lives on the pad – in Army accommodation and in the married quarters. It's another thing that marks him out as being a misfit, for the rest of us are very much unattached.

'So, erm, Dave, you were in SL with 1 PARA, weren't you?' Pete asks.

'Yeah, I was.'

'It was a NEO, wasn't it?'

'Yeah.'

SL is short for Sierra Leone, a nation in West Africa that had been torn apart by civil war. My battalion, 1 PARA, was sent there a few months back to carry out a non-combatant evacuation operation (NEO) – in layman's terms, pulling out all British and allied civilians. The rebel forces were poised to take the nation's capital, which would have caused a horrific bloodbath. We were flown into the teeth of that conflict to get our people out, and to stop the carnage.

'You'd have to be a fire-pisser to be on that one,' Pete remarks.

'A what?'

Pete mimes as if he's holding his cock. 'Someone who pisses fire.'

'Fair enough.' I raise the obvious question. 'So, mate, why're you doing selection?'

Pete knows why I'm asking. He's an older, married family man, and he's clearly a well-established regular Army kind of a bloke.

He shrugs. 'Last shot to do something exciting ... I love the Guards. I'll always be true to my roots. But I don't exactly think they'll make me RSM, 'cause I've had more than a few run-ins. Pathfinder selection – it's my last chance at being a fire-pisser.'

The crack with the guys is good and morale is high, but none of the torture has started yet. Plus there's something else that I'm painfully aware of. I'm not just here to undertake Pathfinder selection. I'm here to see if I can make it through as second-in-command (2IC) of the unit, and that's the added pressure that I'm under.

By midday all forty of us are present and correct. We head for the cookhouse, each of us carrying our own plate, mug, knife and fork. Sennybridge Camp is a temporary kind of set-up, and too much of the Army-issue cutlery has been nicked by those who went before us. These days, if you want to eat you have to bring your own tools.

We queue for food. It's hot dog and chips and we pile it high. There are a couple of urns, one serving coffee and the other tea. It's the cheapest, shittiest brew the Army can find, and whichever you choose it all tastes pretty much the same.

As we move off with our brews I spot a row of familiar figures, but there's not a flash of recognition amongst them. They're stony-faced and pretending they don't know me.

One is Lenny, the present 2IC of Pathfinders. He and I were on the piss together directly after Sierra Leone, and we got so hammered we woke up in bed together. I actually thought he was a bird at first, that's until my hand felt the stubble on his jaw. But right now he's acting as if he's never set eyes on me before.

Then there's Gavin and Tricky, two more PF stalwarts that I know well. But right at the moment they're the Directing Staff (DS) on selection, and they're here for one reason only – to beast us through the weeks of hell to come. In fact, the entire Pathfinder unit has pitched up so as to better handle the murderously intense pace of what's coming.

The PF lads have got their own, separate accommodation block and their own separate showers. To a man they're pretending they don't know me. I don't try to greet them, either. I understand there can't be even a hint of any matey-matey shit between us. No special allowances. Zero favouritism. No exceptions made for any man who doesn't make it through of his own accord.

The Pathfinders is an incredibly tight-knit unit and it only takes the best. It consists of six, six-man patrols – so thirty-six fighting men in all. Together with support staff – engineers, signallers and the like – that makes it a sixty-strong unit max. It may be small but it's perfectly formed, for Pathfinders are the most highly-trained and specialist mobility troops in the world.

Unlike the SAS and SBS, who are trained in all facets of anti-terrorism, anti-insurgency, regular and irregular warfare, Pathfinders train relentlessly for one thing only: insertion deep behind enemy lines on recce, capture, demolitions or kill missions. That's why The Pathfinders were originally formed, it remains the *raison d'être* of the unit today.

Pathfinders are experts at HALO (High Altitude Low Opening) and HAHO (High Altitude High Opening) parachute jumps, as means of covert deep penetration insertion. Via HAHO they can open their chutes at the kind of altitude airliners cruise at and drift silently and unseen for miles towards a distant target. Via HALO, they can skydive from very high altitude, as a fast and invisible means of getting onto the ground.

HALO and HAHO are the bread and butter of what The Pathfinders do, and it's what they're renowned for. I've seen the unit on exercises HALOing into a drop zone, arriving James Bond-like out of the silent and darkened heavens. It's that which first made me want to join the unit. But Pathfinders are equally highly-trained for insertions by foot or via light, off-road vehicles far behind enemy lines.

We get the food down us, and there's a lot less piss-taking and high spirits now. A massive bloke rises from the Pathfinders' end of the cookhouse. Stan Harris is the PF Platoon Sergeant. He's a giant of a Yorkshireman with a face as hard and as grey as a chiselled crag.

He's also a living legend in these circles. Amongst the many feats of soldiering he's renowned for, he won the Military Cross when The Pathfinders took on rebel forces in a pitched battle in the Sierra Leone jungle.

'Right, all youse want to join The Pathfinders, the first event is the eight-miler,' he announces, with zero ceremony. 'You must be with the DS at the end of the tab. If you're not, it's a fail.

'This is not like any other course in the Army.' He eyeballs the lot of us. 'If you're sick, lame or lazy, at any point you can voluntarily withdraw – VW. None of us is here to motivate you; if you want to go back to Battalion and do guards and duties with your mates for the rest of your life, then you're more than welcome to go.

'This isn't a face-fits unit,' he continues. 'There are some right criminal-looking bastards in the PF. We're looking for a few good men – those who can survive and deliver against all odds. All of us here in the PF – you call us "Staff". No one wears rank in our unit, so you don't need to worry about that. PF selection is fast and intense. It's not like the SAS, where all you've got to worry about for the first five weeks is tabbing. We've only got youse for six weeks, so after your tabs you've got lessons and more tests, and then if you're lucky you might get your head down.

'I'm sure you know the basics, so I won't waste any more of my precious breath, 'cause by the end of today some of youse won't be here.' He pauses for a long second, just to let the words sink in. 'If you do pass selection, you'll go on to continuation training, including combat survival and resistance to interrogation. You're on probation for the first year, in which time you must pass your HALO and HAHO courses, plus your comms and mobility cadres.'

He glances at the watch strapped to his massive, hairy wrist. 'It's 13.45. The armoury is two blocks down from your accom block. Go draw your weapons. Be on the parade square at 1400 hours with Bergens in front of youse, ready for weigh-in. If you're not at minimum weight we'll add it to your Bergen, plus a big rock so you'll be over weight for the tab. And remember, everything in your Bergen must be useful kit for winter in the mountains.'

For a moment his laser-eyed stare sweeps the room. It comes to rest on Pete. 'Well done, Sergeant Terry. You've just volunteered yourself to be in charge of the tea urn roster. Perfect work for a Guards sergeant. Make sure everyone takes a turn, and make fucking sure every time we go out there's two on the back of each of the four-tonners – that's one for you lot and one for the DS. If anyone forgets the tea urns I will be extremely pissed off and you'll be going up and down an additional mountain. Now, get away.'

We split.

The atmosphere has utterly changed. It's silent and tense and there's a real urgency in the air. I've got serious butterflies in my stomach, and I'm worried about whether I should have eaten as much as I have. I know I'll need the energy, but doing a forced march like what's coming on a full stomach can easily make you puke.

We head for the Nissen hut, grab our Bergens, then there's an argy-bargy at the armoury to be first to draw weapons. We're each issued with a dummy SLR – an ancient, self-loading rifle. It's the kind of weapon the British Army soldiered with a few decades ago, and we've only got it for the weight and the discipline, plus the added realism. But woe betide anyone who disrespects their weapon ...

Until recently, those doing selection used to be issued with real assault rifles. But too many were lost during the more extreme stages of selection, high on the hills and in atrocious weather conditions. Search parties had to be mounted to bring in the lost kit, and it all got a bit too much – hence the introduction of the dummy rifles.

We form up on the parade ground in three ranks, with our Bergens propped in front of us. Some of the blokes have laid their dummy SLRs on the ground beside their packs. It's another thing that Jack Quinn had warned me about: unless you're sleeping, you never, ever let your weapon leave your hand, and even then it's got to be just a quick grab away.

Stan Harris stops dead in front of the first bloke who's committed this heinous crime. 'First fucking thing is this,' he yells into the offender's face. 'In the PF you NEVER, EVER put your weapon on the fucking ground. If you EVER need to put your weapon down rest it on your feet or your pack.'

'Staff,' the offender confirms, grabbing his dummy rifle.

'Your weapon must at all times be within arm's reach,' he continues. 'If you fuck up, we run a fine system. You'll be fined every time, and you'll soon fucking learn. Money goes into a fund and we drink it in a piss-up at the end – that's for those who pass. Anyone got a problem with that?'

Silence.

'If I catch anyone using their weapon as a walking stick when you're out on the hills tabbing, you'll be RTU'd, no messing.' He turns to a lean and hard-looking bloke beside him. It's Tricky, his fellow DS. 'Time to weigh in their kit.' He turns back to us. 'You lot – remove your water and food.'

We're each supposed to start with a Bergen laden with 35 pounds of kit, that's not counting water and food. As the days progress, we'll keep upping the weight in increments, until we're tabbing under a crushing load. The DS will keep checking us at the start and end of each stage to make sure no one's shirking.

As we pull out all the scoff and the bottles from our Bergens, most blokes are carrying high-energy drinks and protein bars. But I always have at least one Ginsters Cornish pasty in my Bergen. It's real, hearty food and I've got it as a special treat. Just the knowledge that it's in there can prove a real boost to morale.

Tricky sees the pasty, and shakes his head in disgust. 'What – the fuck – is that?'

'Ginsters pasty, Staff.'

Tricky lets out a snort of disbelief. 'What, a Ginsters Cornish pasty as recommended by the British Olympic Committee?'

'Staff.'

No one so much as sniggers. We all of us know that if you laugh at the DS's jokes, they're just as likely to turn on you.

Tricky and I know each other from the Sierra Leone op, plus we've been out on the beers together. But right now I realise that the DS are very likely to give me a doubly hard time. Firstly, so as to be absolutely certain they are not showing any favouritism, and secondly because I am trying for the 2IC's slot in their closely-guarded unit.

I decide I'm going to have to try to be the 'grey man' here – the bloke who does nothing to get himself noticed or singled out still further. That way, I might just escape from the worst of the DS's ire.

We weigh in fine with our Bergens, all apart from the one bloke who's a kilo under. Tricky glances at Stan Harris, who indicates a sizeable boulder lying at the edge of the parade ground.

'Right, go fetch that fucking rock,' Tricky tells the offender.

I can see the sheer panic written on the bloke's face as he realises what's coming. He scuttles off, lifts the rock, brings it back and Tricky piles it into the top of his Bergen. He gets the scales and weighs it for a second time.

He smiles. 'You're two kilos over. Tough shit. I'll be weighing your Bergen at the end of the eight-miler, and it'd better be the same fucking weight.'

'Right, enough fucking around!' Stan Harris yells. 'On the back of the four-tonners!'

We double-time it over to the battered khaki green Army trucks. Two are needed to carry the forty-odd blokes starting selection. The tailgate on a four-tonner is heavy, and it takes two blokes to unlatch the first one and lift it down. We're about to start mounting up the truck, when Stan Harris stops us with a look that could kill.

He's staring into the nearest truck with eyes like murder. 'Fucking Guards sergeants ... So, tell me: who's forgotten the fucking tea urns?'

The PF Platoon Sergeant has got lock-on with Pete already. On the one hand I feel sorry for him. But on the other, I know I'm going to have to give Pete a wide berth from now on. If you're mates with the guy who's got lock-on from the head DS, you'll likely get hit in the back blast.

'Staff!' Pete yells, acknowledging his failure to sort out the tea roster. He turns to Jez and Al. 'Lads, let's get the fucking urns sorted.'

Jez – 'The Colonel' – has already got his Bergen and dummy rifle loaded onto the four-tonner. He turns and makes a run for the cookhouse, but he's left his weapon lying where it is.

Stan Harris practically explodes. 'WHERE THE FUCK IS YOUR FUCKING WEAPON?'

Eyes bulging, Jez stops in his tracks. 'Staff!' He runs back, grabs his dummy SLR, and turns to go and fetch the tea urns.

'What's your fucking name?' Stan Harris barks after him.

'Rowlands, Staff.'

'Fucking *Rowlands*? Sounds like a poofy bloody officer's name!'

'Staff.'

No one is laughing. No fucking way. And no one answers back.

All it takes is for one of the DS to decide he doesn't like you, and you'll get beasted half to death by the lot of them.

Jez returns with a tea urn under one arm and his rifle under the other. We mount up the four-tonners. As Jez climbs aboard he's got a box of sugar and a carton of milk balanced on top of the tea urn. Predictably, the whole lot goes over.

Luckily, the milk's unopened, but the sugar ends up scattered all over the bed of the truck. Before the DS can notice Pete scoops it up as best he can and throws it into the tea urn, presumably working on the assumption that the mud and grit will sink to the bottom, whereas the sugar will dissolve.

'Fucking hell, lads,' he hisses, 'use your fucking heads. Don't bring the fucking sugar and the urn separate. Dump it into the urn back in the cookhouse, and bring it like that. Otherwise, it'll keep getting knocked over and we'll keep having shit in our tea.'

I take my place on the hard wooden bench by the rear of the truck, so I can keep a check on where we're going. I quickly realise my mistake. As soon as we're under way the wind starts whistling in through the open canvas back, and it's freezing.

There's a heavy, oppressive silence as the four-tonner trundles along this narrow country lane. No one's chatting now and there's zero crack.

It's day one of PF selection, and we know we're going to get thrashed.

*

CHAPTER TWO

We thunder through the slate-grey streets of Sennybridge village, and as we head into the open hills someone remarks: 'Anyone know where we're going?'

'Sennybridge Training Area for the eight-miler,' a voice responds.

'So how long do we have to do it?' someone asks.

'You get two hours in the regular Army. But right now the max time we'll get is one hour thirty.'

'Fucking hell, that's quick.'

'Yeah, but they can go a lot faster. Remember what the DS said: keep up, or you're out.'

'In the regular Army the eight-miler's done on tracks and roads. This PF lot, they go cross-country and through all kinds of shit . . .'

I keep quiet. I'm not really listening. I'm trying not to get psyched out by the talk. I think back over all the murderous preparation and training I put in: the countless nights camped out in the cramped confines of my battered BMW 3 Series, after a long and lonely day spent tabbing across the rain-lashed hills.

The four-tonner rumbles over a cattle grid. I tell myself that I have to pass this first test – the eight-miler. If I fall at the first hurdle, all the pain and discomfort of training will be as naught. It was always raining back then when I was training. Always. And just to make us feel at home a fine drizzle has started to fall now.

Sennybridge Training Area sits on the fringes of the Irish Sea, and the winds blow in from the south-west after 3500 miles of Atlantic Ocean. The sea air's cold and damp and burdened with moisture, all of which starts to fall just as soon as the cloud mass hits the mountains, hence the permanent fog and the rain. It's like Mordor, but without the Elves for company.

The four-tonner starts to labour up this steep incline. The noise of the engine and the rhythm of the rocking truck becomes strangely comforting, for it means the pain hasn't started yet. There's the reek of diesel fumes drifting up from the exhaust, as we creep up this hill for two long miles.

As long as I have that sound in my ears and that smell in my nostrils, I know it hasn't started yet. When they stop, I'll know for sure that pain like nothing I've ever experienced is about to come.

With a crunch of gravel we grind to a halt. No sooner have we done so than a voice announces: 'Dismount and form up in three ranks!'

The DS are there before us. They've made their way here in the PF's lightweight, all-wheel-drive Pinzgauers. I take a place at the back of the three ranks. Being at the rear of the pack can mean you get held up by the slow-coaches, which means you have to work harder on the tab. But my main priority right now is to be the grey man, and not get myself noticed.

I stand there in total silence, my Bergen on my back and my hands on my weapon. Rain starts to drip down my sodden features. It isn't that heavy yet. It's a fine, drifting skein of grey that blankets out the sun, but somehow it is very, very cold, not to mention wet.

I tell myself I won't speak unless spoken to – not even to the blokes I know who're standing nearby.

Silence is anonymous. Silence is safety.

Tricky takes his place before us. He's the DS pacesetter, the bloke who's going to lead the eight-miler. He's got a massive Bergen on his back, and he appears to be fit and muscular as fuck. He's a Jason Statham look-alike, with piercing, frozen, ice-blue eyes. I'm taller than him and bigger, but he's definitely not the kind of bloke I'd want to pick a fight with in a bar.

To one side of us the entire Pathfinder Platoon form up as one phalanx of steel-hard, Spartan warriors. They look utterly, deadly serious. No one is dicking around, whether they're here to be tested or they're here to lead the torture. I see Tricky glance at this big, chunky diving watch that he's got strapped to his wrist.

'By the left, quick march,' he announces, with zero warning.

And then he's off like a shot from a gun.

The pack surges ahead, trying to keep it together and to keep with him. I feel someone's rifle crash into my legs and I almost stumble over. We've not found our rhythm yet as a group, or spaced ourselves out into a formation that works. We're just a gaggle of worried, nervous, pumped-up blokes trying to keep up – and then we hit the first incline, this one mercifully going downhill.

'Break into double time!' Tricky yells from the front. 'Double march.'

I see him haring off down the hill and basically he's running. My shins haven't even had the time to warm up or properly loosen yet, and I can feel the tightness in them as I pump my knees and force my legs to fly.

The forty of us stick together as one pack for the first couple of miles. I'm beginning to think that every one of us will make it through this first test. But it's then that we hit the first uphill section, whereupon Tricky barely slows. We hit the flat again, and he's going at a fast jog. Then we're on to a downhill section once more, and he's practically doing a 100 metres sprint.

He keeps it going without let-up for a good three miles, and the pack starts to thin noticeably. Behind us are the 'jack wagons' – a couple of bog standard Army Land Rovers. They're creeping along at the rear, so as to pick up anyone who decides to can it – to voluntarily withdraw.

I can't believe anyone will do so on this, the very first day, but there's no telling.

All around me figures are gasping for breath, their lungs heaving painfully. In spite of the cold and the wet, we're pissing sweat from out of every pore. For mile after mile Tricky maintains the punishing speed, and just when I figure he can't keep it up any longer, he ups the pace still further.

He's bolted off ahead of us, running and running like a hare.

I remember Stan Harris's words. I can hear them playing through my head: *You must be with the DS at the end of the tab to pass. If not, it's a fail . . .*

I'm thinking to myself: fucking hell, I've done the forced marches in P Company – the PARA Regiment selection course – and I thought they were hard. But right now Tricky is going like the proverbial bat out of hell. The human body just isn't designed to keep up this kind of pace over this kind of terrain, under this kind of a load.

We're still on metalled roads right now, which makes for even, steady going, but the hard impact of boots thudding into tarmac makes my shins feel like they're about to snap. My lungs are burning like they're on fire, my legs are aching as if knitting needles are being rammed into them, and my guts are churning like I'm about to throw up.

It's then that I glance up momentarily, and I realise I've caught up with the leaders of the pack. Tricky's called a momentary break for water. He's standing there looking like he's barely breaking sweat. Al reaches the stop just a few paces ahead of me, and as he pulls to a halt he lets his weapon fall to the roadside.

'Pick your fucking weapon up,' Tricky snarls. 'Rest it on your boots if you have to. Only then do you get your water out.'

'Staff,' Al acknowledges in a breathless gasp.

It's one of the few times I've ever known him take such harsh criticism without making some kind of a wisecrack, or without using the f-word. Right here and right now, he knows it would be fatal to do so.

I'm bent double, leaning my weight on my knees while I try to catch my breath and get my heartbeat under control. My pulse is pounding like thunder in my head. I glance at Pete. He's got a bright red face like he's about to have a heart attack, and his hair is soaked through – whether with rain or sweat or both I can't tell.

I grab my water bottle and neck a few greedy gulps, trying to replace some of what I've lost. Behind us, the last of the stragglers are limping into the water stop. But no sooner have they reached us than Tricky straightens up and he's off once more.

'Bring to quick time – quick march!' he yells.

We're left in no doubt that he means everyone. You falter here, you're done for – and that includes those just in. The stragglers won't have time for even a sip of water or a few seconds' precious rest, and that's just the way it is.

Keep with the DS. If not, it's a fail.

Tricky hammers onwards up a long and steady hill, burning up the miles. I feel my shins cracking and crunching, and my back is aching like hell under the load. It's then that he reaches the top of the climb, and breaks off from the tarmac to head cross-country.

The path weaves down a very steep and uneven slope. The grass has been cropped short by grazing sheep, and it's soggy and slick underfoot. There are sections you can't afford to go straight down, and I find myself zigzagging crazily back and forth across the terrain in a desperate effort to retain my footing.

From behind me I hear a burst of wild yelling and cursing. Someone shouts 'fuck' as they fall, collapsing into a flurry of spinning arms and legs. The bloke's dropped his weapon, and it's tumbled off downhill. I see him get to his feet and go charging after it, in a desperate effort to retrieve it and keep with us.

I don't recognise who it is. The DS completely ignore him. I've got no option but to do likewise. If I pause here in an effort to help the bloke, then I'm finished.

Tricky reaches the bottom of the incline, and surges ahead into a boggy, marshy area. I follow, quickly sinking to my knees.

Evil-smelling water and a thick slurry of dark mud pours into my boots. I feel the cold, sticky wetness seeping into my socks, and filling out my Lowes with extra weight that I just don't need.

A bloke behind me goes into a slide and ends up face down in the bog. He comes up covered in shit, and with his dummy rifle dripping gunk from either end.

By force of will I drag my legs through the mire and onto the far side. As I clamber onto solid ground my muddied feet are sliding about inside the slippery wetness of my boots. I know for sure I've got to tighten the laces next time we stop, or I'm going to badly twist an ankle.

A dry pair of boots retain their rigidity and shape over many miles. When sodden and mud-soaked as mine are now, the leather starts to lose its form and goes sloppy. I've got to tighten the laces extra hard, so as to compensate.

I struggle up the steep incline, pushing myself against the pain and the agony to keep with the pack leaders. Behind me the blokes are spreading out still further, so that they're strung across the rain-soaked, grey emptiness of the valley.

Pete and I stick doggedly to Tricky's shoulder. We fight against the pain plus the loads that we're carrying, so as to keep ten metres behind him. We climb and we climb. For a while Pete is ahead of me, and then I overtake him. As I do so I can hear his breath coming in tight, gurgling, wheezing gasps. With all the ciggies he smokes it's a miracle he's still breathing.

I see Tricky throw a momentary glance over his shoulder. It's piercing, and utterly contemptuous of those falling behind. And then he's powering on. I am just about keeping up, but still I'm worried. If it's this tough on day one, how will I last the weeks to come?

I sense Pete on my shoulder. He's labouring hard, his breath coming like a steam train puffing fire and sparks as he chugs up the hill. He draws level with me, and I can read the utter, unshakeable determination in the tense hunch of his shoulders. I figure his

Army-issue boots must be sloppy as shit in these kind of conditions, but he's still able to pull ahead of me.

I settle into the lee of Pete's form and stick doggedly to his heels. By now I figure we must have done approaching seven miles of the eight-mile forced march. My eyes keep scanning the ground underfoot as my boots pound ahead, kicking up spurts of dirty water from the sodden earth. I'm searching for any breaks in the terrain on which I might twist an ankle or take a fall.

I risk a fleeting glance upwards to the front, blinking the rainwater out of my eyes. Sure enough, a mile or so ahead of me I can just make out the distinctive forms of the four-tonners pulling to a halt. They're there to collect us at the end of the march. They have to be.

That sight alone proves a massive boost. My pace quickens. I can make this. For sure I can. No dramas.

I thrash myself over the next half a mile, and then Tricky starts to slow his pace. It's a sure sign we're almost done. The distinctive form of the trucks draws ever nearer. Their silhouette grows blocky and firm on the horizon. I sense others catching up with us, as Tricky slows to a comfortable walk.

We've done it. We're home.

I glance behind me, across the gaping void of the valley. The rain is heavy now, sweeping in dark curtains across the terrain we've just covered. I can see the odd figure a way back in the distance, with here and there a DS helping them onto the Land Rovers. It's amazing: we're this close to the end, but still they've decided to jack it and they're finished.

With a last burst of effort Pete and me stumble around to the rear of the four-tonners.

'Fucking – made – it,' he gasps, as he doubles up, clutching his guts.

'Fucking – killer,' is about all I can manage in reply.

But inside I feel this sense of total elation that I've passed the first test on Pathfinder selection. I'm about to dump my Bergen in the rear of a truck, when I hear the cough of an engine starting.

There's a belch of thick, dirty-black diesel smoke as the four-tonner pulls away.

Tricky doesn't say a word. He doesn't even look at us. I glance at him, but there's not the slightest change in his poker-faced expression. All he does is straighten his back and start marching ahead again, following the direction in which the truck's heading. In no time he's double-timing it along the dirt track, as the four-tonners disappear into the gloom.

I know that unless I move it, right now, then I'm done for. I've heard about them doing this. It's a stalwart of the kind of mind games they play on selection. It's called the 'sickener'. Jack Quinn warned me to expect this and to be ready, but it's funny how the mind chooses to forget such warnings when the body is totally and utterly bollocksed.

For a moment I'm almost beaten. Then, with superhuman effort I force my mind to accept the sickener – the initial flood of relief followed by the dark and brutal sense of let-down – for it's always your mind that will break you. I tell myself that my body is able to last this extra lap, and so it is that I get myself moving.

I force my legs to un-seize themselves. Beside me, I see Pete doing likewise. I burned myself out on the last mile that we'd done, trying to stick with Tricky and Pete and get to the trucks. This last stretch – the sickener mile – is really going to kill me.

There are figures ahead of me now – the blokes who've paced themselves better. Somehow I force myself into a quicker pace to keep with them. I can hear taunting voices to either side of me now, ringing in my ears. There are DS lining the route, and they're piling on the pressure big time.

It's evil.

'There are no four-tonners. You've taken too long. We've sent them back to Camp.'

'There's a nice warm pub a couple of miles away in Sennybridge ...'

'The jack wagons'll drive you direct to the Sennybridge Arms ...'

'A massive plate of chips and a few pints of Guinness – what are you waiting for ...?'

I tune out the voices. I keep the legs pumping. I force-march onwards through the tunnel of driving rain and the gathering gloom.

Tricky slows for a second time. He walks the last quarter of a mile. And this time, when we reach the trucks they stay right where they are. As I hobble into the finish – the real finish – there's a couple of DS writing down our names and our times.

'Right, get some water on,' Tricky announces, his voice a flat monotone. There isn't the slightest hint of a well done or even the barest encouragement in it. 'Form up in three ranks.'

'Shout names,' another DS instructs us. He points at the front row first, from right to left. Once I've yelled out my name, I'm finally allowed to clamber into the sanctuary of the four-tonner.

I ease myself out of my Bergen. My T-shirt is piss wet through with sweat, as is my pack. There's a sore that's been rubbed into either side of my hips, due to the Bergen being so heavy and the pace being so horrific. In fact, I have never moved so fast in all my life.

This time, I go and take a seat at the very front of the four-tonner – the warmest place possible. But still I know I'm going to be wet and cold for all of the long drive back to Camp.

I glance around as figures pile aboard. Pete is first amongst them. No surprises there: I don't know what would break the bloke. Al and Taff are close behind. Mark the Kiwi has made it, and even Jez pitches up eventually. He may look like a short and somewhat roly-poly Colonel figure, but he is clearly made of sterner stuff, and he's starting to earn himself a grudging respect.

As the truck pulls away several spaces on the benches remain unoccupied, marking those who have jacked it. It's Day One, Mission One, and already we've lost a good number.

It's a long and miserable ride back. We're quiet as mice, and we're enveloped in the thick cloud of steam that forms as our sweat evaporates into the damp air. Someone tries to get the nozzle on the tea urn to work, but either their fingers are frozen or it's seized up completely.

It's Pete who intervenes. 'Lads, lads, don't fuck about. Open the lid, get your mug and scoop some out.'

We do just that, and a mug of tea has never tasted so good.

In spite of the injection of sugar and the warmth, the cold in the wagon is piercing. I rip off my smock and my T-shirt. The latter is soaking wet and it's freezing to my body. I put the smock back on, and a green duvet jacket over that. Even so, I huddle closer to the body of the truck cab, to shelter from the wind and the cold.

By the time we're back at Camp it's pitch dark. My legs have seized up completely from the exertion of the eight-miler, followed by the inactivity of the drive and the cold. As the truck crawls through Camp I try to massage some life back into them. We pull to a halt and I fall out of the four-tonner like an old man, my legs half collapsing under me.

'Right, lads, drop your weapons off at armoury, then shower, and scoff's at six-thirty,' one of the DS tells us. 'Map-reading test is at seven-thirty in the classroom next to the accom block. Bring a Silva compass, pen and pencil. And a protractor.'

We've been dropped on the parade ground. Together with the others who've survived the eight-miler I hobble off in the direction of the armoury, and thence to the showers.

There are five shower heads in the communal block for the thirty-five of us who remain. One shower head dribbles out a rust-brown trickle of water, before it stops completely. The other is stuck on permanent cold. That leaves three working showers for the lot of us.

As we queue to wash I think about the blokes who've jacked it. Right now they'll be in the office with Lenny, the Pathfinder OC, getting a formal interview. When we turned up at Camp we had to hand in our medical records, to prove we were fit and well enough to undertake selection.

One of the blokes who's jacked is a fellow PARA, and I can just imagine what Lenny will be telling him. *You're being formally RTU'd. Get your medical docs from the clerk, make your bed and don't leave any shit behind. Take your sheets and dog blanket back to stores, then you're done.*

It will be as blunt and as unemotional as that. These blokes may just have failed at their dream of a lifetime, but that means bugger all to the DS. If you can't make the grade The Pathfinders don't want you, and jacking on day one really isn't the best way to make a positive impression.

It would be different if a bloke had lasted through to the final week, and picked up a horrific injury that meant he just couldn't continue. Then Lenny might show some real sympathy and invite him back to try again. But if you fell at the very first hurdle, you clearly weren't serious about it in the first place.

If you get RTU'd on day one of selection, you have to return to your regiment and face the music from your mates. And you certainly haven't earned yourself a place in one of the most elite and secretive military outfits on earth.

From the showers I head directly to the cookhouse with Pete. I know he's in the firing line and that I ought to avoid him like the plague, but I'm warming to the bloke. Anyone who can do what we've just done today in regular Army boots has to get my vote. He's a no-nonsense, no-frills, tough as fuck soldier, and he doesn't give a shit.

I can't help but like him.

In any case, sooner or later I figure I'm going to be in the firing line myself, regardless of whom I choose to keep as company. I'm the only officer on selection, and I'm slated to be 2IC of the unit, that's if I pass. I'm bound to be under the spotlight. The DS can't help but want to beast me, and I figure Pete is the kind of bloke who'll stick with me when it all starts.

Typically, the food is shit. It's dry beef burgers fried hard as rocks, with potatoes and green veg boiled to a mush. Most of the blokes have bottles of Hi5 energy drink to wash down the scoff, and we're stuffing slices of bread down us in an effort to pile on the carbs. But it's going to be impossible to keep our weight up, even if we eat like we're doing until we want to vomit. We need the carbs for the energy, but six meals a day wouldn't make up for what we're going to burn.

There are hard green apples and tiny yellow oranges to complement dessert, which is a rubbery bread and butter pudding. I tell Pete he should use some of the pudding to re-sole his boots, 'cause it's tougher than whatever the Army uses.

It raises a quiet laugh, but there's almost zero crack now. We're all of us aware that if we keep losing blokes at the rate we've done today, there'll be no one left at the end of selection.

From the cookhouse we head as a pack for the mapping session. The classroom is set higher up the hill, and it's half hidden in the dampness and the murk. It's another chicken hutch with a lone radiator bolted to one wall, one that is barely working. As I enter the place I can feel the bare cold seeping into my bones.

Our DS for this evening is a PF bloke called Corporal Cavill, or Cav for short. But we only know his name because one of the 3 PARA lads recognises him from before he joined The Pathfinders. He certainly doesn't introduce himself to us now, for you're basically a nobody until you've passed selection and joined their number.

We sit at individual desks, like we're being tested in a school exam. The DS hands out two sheets of A4 paper, which are stapled together. On those are printed various mapping exercises. It's our task to complete them within the set time. He tells us to grab a particular map sheet from a stack piled before us and he sets the clock running.

Rows of blokes hunch over their wooden desks. It's quiet like you can hear a pin drop. Our Arnie look-alike is still with us, and it strikes me as being absurdly funny seeing this monster bloke hulked over his tiny desk.

I know I'm going to find this part of selection easier than most, but still it's a massive effort to force my tired mind and my aching body to focus on the task in hand. I've got a belly stuffed to bursting with warm food, and my body craves sleep. Instead, I've got to concentrate on some seriously abstruse navigational problems.

Question One is easy enough: 'What is the bearing of the A-to-B on grid ref 784639?'

For me at least it's a cinch. In 1 PARA I commanded 1 Platoon, A Company, so I had a good twenty-eight blokes under me. Mostly, the privates wouldn't carry a map when out on operations. The sergeant and the corporals would, but the average rifleman was there to fight and to follow orders. Mostly, the bigger picture stuff like mapping was left to those in charge.

The questions get harder as I work my way down the page. There's one that's a real mind-bender. I've got to work out the GMA adjustment for a particular set of maps. Every map has an incremental variation – it will be out of kilter by a fraction in relation to the terrain it represents and true north.

The GMA variation increases year by year. It's measured in 'mills' – there being 6400 mills in a full circle. To calculate the present GMA you need to check the year of manufacture of the map, and work it through accordingly. The GMA question proves a real challenge for me, and it'll be a total head-twister for some of the junior ranks in the classroom.

Then there are the speed-equals-distance-over-time calculations. You work on Naismith's Rule, that the average walking speed of a human being is four kilometres per hour. You add time on to that for the gradient being crossed, piling on a minute for every ten-metre contour.

It's complicated stuff, and I can see the lads in front of me scratching their heads over their pocket calculators. Once I'm finished, I work through all the questions one more time, for it's easy to make a mistake. I'm done and dusted well within the 45 minutes allowed, and Pete finishes at about the same time as I do.

We hand in our work and we're free to leave. Together, we head back towards the accom block, and all I can think is that I really need to get some sleep. I leave Pete at his bunk next to the door, telling him I hope he gets some rest with that banging and crashing to and fro all night long.

'You've never had to share a bed with my missus,' Pete remarks. 'A few years of that and you could sleep through bloody anything.'

Sure enough, just as soon as Pete gets horizontal I hear him start to snore. The door bangs and smashes a good few times as blokes return from the classroom, but there's not the slightest break in Pete's breathing. I lie there trying to get some sleep and feeling relieved that I am not next to the bloody door. I think back to the last time I'd sat behind a hard, bare wooden desk, with weeks of exams from hell before me. It was back in my schooldays.

I'd long reached the stage when I felt there was no point in school any more, and I really did not want to be there.

*

CHAPTER THREE

I grew up in Middlewich, a town to the south of Manchester. The neighbouring, rival town was Winsford. Winsford was created in the 1960s to cope with the overspill from Manchester and Liverpool. Many of the people in Winsford had scouse accents, and it crept into our town.

Middlewich was full of 1970s housing estates. My family lived on one of them. No one was particularly affluent, and the furthest anyone would travel to work was to one of two neighbouring towns. With Warrington and Northwich close by, there was a lot of industry, including British Salt and the ICI chemical factory.

Mostly, people on our estate were blue collar and working class, and back then neighbouring Winsford was plagued by unemployment and a high crime rate. I had mates from Winsford, but I'd always have to watch my back whenever I went there. Back then there was a lot of fighting, and people would get bottled and all kinds of shit.

I spoke with a Cheshire accent, which is much softer and more rural than a scouse one. Just as soon as I opened my mouth the lads in Winsford would know that I wasn't from 'their' patch. If they clocked that I was from Middlewich, then I was from the 'posh' town and that made me fair game.

My grandparents hailed from Liverpool itself, as did my mum and dad. Dad grew up in a tiny terraced house as one of six kids. He shared a bedroom with three brothers, and he had to work hard to make it out of there and into university, and to qualify as a teacher.

My parents had never forgotten where they'd come from, and they taught me to make the most of what we had. Mum had a strict weekly budget for feeding me and my two sisters, but putting good food on the table was a priority and there were many who were worse off than us. And for just about everyone – myself included – football was our life.

Manchester and Liverpool produced some of the most influential football teams in the world. Not surprisingly, most boys growing up in the North-West wanted to be professional footballers. The guys in the top teams had hero status, and many families had their pictures all over the house. I had one boyhood friend whose parents kept a framed photo of the entire Liverpool football team above their bed.

In the summer of '86 Liverpool won the FA Cup Final *and* the League. I was eight years old at the time, and this was about the biggest event in my short life. Mum bought me a Liverpool tracksuit top to celebrate and that became my uniform. I truly believed in them: they were my heroes. And I believed that I could join their number, the exalted few.

The whole of Liverpool and the surrounding towns came together. It was like the second coming of Christ. The factory workers and the dockers needed something to believe in and something to brighten their lives. Thatcher was in power back then, and she was closing steel factories and mines left, right and centre. It was as if there was a war being waged on the working man.

The Liverpool footie team – those unbeatable heroes – had just become the thing that we could all believe in.

My Grandpa on my mother's side had a friend who worked at Anfield football ground. Joy of joys, occasionally he would get Grandpa and me some free tickets. We'd get the *Liverpool Echo* and scan the fixtures list for the games we really wanted to see. Grandpa didn't want to read about the crime rate going up or factories closing: he wanted to read about our gladiator heroes.

Grandpa lived with Nan in Huyton, a suburb on the outskirts of Liverpool. He was a salesman with Rank Hovis McDougall, the food people. He had time on his hands when travelling away on work and he spent it reading. He devoured true stories and current affairs, and he was largely self-educated.

He'd travelled the world while serving as a sailor in the Second World War, and he'd seen real suffering. His priority was to make a better life for him and his family. Mum loved him to death, and she encouraged me to spend time with him. He'd sit me on his knee as a young boy, and tell me stories about the war and his exotic travels. He'd collected banknotes and postcards from all these exotic places in the Far East, and he'd use them to illustrate his stories. That really brought them alive for me.

Grandpa was careful with his money, plus he was big into his cars. One of my earliest memories was of him taking me out for a drive around the motorways that encircle Manchester and Liverpool in his new Ford Capri. I sat in the front and begged him to put his foot down. 'Go on, Grandpa, go on!'

He got the Capri up to 100 mph, which was totally thrilling for a young kid like me. I had complete trust in him, but my Nan was going apeshit in the back. That Capri was his all-time favourite. It was bright metallic green – a real Starsky and Hutch kind of a motor. It was a working-class hero's kind of a car.

One day he lent me his medals, so I could use them to do a talk at school about the Second World War. After the talk he allowed me to keep them for a while, and that was a real big deal. But with no tradition of military service in our family, it never occurred to me that I might want to follow in Grandpa's footsteps one day and become a soldier.

I had mates whose families didn't own a car, so going for a drive was a real treat. But fuel was expensive, and so mostly I'd walk the mile and a half to school. I'd rendezvous with my mates at the corner shop and spend some of my dinner money on sweets, but all the time I'd be thinking about the footie we'd play during break.

I could handle most positions. I was a good striker and a great goalie, in part due to my size. We played on concrete, for the pitch had to be kept for special occasions. We'd put down a couple of jumpers to mark the goal posts and I'd regularly dive onto the concrete, because I was so determined to stop the ball going in.

Like most of the boys at Park Road Primary, I truly believed I was going to make it as a pro. There was a girl in our class who said she was going to be a *Sun* Page 3 model. She was only average looking, but with the typical innocent exuberance of youth we all pretty much believed her.

There was a fierce rivalry between myself and another kid in my year, a guy called Dale Thain. His father was a football coach, and he saw it as his God-given right to be the best in our year at sports. He hated it when I kept winning the sports day races, and especially when my mum also beat his mum in the ladies' sprint!

He grew aggressive with me on the football pitch. At one point just prior to high school he and I were out training together. We talked as lads do about what we wanted to be when we grew up. He told me for the umpteenth time he was going to be a pro footie player. Then he spoke about friends of ours who just 'wouldn't make it', and in the same breath he said the same about me.

Years later I'd remember Dale Thain's words, when there were other naysayers who said I'd never make it in the military. There are always people who are intent on bringing you down. There are always those who are jealous and will try to discredit and undermine you, and put doubt in your head. I learned not to listen to them. If I burned for it brightly enough I'd get there.

Anyhow, by the time Dale was trying his best to put me off football, horse riding had already started to take over as my driving passion in life. We lived in a brick-built box of a house that was set on a postage-stamp square of garden. Dad had built a climbing frame out at the back and I loved it, but there was zero room for indulging my mum's real passion in life outside of our family – which was horses.

Ever since she could remember mum had always loved horses. She had grown up with a farmer's horses in the field next to her home. She'd helped out on the farm and learned to ride that way. She'd been denied the joy of owning a horse as a kid, because her parents couldn't afford it, but she was forever talking about horses.

My mother is incredibly sociable and she was always out meeting people. She ran into this person who owned a horse but didn't have the time or the inclination to ride it much any more. Mum didn't hesitate. She volunteered to be the horse's surrogate owner. Of course, she couldn't leave her kids at home when tending to the horse, so she started taking us whenever she went to the stables.

Mum was dynamic, loving and supportive, and she really wanted us to enjoy the horse as she did. Dad was patient, practical and creative, and in time he'd put his skills into helping us have our own horses, and all that goes with them. But everything has to start somewhere, and right now we started by being that horse's surrogate owners.

The horse was kept at a livery yard – a place where you had to pay to have it stabled. The seriously wealthy would own and operate their own stables, of course, so this was the kind of place to meet the poor man's horsey types. It was peopled by horse dealers, blacksmiths and farriers, and they were some of the most colourful characters you could ever meet.

We befriended a trainer called John. John hailed from a council estate, and he'd started off as a groom before making it as a trainer. He spent a lot of time and effort teaching me how to ride and he became an important part of our family.

Learning to ride was an incredible experience. It required something very different from booting a ball around a field, and I took to it like the proverbial duck to water. There was something totally exhilarating about galloping along on horseback, and I loved working so closely with a real, live animal, one that embodied so much athleticism and power.

One day I cheekily said to mum: 'So, when can we get our own horse?'

I saw this look in her eyes. She had asked the same question of her parents, but they just couldn't manage it financially. Mum decided there and then to make it happen. She saved up £500, which was a lot of money for us back then, and with that she purchased a tough little Welsh mountain pony called Sid.

Having opened my mouth and asked that question, I now had to get one hundred per cent involved. At first it was John who trained me on Sid, but just as soon as I started to show some real promise mum took over.

To me, riding a horse was a manly thing to do. My dad's favourite film was *Once Upon a Time in the West* – the ultimate cowboy movie, which dad and I had watched countless times. The men were hard as nails. Henry Fonda played the baddie, with his steel-blue eyes, Charles Bronson the avenging good guy. The women in it were real women and they fell in love with these all-male heroes.

Dad explained to me why that movie was such a classic. The characters were real and battle-worn, and they were the ultimate genuine tough guys. They went out as small, maverick teams of blokes into the wilderness, and were up against the harsh, unforgiving elements plus their enemies.

Lawrence of Arabia, starring Peter O'Toole, was our other all-time favourite. Lawrence was the ultimate young, maverick, renegade British officer, one who wouldn't take no for an answer. I always remembered the scene at the end where he died on a motorbike speeding through the Dorset countryside, yet feeling totally unencumbered and free. That was exactly how I felt when out riding horses.

I took to Sid instinctively, as did my two sisters, who are both younger than me. Owning a horse is a very physical thing. There's all the grooming, the mucking out, the feeding morning and night, plus the exercise the animal needs. I'd be up early before school to feed Sid, and I'd be down at the stables directly afterwards to take him out for a run.

Eventually, dad managed to buy a small plot of land three miles from our house. We had no money to employ proper builders, so as a family we made our own stables and a barn. Now that we had a small ménage, things started to get more serious. I started to travel with mum all across the country, competing at showjumping events in the Juniors – the under-sixteens.

This was a whole different world compared to the one I was used to. In the UK showjumping is dominated by a handful of very wealthy families. It's a hugely expensive sport, and it wasn't unusual for me to be up against those who'd spend £75,000 on a pony and coaches and grooms for the year – and all to support their ambition for their child to be the best.

I learned pretty quickly that money most certainly can buy success. But I also learned that even without a lot of ready cash, with disciplined training and a good dash of cunning I could still beat those for whom money was no object. And so it was through horses that I first learned to train hard and fight hard for what I wanted, something which would stand me in good stead for the military.

My parents put everything into this family dream. We worked together as a small, close-knit team, and for no significant financial reward. I was competing against those who had blank chequebooks with which to buy the best horses, and with which to run enormous horsebox camper vans-cum-homes, ones that would cost more than our house had.

Together with the thoroughbred horses that those vehicles carried, they'd be taking to the road with a fortune in animals and equipment. We'd turn up at competitions driving a battered Land Rover towing a dented old horse trailer, and with Sid waiting patiently inside.

My mum and I would put in months of training, with her coaching me relentlessly, and all leading up to a few hours in the arena. I'd take Sid around a course of wooden rails and other jumps, trying not to knock any down or have any falls or refusals. And against all the odds, Sid and I started to win.

Eventually, there was one event where I made a silly mistake in the first round, one that resulted in me not going through to the finals. Mum and I argued about what I had done wrong: my selection of path and approach had meant that I'd knocked a post down.

Mum was working full time as a teacher, bringing up three kids, training me in her every spare hour and driving me around half the country to compete. We were a fantastic team, but it was now my time to learn that once you were in the arena you were there alone. I had to figure out for myself just what I had done wrong, and stand on my own two feet if I really wanted to win.

It was a watershed moment.

I went on to compete in a Junior Championship and I did win. I'd learned that I needed to be self-reliant and absolutely single-minded to succeed. Eventually, we managed to buy a delivery van – a decommissioned Big Green Parcel Machine truck – and convert it into a horsebox. But as with the stables, it was a long-term project with my dad doing all of the hard labour.

It reached the stage where I was in my teens and riding horses for rich owners whose daughters had grown more interested in partying and boys. But the real buzz, the greatest kick of all, was beating them at their own game, and using little else but determination, skill and cunning. After Sid, all the horses we ever bought came from Ireland. We never spent more than a few grand on one, and we'd take these wild, spirited Irish gypsy ponies and turn them into champions.

Under our tutelage they'd go from a fairly worthless steed to one that could beat ponies that had cost their owners a fortune by comparison. That taught me an invaluable lesson for the future: you could fight against all the odds and you could still win the day.

My parents were Catholics, and that helped get me into the Catholic school in the neighbouring town, one that was far better than the local comprehensive. The rough kids in my neighbourhood didn't like us in our smart brown St Nicholas's school blazers, and they liked me even less when they saw me out riding horses around the local lanes and fields.

To them, horse riding was a 'poofy' thing that only 'snobs' did. On more than one occasion I took the taunts they threw at me, as they cycled past on their bikes. But one day I snapped.

I'd been out hacking with one of our ponies – one that we'd only recently broken-in. A couple of local kids came charging past on their bicycles. They were around fourteen or fifteen, so a good year older than me. They circled around and started riding their bikes right up to me and the pony, then slamming the brakes on.

As the bikes skidded on the loose gravel, the pony shied and almost bolted, but still they kept on doing it. If the horse threw me here on this road I could fall and break my neck. I knew of someone who'd died that way quite recently. If the horse kicked out with its iron-shod hooves, it could easily kill both of them.

I was wearing a red-and-white striped Puffa jacket, but it had faded to pink with age and the sun. They kept taunting me that I was wearing a pink jacket and that I was a horsey, snobby 'gay-boy'.

Eventually I saw red. I stopped, dismounted, looped the reins around a branch and stood to face them. I was in hand-me-down riding jodhpurs and boots, plus I had a safety hat. They were in tracksuits and trainers. They came at me like it was a dead cert they would smash the fuck out of me.

It didn't happen that way.

One of my primary school mates had a father who was a seriously hard case. He'd once given us some advice. If ever one of us was alone and surrounded by a gang of boys, we should pick out the ringleader and waste no time in head-butting him, and not stop smashing him until he went down. That way, the rest of the gang might well back off.

I'd never forgotten those words, and they came banging into my head right now. I stepped forward and my riding helmet made a smashing, crunching impact on the nearest of my two tormentors' noses. I was so wound up with anger at what they had done that within seconds I'd given the lad a good battering. Seeing the mess that I'd made of his mate, the other kid turned and ran. That was the last trouble I was ever going to have from them, or anyone else on my estate. Riding horses had taught me to really burn for what you wanted in life, and to fight hard and fast and dirty when needed.

That was a crucial lesson I would carry with me into the military, and into selection for The Pathfinders.

*

CHAPTER FOUR

keep my boots by my bunk. They're within arm's reach, so that when we're woken in the midst of the night by a screaming mob of DS intent on dragging us out for yet more torture, I can grab them almost without thinking.

In fact, I've brought two pairs of Lowes with me, both of which are well worn in. The pair I've used today are in the drying room. I've removed the inner soles and stuffed them with newspaper, for the leather is piss wet through.

The drying room is chock-a-block. It's crammed full of all the soaking wet gear from the blokes who've made it this far. The secret is to get your boots near enough to the steaming-hot pipes to dry them, without roasting them to a rock-hard and brittle uselessness.

But even with taking such precautions – switching my boots daily – I know they won't dry completely, and my feet will stay wet through most of the time. It's day six of selection, and already the punishment is really starting to show on our bodies.

There are blokes like Pete who only brought the one pair of shitty Army boots, and by now their feet are practically mummified in zinc oxide tape. In fact, some of the lads may as well have wrapped themselves from head to toe in the stuff, they're falling apart that much.

Zinc oxide is this white, breathable plaster tape. Even with switching my boots daily, I've still had to wrap each of my toes in the stuff. I've also done the back of my heels and the whole of my inner thighs, which are chafed to a raw redness. Plus I've done most of my lower back, where the weight of the Bergen thudding up and down has rubbed it to a bloodied mess.

Each morning I do the ritual. I get out a fresh roll of zinc oxide and I slap a new layer onto those parts of my body that are falling apart. And late at night when the physical and mental abuse is finally over for the day, I de-tape myself so that the parts of me that are blistered, bleeding and sore can breathe.

Each night Pete has to phone home to check in with the wife. He has to climb the hill above the classrooms in the pissing rain to try to get a signal on his mobile, and even then he can barely get the one bar. She knows he's volunteered for this insane punishment, so she's hardly showing any sympathy. It's sheer misery for him.

As for me, I don't have a regular girlfriend right now. I've been dating this chick but it's hardly going anywhere, with me away for weeks on end on selection, or off on operations overseas. In a way I'm glad. While Pete is out treading the rain-lashed hill trying to phone home, I can lay my battered body on my wipe-down plastic mattress.

It's like paradise.

The dropout rate has been fierce. If it keeps going like this, we'll soon be down to just one truckload of blokes. I get talking with the 3 PARA lads – that's Taff, Al and Jez 'The Colonel' – about why so many are failing. We put it down to the lack of training. It's the old adage: fail to prepare, prepare to fail.

They ask me why they didn't see me in Camp on any of the training sessions they did prior to selection. Basically, the 3 PARA lads would check into Sennybridge Camp and go training in pairs, as you're supposed to, and they'd log their route maps at the Camp office before each day's session.

I tell them that the CO of 1 PARA wouldn't allow me any time off to train. The reasons why were complicated, but it meant that I was forced to prepare for selection in my own time, and pretty much alone, and keeping well below the radar.

I took to driving up to the Brecons on a Friday evening directly after work, parking my BMW in a hedge where it couldn't be seen by anyone and kipping in the car. I'd go out alone the following morning and tab over the hills. I'd get chips and beer in a local pub that night, kip in the car, and tab all day Sunday, after which I had the long drive back to Dover Barracks for Monday morning.

'Fucking hell, that's fucking insane,' says Al.

'You're lucky you didn't fall asleep at the wheel,' says Taff.

Jez shakes his head in quiet disbelief. 'Dave, mate, that's way out of order.'

I knew that if anyone saw me kipping in the car, or out tabbing alone, and they recognised me, I'd get reported. If that happened, I'd pretty much get booted off selection before it had even started, for there are strict rules and protocol about how you are supposed to go about training. So if ever I met a pair of blokes out on the hills – doing their prep for selection just as I was – I'd put my head down, barely grunt an acknowledgement and press on.

'You're fucking cracked,' says Al.

'Insane,' says Jez.

Taff nods his agreement.

We've been up before first light on each of the mornings, getting beasted. I dress in cycling shorts worn under a pair of normal running shorts, to try to help with the chafing. If you run the London Marathon, you have helpers along the route handing out tubs of Vaseline. You rub it around your thighs and bollocks to help cope with the sweating and the friction, which can rub you raw.

Here, we're doing the equivalent of a marathon every day, but over horrendous terrain and in appalling weather, and carrying a bloody house on our backs. Yet you won't exactly find the DS handing out tubs of Vaseline as we go. Either you tape-up, man-up and prove you can take the punishment, or you VW.

For those pre-dawn PT sessions I wear a long-sleeved Helly

Hansen lifa vest – one that wicks away the sweat – under my maroon PARA Reg T-shirt. It's there to help ward off the intense cold. For the first few minutes we're out on the parade ground, doing sit-ups, press-ups and short bursts of sprinting, our breath forming a thick cloud of mist in the freezing air.

But just as soon as we move off for the first run of the morning, I rip off the HH vest and I'm down to my maroon T. We run as a pack for an hour and a half with no water stops. It's fast as fuck and we're moving over punishing ground. At various points the DS halt and we're forced to sprint up and down a hill.

Then comes the order we're all of us dreading. 'Right, pick a partner!'

This is where the strength of character side of us is really tested. We are being examined on every facet of our make-up, both physical and mental, and if any of the DS spots a streak of selfishness or naked self-interest, that can get us binned. You can last the course physically, but you can still get rejected in the end because you're not the kind of bloke they want in The Pathfinders. It's their club that you want to join.

You have to choose a partner of approximately your own size. If I tried to do what's coming teamed up with Taff, I'd deserve to get myself binned, and for sure the DS wouldn't fail to notice such jack behaviour. Sadly, there is only one bloke who's about the same size as me. You've guessed it: the Royal Engineers monster.

I hump eighteen stone of angular bone and muscle onto my aching shoulders. *The bastard.* We're ordered to set off uphill, and to keep with the DS. Bloody Arnie keeps slipping and sliding on my back, and I have to keep stopping and humping the colossal weight of him up into the fireman's lift once more.

I'm totally fucked by the end of the first five minutes. I've got rivulets of sweat pouring down my face, and it's going down my back in torrents. I know we've still got an hour twenty-five of this to go. Thankfully, I also know that there's a very good reason why they've made the fireman's carry a key plank of PF selection, and that makes it just a fraction easier for me to deal with.

If I do make it through to The Pathfinders, I'll very likely get deployed on operations far behind enemy lines and in a small team of six operators. At that point we're almost inevitably going to come up against an enemy in far greater strength – so at platoon or company level. We're more than likely going to be heavily outnumbered and outgunned.

For that reason, the standard operating procedure for a PF patrol which comes into contact with the enemy is to put down a wall of intensive fire, and then to break fire and withdraw as quickly as possible. And if one bloke has been shot and wounded in your six-man patrol, you need to be ready to hoik him onto your shoulders and manhandle him out of there.

Knowing why I'm doing this helps with the burning pain of hefting our Arnie look-alike up and down the hills. Over the days I've realised that if I don't flap too much and accept what's coming, I can zone out the worst of the agony. I accept that I'm getting Arnie and that it will hurt like fuck, and somehow that makes it easier to keep moving forward under such a punishing load. Your body can prove far more capable of taking punishment than you ever imagined.

By mid-morning we're back from the first round of the day's torture, and we're straight into the classrooms. The PF believe in joint training, instruction and testing as you go. We each of us need to go through the navigational exercises and pass, to prove we're capable of being thrown onto the unforgiving hills in the midst of a bitter winter.

Pretty soon we'll be moving into week two, which is Hills Week. We'll be setting out in small groups or alone, and with stupendous loads to carry over mind-boggling distances and daunting terrain. It's too dangerous to send blokes out to do that unless they've proved that they're capable of finding their way through the trackless, wind-bitten wilderness and back again.

Over the years men have died on elite forces selection, and that doesn't serve anyone's interests. Hence we carry real, vital, cold weather and survival gear in our Bergens, and we have to prove we know what we're doing before they finally unleash us over the worst of the hills.

While there is no active encouragement in Pathfinder selection, the DS will throw you the odd tip now and then. That's the instruction part of selection. If we're mapping out a mission and a route to take us from A to B, the DS might point out the shortcomings.

'Fair enough, but see there's a sheep track which parallels your bearing – take that, as it's much the easiest route to walk.'

After a lunch that is crammed down us, we're into the four-tonners and out for yet another forced march into the teeth of the cold wind. We're each given a map, but we're not told where exactly we're heading. I always try to keep a watch on where they're driving us, so I can pinpoint exactly where the start point is today.

We head out on a long drive north-west. We're a good hour in the back of the four-tonner, and I just know for sure where we're going. We're headed for the Elan Valley – the Valley of the Shadow of Death, and a place where you sure as hell should fear the kind of evil the terrain and the weather can throw at you.

Only a person who's never tried to tab across the Elan Valley won't fear and respect the place. It's a nightmare.

Sure enough the truck pulls up at the head of the Valley, a place of swirling clouds, hanging cliffs and thick, disorientating mists. It's a place that I know intimately from my lonely training sessions. The tailgate goes down and by now we're being called off the back of the trucks by individual name.

But today, there's one lad who simply refuses to get down. Perhaps he knows the Elan Valley, and is dreading it so much he just doesn't want to go there. Or maybe he's never set eyes on the place before, and he hasn't in his worst dreams imagined that such a place could exist in the length and breadth of this great country of ours.

That young lad proceeds to VW himself. We haven't even set foot in the place yet, and the Elan Valley has defeated at least one of us today.

It's a ten-miler that we'll be doing, and the weight's just gone up to 50 pounds, minus water and food. My legs are feeling strong but tired, and I'm onto the sachets of Lucozade gel by now. I suck one down greedily as I stare into the swirling morass of the Valley, tumbling waterfalls plunging from rock faces to left and right high above us.

My thighs seem to be growing accustomed to the weight. I'm starting to feel more like a machine that eats up the miles. But the kind of prolonged punishment that we're taking here can defeat just about anyone. Unbelievably, we lost Arnie at the end of this morning's PT sessions. Right at the end of the run he twisted his knee and it ballooned like a football.

The bloke is as hard as he looks and he refused to VW. Lenny called him in for an interview, and to try to assess his injury. Arnie argued that he was more than happy to continue. Lenny overruled him. It's a rare exception when the DS refuse to let a bloke go on, for those are exactly the kind of qualities that the PF burn for.

Lenny told the Royal Engineer bloke what was pretty obvious really: if he tried to carry on he'd do irreversible damage to his injured leg. Most people fail themselves. Arnie had refused to, so Lenny was forced to fail him. But he told Arnie to come back and try again when the leg had recovered. The Pathfinders run a summer and a winter selection. If he's fit again by the summer I'm sure Arnie will be back, and with the body and the will to conquer.

In a way I'm relieved. It means no more carrying his monstrous weight up and down those never-ending hills. But on the other hand I'm sad to see him go. Arnie was made for the PF. But Lenny was right. With an injury like that he wouldn't have lasted another day.

Arnie's spoken to no one about it and he's left without a word. But still the news has filtered out to those of us who remain. Arnie had looked indestructible, but just like that he's gone. And with the young lad who's just VWd at the start of the Valley, that'll be two more empty bunks in the Nissen hut tonight, and maybe more.

As we step out into the Valley I can feel my arse chafing badly. I finally gave in this morning and taped it up with zinc oxide. Having a permanently wet bum crack can do bad things to your posture, not to mention your ability to keep walking under a crushing load. But taping up your arse in front of a load of other blokes is still somehow embarrassing.

I pop a couple of Ibuprofen, so as to dull the pain. I've got a bulk supply in my medical kit stuffed deep in my Bergen. In spite of all the precautions I've been taking my feet are badly blistered, and as I start walking I can feel my damp socks rubbing the blisters into a pulp. There's a massive blister on the ball of my left foot, so it's not exactly as if I can keep my weight off it.

The ten-miler through the Elan Valley has to be completed in an hour thirty-five, less if the DS really push it. Unless you've trekked the place, it's hard to understand what an insane pace that means they'll be setting.

We're seven miles in and we're ploughing across a hillside of what we call 'babies' heads'. These are tufts of indestructible bog grass that grow in clumps dotted all across the Valley. The clumps are each roughly the size and shape of a young child's head, hence the name. And of course, they make for horrendous going.

Charging across a field of babies' heads at full tilt someone is bound to twist an ankle. It's freezing cold and the rain starts to turn to sleet and snow. As I plough through the gathering storm, I feel as if I have severed every last tie with civilisation. I am a wild animal heading into the dark heart of the Valley, and man do I fear its evil.

Tricky is the DS leading this forced march. Pete – the stubbornest bloody soldier ever to walk this earth – is next. I stick doggedly to his shoulder, 20 yards behind him. I keep catching him, but then he finds an extra spurt and surges ahead. His bright red face is melting the snow and ice as it hits him. It's dripping down his forehead, the heat throwing off a cloud of steam. He is a big, strong, unbreakable kind of a bloke, but even he looks fucked. I tell myself I'm glad I can't see how I look.

I lean forward into the weight of my pack. Tricky's still in my sights, which is good. The belt strap of my Bergen is vice-tight around my waist, in an effort to stop the pack shifting about, but I can still feel it sawing into me, rubbing away at the zinc oxide tape and working through to the bloody flesh below.

The tape can't adhere properly to my wet and sweat-soaked back. The salt in the sweat works its way into the wounds, and it stings like hell. I try to zone out the pain by dreaming about food. I had a massive cooked breakfast this morning, and an even larger plate for lunch. And for this tab, for this foray into the Valley, I've allowed myself to carry the ultimate in comfort food – a Melton Mowbray pork pie.

I don't give a fuck what Tricky says: the next stop he calls, I'm scoffing it. I opened a couple of cans of Coke over lunch, and allowed them to go flat. I've decanted them into a water bottle. That way, you can neck the sweet, sugary caffeine-filled liquid almost without stopping. That's my morale-booster of last resort.

As I march I find that I've got the words of the Fallschirmjäger song running through my head, over and over again. It was composed for German paratroopers during the Second World War, but every British PARA knows it off by heart. There's an odd kind of a respect between the two airborne units, one that was born out of the blood and guts of that war.

'There's blood on the parachutes ...'

I first learned the Fallschirmjäger during P Company selection, but there have been a few muted renderings of it late at night in the Nissen hut over the past few days. Anything – in an effort to keep our morale from flagging completely and our spirits from falling through the floor.

Tricky's pulling away from me now. Between him and me there's the solid figure of Pete pounding onwards. I glance uphill and to my left, and I see a group of figures overtaking us and powering onwards into the gloom. They're plastered in frozen mud, and they are laden down with packs just as heavy as our own. It's The Pathfinder wolf-pack, every member of the unit having opted to join us in this march across the Valley.

Carrying the dummy rifle is a total bitch. I try to keep swinging it to help with the momentum, but I'd far prefer to be able to use my hands to grab the shoulder straps of my Bergen, to help with the load. As I watch the Pathfinders disappear into the distance, I feel small and bent double, like a broken old man, there's so much weight and embuggerance upon me.

The bulk's been dropping off of me during the past few days, as my body starts to consume its own mass like emergency fuel. By contrast, the Pathfinder blokes seem massive in comparison. They've got incredible upper body strength, as a result of doing endless rounds of fast-roping from helicopters, plus HALO and HAHO jumps.

The PF pack is tight and together and it's working as one machine, one living breathing animal of war. They appear to me like Range Rovers powering through the terrain, while I feel as if I'm a clapped-out Ford Escort, one that's fast running out of fuel and oil.

The Pathfinder pack had set out after us on the same route as we are following. They're using selection as an excuse to get in some seriously testing additional training. I'm totally fucked and my back feels broken, and I've looked up to see that lot of invincible warriors go powering past.

But in a strange way I find it uplifting. I burn to be amongst their number, and I know that each and every one of them has been through the hell of what I'm going through now, and made it out the other side. There's no other way into their number, and that's the challenge and the very beauty of it all.

Seeing them surging ahead spurs me onwards. I don't know what it's done for the others – for Pete before me, and Al and Jez directly to my rear. It may have done the opposite. It may have made them feel isolated and unworthy. But for me, it's simply a question of how much you really want it and how far you're willing to go.

It's the first time I've seen The Pathfinders moving as one unit. There's a tendency to think that PF and SAS are all big, monstrous blokes. For sure, there are some real Arnie look-alikes in their number. But there are just as many smaller, leaner guys too. It's the inner confidence shining out of them that makes them look so impressive. Who wouldn't want to join them?

Not a man amongst them wears any mark of rank or insignia. If anyone is captured by the enemy, they want to be carrying nothing that might give away who or what they might be. I know that if I get through this I'll be second-in-command of one extraordinary bunch of warriors, and I absolutely cannot allow even one of them to see me fail.

Up ahead Tricky begins to slow. He went fast as fuck at the start, to weed out any remaining slackers, but finally he pulls to a halt beside the four-tonners. There's no sickener this time, which is kind of fortunate. I can't stand. My legs are moving involuntarily, twitching and shivering and spasming of their own accord.

I collapse into the open truck back and wait for the rest to come in. Taff has been right behind me all the way, pushing me onwards at every turn. He marches in, and as he does so he mouths at me 'NO FEAR'.

We sit together and wait for the rest of the pack. I feel an overwhelming sense of achievement as we stare into the plunging void behind us, one that's a flurry of thickening sleet and snow. I've made it through the Valley and I've passed week one of selection. And I was one of the very first in.

Al is next in. The bloke's hard as nails and he's just too solid and concrete to feel very much pain. Mark the Kiwi is close behind him, his big horsey teeth showing as he gasps for air, his hair plastered in sweat across his forehead. I wonder for an instant if he wishes now he'd taken up the place they'd offered him as a trainee officer.

Jez marches in on Mark's heels, his bald head shining dully

through the gloom. No doubt about it, the guy's a real trier and he's not one for giving in. But he still looks completely out of place in this environment. Fittingly, his nickname here on selection has fast become 'The Colonel'.

We count the last of them in. We're down to eighteen blokes. Week one is done and dusted, and more than half of those who started selection have been culled. At the end of the ten-miler through the Elan Valley the jack wagon's pretty much full to bursting.

We drive back to Camp. I feel exhausted but elated. It's a Friday and there are more weeks to go, but week one has done what it's designed for. It's seriously culled the pack. Come Sunday it'll be Hills Week, when we're unleashed into the mountains alone and with miles of trackless terrain to navigate, and regardless of the weather conditions. But at least I'm through week one.

Stan Harris gathers those of us who remain on the parade ground. It's dusk, and the odd flurry of snow whips around our faces.

'Right: week one down,' he announces. 'For those who remain – make sure weapons are clean and handed in to armoury. Shower. Then get the fuck out of Camp. If you're an orphan, you can stay in the block.'

'Orphan' means you have no family to go to, or no wife or girlfriend. That's pretty much me.

'Report back 'ere for scoff at 0800 hours Sunday morning, when you're going out for your first real walkabout. Bergens start at 45 pounds. There'll be a notice up on the board from Saturday night for what maps you need. You've got three walkabouts, then Test Week starts proper.'

He pauses, and there's maybe just the hint of a smile. 'That's it. Fuck off. You're good to go.'

*

CHAPTER FIVE

━━━━━

A mate of mine at high school had started competing in speedway. I'd go to watch him, and I'd see him flip his motorbike and come off and break the odd bone or two. Speedway was fast and exciting, but to me there wasn't anything like the same teamwork or skill involved as there was when working with a live animal.

Our entire family pitched in to nurture and train the horses. That meant that the pressure was higher, but so was the intensity and so were the potential rewards. What I loved most was that there was no rank or status or cash advantage when you finally got into the showjumping arena. That was the greatest leveller of all.

As I rose in the sport I loved to go up against those mega-rich competitors and beat them at their own game. I thrilled to feel the horse's stride and its rhythm, and to become as one with the animal. That was the secret to winning, the key to succeeding against all the odds.

In showjumping the first round is generally a non-timed event, when all you need to worry about is scoring a clear round – making it over the jumps. Round two is the jump-off, which is run strictly against the clock. It involves much tighter turns and much greater speed, as horse and rider push themselves to achieve the fastest round.

A variation on the theme is the Puissance. You start with a jump which is basically a wall made of heavy wooden blocks. Each round the wall keeps going higher, and you have to keep getting your horse over it. The Puissance is a game of nerves, pure and simple. One day my mum explained all of this to me, before telling me: 'David, you'd be good at this. You really would.'

It was great to have her say that to me. In her view, I'd be good at a game of nerves like the Puissance. It boosted my confidence and it inspired me. In the Puissance the horse almost never refuses a jump. It's the rider that does. Or rather, the horse can sense that the rider is bottling it, and so it in turn baulks at the jump.

Sure enough, I loved doing the Puissance. It led on to me competing in the Pentathlon, in which you run, swim, shoot, fence and ride horses. I could turn my hand to fencing out of pure athletic ability, and running and swimming too. But pistol shooting truly had me stumped. It required mastering a weapon, a machine, and that requires serious levels of training that I just hadn't had.

The name Pentathlon comes from the Greek word for 'five' – *pent*. The discipline originated in ancient Greece, and it consisted of the five key skills that the Ancient Greeks determined were crucial in battle. It was real Jedi Warrior stuff, and the modern form of Pentathlon was based upon the skills needed by a 19th-century warrior working behind enemy lines.

But with shooting, the harder I tried the worse I seemed to get. I found it hugely frustrating. If you tried too hard you'd snatch the shot. What you needed to do was relax into the shot and gently squeeze the trigger, with your hand and arm providing the vice within which you achieved deadly aim. That's the only way to reliably hit the target time after time, as opposed to snatching at the trigger. But I hadn't learned any of this yet, and my failure to master shooting really got to me.

I was fifteen years old when I had to do work experience at school, and while most of my mates went to shops and offices around the area I did mine with a horse dealer friend. Simon Ferguson was of Irish origin, though he'd been brought up in Manchester, and he worked me half to death. The guy had to graft to turn a profit, so I figured it was fair enough really.

I was exercising five ponies a day, plus mucking them out and feeding them. Some of the horses were like wild bulls. It was my job to break them in – to tame them – and I got thrown just about every day. While my mates were office boys making tea, I was lifting bales of hay or getting tossed through the air. I needed two baths every evening to get rid of all the muck, and to soak my aching limbs.

Simon Ferguson was a great trainer with buckets of experience, so even as I worked I was gaining invaluable know-how. He was also a one in a million character. He was obnoxious, rude and gobby, but he'd have my mum and me crying with laughter. He had jet-black hair and was missing a couple of front teeth. He was also tough as old boots, a real pirate and a renegade.

He took me to all these posh, horsey shows, and he just didn't seem to give a damn. He'd see a fit woman dressed in figure-hugging jodhpurs and he'd yell out in his thick accent: 'Oi! Just look at the arse on that!'

It was exactly what every other man present was thinking, but would not ever say. I loved those weeks I spent with Simon. They were a real education for me. The hard intimacy with nature, plus the physical exertion and the closeness to animals really did it for me. I loved the adrenaline-rush of it all. But it was clear to Simon – as it was increasingly becoming to me – that my days of competing on horseback were numbered.

I'd grown too tall and too heavy, and several times my feet hit the poles and knocked them flying. I'd cracked my ankles on the jumps, because the horse just couldn't lift my bulk high enough. I was now amongst the top dozen Junior showjumpers in the UK. I was Central Scotland's Junior Champion. I'd even competed at the Horse of the Year Show in Wembley, and come fifth in the British Juniors.

I had more than proved I could hold my own with the best. I was competing against famous families who had generations of top showjumpers behind them ... and I was winning. But once I turned sixteen and went into the Seniors the whole ball game would change. In the Juniors, I could take a pony that cost less than a grand and beat a horse that cost a hundred times that. But not in the Seniors.

At that level the competition is international. You're up against wealthy Arab sheikhs and you need either serious levels of cash or a major sponsorship deal to compete. It's like the equivalent of going from go-kart racing to Formula One. And even if I could somehow rustle up the millions I'd need to compete at that level, it still didn't alter the fact that at six foot two and growing I was simply getting too big.

The let-down was massive. I hadn't in any way failed at what I loved. In fact, it was my body that had outgrown my dreams.

I was sixteen years old when I was forced to seriously ease off on the showjumping. I hungered for a new challenge to fill the void, and school – academia – really wasn't doing it for me. I'd done pretty well so far, taking two GCSEs – Maths and French – early. Mum and dad were pushing for me to go on to university. But I was bored of sitting in classrooms studying all day long.

My speedway mate was older than me and he had a car. I looked bigger and older than I really was, and we started going clubbing. We'd drive into Manchester and go to The Haçienda and rave the night away, or we'd hit Cream in Liverpool or Kinetic in Stoke-on-Trent. I had a bit of cash due to my showjumping wins, and he had his from speedway, so we ventured out into the wider world, which comes complete with all its dangers.

One night we were out on the town in Northwich and hanging out in a park. Parts of Northwich are quite rough and rival gangs would rove about during the hours of darkness. The park was full of fifteen- to eighteen-year-olds drinking cheap booze, and I was used to the odd fight kicking off. But this night it really blew up big time, in a massive football hooligan style street battle.

Weapons were involved – coshs, iron bars, knives and

knuckle-dusters – and mates of mine ended up a real mess. I remember thinking to myself: *This is getting well out of hand. Sooner or later someone's going to get hurt bad, or even killed.* A lot of my mates were leaving school to take up apprenticeships in the local factories. I figured I needed to get out of town and away from the kind of trouble that was brewing, but I didn't have a clue as to how or where.

Mum encouraged me to go to a nearby careers fair. There were reps from all the usual industries giving their patter, but none of it did it for me. Then I came across a stand put on by the Army. Compared to the rest, the Army's was Gucci and slick. There was a man and a woman presenting the military's case, and they struck me as being smart, charismatic, confident and self-possessed.

But what really gripped me was the sense of adventure and of getting into the wild outdoors. They asked me about my grades at school, and they told me with grades like that I should try for an officer candidacy. They told me that the Army's sixth form college was the place for me, and as far as I could tell it sounded like it would cover all of the bases.

I could sit my A-levels, which would keep my folks happy. I'd get well into the outdoors and the adventurous life, working in small teams on the military exercises. I could opt not to go on to university, but instead go direct into one of the Army's undermanned corps.

'If you join us you'll get to see the world and travel to lots of exotic places,' the recruiters told me. 'You'll do water-skiing, skiing, parachuting, even surfing if you want. You only have to commit to three years, and there are a whole range of regiments with different functions that you can choose from.'

I was sold. I'd started to see some of my mates getting into serious trouble fighting, or with petty crime, or even dealing drugs. This was my ticket out of all of that.

Being teachers, my parents had several weeks' holiday every summer. We'd move as a family to Abersoch, a fishing village on the Welsh coast. We'd camp and I'd spend the time out scaling the sea cliffs and fishing with my dad. We'd climb a cliff, drop down to a deserted cove and knock limpets off the rocks to use as bait. We'd hook out the flesh with a pocket knife, and impale it on the hook.

Dad was big into sea fishing, and so was I. Whatever the weather down at Abersoch, we had to go into the sea every day and swim. That was a family rule. Even if it was freezing cold, the sea would still energise you. A quick dip in the freezing Irish Sea would re-set your clock and get your pulse racing.

My parents had taught me a love of the outdoors, one that I'd taken with me into horse riding. And now I felt I could continue that love affair in the Army.

The Army's Welbeck College was based at Welbeck Abbey, the former home of the 5th Duke of Portland. Basically, Welbeck is an enormous and very grand country house set in massive grounds. As an added bonus for me, one of the UK's first ever riding schools was founded there, one that was second only in size to the Spanish riding school in Vienna. There was even an underground ballroom sited beneath the building, it was that grand.

The first time I went to visit I had never experienced anything like it before. Dad, mum and me drove through these two gateposts topped off with imposing lion statues and down this half-mile-long drive. We pulled to a halt and were met by these students in their smart blazers, going: 'Good morning, ma'am; Good morning, sir,' to my mother and father.

We were shown around the College, and every time an officer cadet walked past we'd get the same treatment: a crisp 'Good morning sir, good morning, ma'am'. It was in stark contrast to my home town, where gangs of kids hung around street corners in baseball caps or hoodies, menacing passers-by and smoking and drinking.

Here you had kids who were determined to make something of themselves. They were fit and healthy and had a wholly positive attitude. The gymnasium was fabulous, there was a great climbing wall, a superlative boxing ring, a fine rowing club, plus a lake to row on, and acres of grounds in which to run.

My parents had never considered that one of their children might go into the military. They had no experience of the British Army, and no friends with kids in the services. It was the early 1990s, and the most serious recent conflict the British Army had been involved in was the Falklands War.

Since then there had been the First Gulf War, during which there were fewer than fifty British casualties. The Cold War was well over, and it was fifty years or more since the Second World War. To them, there seemed little chance of soldiering ever becoming a particularly dangerous kind of career.

You have to do a three-day mini selection course to get into Welbeck. I did mine and we duly got the letter that formally offered me a place. Shortly thereafter I received what looked like a bunch of ID tags in the mail. They were these tough canvas labels, on each of which was printed 'WCK135'. That it seemed was my Army number, and every item of clothing that we had to buy – shirts, blazers, even underwear – had to have one of those sewn into it.

It was now that I started to have some second thoughts. Most of my mates were growing their hair long, dressing in ripped-up denims and getting what seemed like well-paying jobs in local garages or factories, yet I had been given an Army number and was poised to take the plunge into the great unknown.

Mum drove me to Welbeck. She dropped me off, and then she sat there in the car and cried her heart out. I was the oldest child and the first to leave home. I was sixteen, and I was flying the nest and I'm not surprised that she cried. There didn't seem much of a chance that I would get myself killed in the Army, but who knew?

I left her in tears in the car, and took the long walk down a drive lined by serried ranks of tall poplar trees. I was shown to a room with three other new boys. It was spartan to put it mildly. There were four single beds, each with a hard mattress and the ubiquitous

Army dog blanket. I sat on the mattress and opened the bedside drawer. All it contained was a copy of the Holy Bible.

The other lads looked about as clueless as I did. We did the introductions. I was sharing a room with Gareth, Benny and Matt. Gareth had a crooked, broken nose beneath a mop of blond hair pushed over to one side. He was full of bubbling, nervous energy, and he looked a real laugh. He had a thick Brummie accent, and I knew instinctively that he and I would get on.

Benny hailed from Portsmouth, so he was a southern lad. He was calmer and quieter, but again he had a ready smile. As for Matt, he was the serious one of the four of us. There was a nervy intensity about him that gave him a strangely Hitler-esque air. It wasn't much helped by the fact that he bore an uncanny resemblance to the German wartime leader.

Someone came into our room from the Seniors. He was dressed in a blue blazer above grey flannel trousers, with a maroon tie. He announced that we were in Harland House, and that the rival House was York. I didn't have the faintest clue what he meant, but he made it sound of vital importance. He told us to follow him down to the 'stores' so we could draw our 'equipment'.

We filed downstairs and into the basement. We passed by the parade ground, a cobbled area with officer cadets hurrying to and fro and carrying shiny briefcases. The Senior guy pointed out those wearing blue ties. They apparently were from York House, and it sounded as if they were pretty much the enemy.

Kit issued, we were straight into the Basic Physical Fitness Test – the BPFA. In theory, every soldier in the Army does the BPFA every year and has to pass. It starts with a one-and-a-half-mile run. As I glanced around at the other boys, I could see that some fancied themselves as serious runners. They had all the Gucci gear. I was in an old vest and a pair of soccer shorts.

I set off like a bullet from a gun. But this was a 1.5-miler across rough country, with some uphill sections, and I soon started to fall behind. While I was athletic, I didn't have the stamina required for cross-country. By the time I reached the finish I was second to last and the only person behind me was a girl.

I had been knocked down a good peg or two. I knew then that I couldn't busk it here at Welbeck, as I had been doing at school.

We headed directly inside, and were quickly onto the pull-up bars and down on the floor doing press-ups and squats. I didn't score so badly in the gymnasium, for I was naturally strong and had the advantage of my physique. But overall I was somewhere near the bottom of the table, due to my abysmal performance in the cross-country.

One and a half miles was the longest that I had ever run. I felt bad being at the back of the pack and close to being a failure.

I vowed to make it the last time in my life that I was ever there.

*

CHAPTER SIX

With week one of selection done and dusted, all those of us who remain have one precious day off. I drive into Brecon town, my legs cramping up the whole of the way. I eat as much as I can and then I score a trolley-load of bags of ice from the freezer section in Iceland. I also purchase a bath plug from a local hardware store.

I return to Camp. I've read up on how top athletes go about trying to recover from competitions, and I am planning to do the same now. There are only two baths in the whole of Camp, and it's a truism that squaddies steal anything that isn't bolted down. Neither bath has a plug – hence my visit to the Brecon ironmongers.

It is the first day of February as I fill the bath full of freezing cold water, then tip my bags of ice-cubes in. Inch by tortured inch I lower my battered and raw frame until I am submerged, bollocks and all. Needless to say, it is sheer torture, but what it is supposed to do is freeze your outer limbs, as the blood retreats from the extremities of the body to keep the vital core alive.

You have to stay in for as long as you can stand it, and when you get out you're supposed to experience this incredible rush like a real drugs high, as the blood surges back into your arms, legs, toes and fingers. As the blood pumps back into the veins, it's supposed to flush the toxins out – those that have built up during the days of physical abuse – especially the lactic acid. Then you have a hot shower, lie in the ice again and keep doing it for as long as you can.

That is the theory. In practice, it would probably have been less painful to stab myself in the eye repeatedly with a pair of scissors.

I return to the Nissen hut. It's practically empty. There's only a bare handful of us 'block-rats' left. Pete has gone home to the wife, in Aldershot. Al is still there, but I much prefer it with all the blokes and the buzz. I spend the day sleeping, stretching off and watching a war film on a DVD player Al has brought with him. A typical PARA, Al has nothing other than war films.

Come Monday, for the next four days we'll be doing walkabouts on the hills. The concept of the walkabout is one that originated with the Australian Aborigines. At somewhere around the age of sixteen every Aboriginal boy goes out into the bush alone, to walk a route – one of the walkabouts – to prove he is ready to become a man. It is a rite of passage, marking a transition into the adult, warrior phase of life.

The walkabout is also a spiritual journey, for each route is closely linked into the concept of The Dreaming – the Aboriginal spirit worship that is embodied in the landscape. I don't know about the spiritual side of the walkabout in Pathfinder selection, but the concept of the rite of passage rings true: selection is the rite of passage into this elite unit that we each long to be a part of.

At the crack of dawn on Monday morning we set off in one group of nine led by Tricky and Stan Harris. I take the first turn navigating a leg across the Brecons. I have to brief the DS on where I think we are and where north lies, then orientate the map and start leading the stick to point A. I do so using my finger as a pointer, and I've barely started before I get torn apart by the DS.

'What the fuck d'you think you're doing?' Tricky demands, incredulously. 'Everything you do in the PF has to be fucking precise. Exact. Not general. It's crucial you indicate exactly where you are and the route you intend to take. The end of your fucking finger covers a good half a kilometre on this map. It's about as precise as my aim when I'm out taking a shit on the hills.'

'Fine him two quid,' Stan Harris growls. 'He's an officer. He's got to be fucking loaded.'

There's no point saying anything or arguing. I want to join their club, and that makes them right.

'Imagine you're briefing the Brigade Commander for real,' Tricky continues. 'He'll be tired and stressed and he'll have zero time, so he needs exactitude. You only ever use the corner of your compass to mark out a position.' He grabs the map and demonstrates. 'So it's: Sir, north is that way; our position is here; enemy position is here; this is our line of departure for the attack.'

The DS have already banged into us the first golden rule of navigation, which is to trust absolutely to your compass. As long as you keep it away from magnets and from metal, it will never lie. But you can't always simply follow an exact compass bearing, as today's exercise will show.

My leg of the navigation done, Jez takes over. The Colonel seems good enough at map-reading and plotting a route, but it's when we get going that things start to go a bit pear-shaped. I've got my map folded into a see-through plastic map case. It's tied on a piece of paracord to the side pocket of my combat trousers. Jez keeps his map in the same pocket but free. It's blowing a hooley on the tops of the hills. He takes his map out to check and the wind whips it away.

Tricky hammers into him. It's bad enough simply losing your map, especially if you're on your own. You then have bugger all chance of navigating your way out of there, or avoiding the enemy positions. Plus a folded map lost on the battlefield would very likely be found by the enemy. It would give them vital clues. They'd know that someone was out there somewhere in the terrain covered by the folded map, which meant that someone with a map written in English was deep inside their country.

It wouldn't take a rocket scientist to work out that it had to be British or allied Special Forces.

Jez continues with his leg of the navigation. Trouble is, in an effort to stick exactly to his compass bearing he leads the nine of us over some impassible terrain. You can't execute a recce mission like this. You have to adapt your chosen bearing to the terrain and it's often quicker to dogleg around an obstruction, sticking to the contours as much as possible.

It's sheeting down with rain mixed with a splattering of sleet, and if nothing else, going straight up the kind of peaks Jez wants to take us over will freeze us half to death. Then the fog rolls in. No way can we stick to Jez's chosen route, which is the death march from hell.

The DS take over. They steer us along a series of sheep-paths that are just about navigable in the conditions. At least that way we get ourselves off the exposed mountainside where Jez had led us. It's a lesson well-learned, and one you can only really appreciate from direct experience. Adapt the route to suit the terrain, and with a view to what's possible in the weather.

Next, we're broken down into pairs. I'm teamed up with Al, one of the next biggest blokes after me – the reason being that if he goes down with an injury or exposure, I'll have a chance of being able to manhandle him off the moors, and vice versa. While he's not the brightest spark ever, he's as strong as an ox, plus his navigation is bloody impressive, especially for a ranker and a PARA.

Day four of the walkabouts involves Al and me doing a twenty-miler over the Brecons. If you're over the time limit by a small amount they may allow you to continue with selection, because the weather conditions are so atrocious right now. In severe weather allowances can be made. But neither Al nor I want to run the risk, for neither of us wants to get lock-on right now. Test Week starts tomorrow, and that means a black-and-white pass or a fail.

Al and me actually enjoy the twenty-miler. Together, we're a shit-hot team. He's cool as a cucumber across the hills, and my micro-navigation is getting better all the time. A week and a half on PF selection has improved it no end, and my confidence is at a high. I feel more than ready to smash it into Test Week, and get it done.

Thursday dawns and we're down to seventeen men. We've lost just one to the walkabouts. None of the blokes that I've grown close to has binned it, which is a big bonus. Test Week consists of four Test Marches. Each is a Point-to-Point, with the DS manning checkpoints at the highest peaks on the hills. That way, we are forced to follow the most punishing routes possible.

Test March One starts at the Beacons Reservoir, where I slept in my BMW during my weeks of secret, solo training. From there you split into two groups. One does the circuit clockwise, the other anti-clockwise – which is what I get. During walkabout we've learned the rules for the Test Marches. We are not permitted to use any tracks that a vehicle could drive down, and that of course includes roads.

As a Pathfinder operating for real you avoid such routes and go cross-country, and you try to stick to the most inhospitable terrain possible. You do so for a very simple reason. In bogs and swamps, bone-dry desert and impenetrable jungle there are likely to be few other human beings, let alone any heavy concentrations of enemy forces. Isolation and the deep wilderness equates to safety.

In Test Week you are allowed to follow minor footpaths and sheep trails. When moving from point to point you're supposed to scan the way ahead, to pick up on those trails that parallel the way you want to go. Any open path will prove far faster than trying to struggle through thick undergrowth or over acres of punishing babies' heads.

Today's Point-to-Point is very much against the clock. We'll need to average four kilometres an hour, not accounting for the sharp climbs and the plunging descents. The real speed we'll need to go at is far faster. We have to hit a number of checkpoints, whereupon they will radio in our safe arrival and our exact time.

I adopt the plan of going hard early, rather than saving myself for the end. I do so in case I make a navigation error, and have no time to correct myself at the end. Plus I want to get time in the bag, in case I suffer an injury or the weather closes in. That way, I'll have time to play with and hopefully get myself through.

I reckon the real pace we have to average is six kilometres an hour. I'll go hard early and make seven and a half klicks, and ease off to five at the end. I've strapped an external pouch onto the side of my Bergen, so I can keep a pair of water bottles handy and drink from those on the move. If you lose a minute per water stop, ten stops amounts to ten minutes, and that could make the difference between a pass and a fail.

I've got Lucozade in the water bottles, so I can bang down some glucose as I go. I've also got a shitty packed lunch from Camp in my Bergen, including cheap, horrible sausage rolls and Mars bars, but who knows if I'll have the time to stop to neck any of that. At least with the bottles of energy drink I can grab and sup on the move.

I am the last to set off on the Point-to-Point. The DS hold me back until the end, because overall I've come first on most of the previous Test Marches. I'm actually ahead of any other bloke on selection, Pete included. The Point-to-Point is 40 kilometres, and the route starts by going directly up this massive, awe-inspiring feature that looms over the Beacons Reservoir like an apparition: the infamous Pen y Fan.

It offers a near-vertical climb up this massive, sugarloaf-shaped dome of a mountain. The most direct way to tackle it is to zigzag up the face all the way to the summit. You move across the face of the hill, taking short ten-metre legs that switch back across each other, and while doing so you're always on the lookout for short sections of sheep trail that will help you climb.

I've trained here repeatedly, so I know 'The Fan' very, very well. It's one thousand metres straight up, and it's a killer. You reach the summit, only to find a precipitous slope plunging off into the gloom on the far side. So steep is the drop that you can't even see the lower sections, for they're shielded from view by the gradient above.

But what makes this the worst is that the drop bottoms out at a stream, whereupon there's a second thousand-foot climb to a further peak, which is almost exactly like the first. With dark humour the PF lads call this 'VW Valley'. It's shaped in profile like a V or an inverted W, but more to the point this is where so many on selection decide to voluntarily withdraw.

It's impossible to slide down the slope, because you'd quickly spin out of control and kill yourself. You can't drop your Bergen, either, because you'd never find it again, or it would tear itself to pieces. All you can do is thunder down the incline, trying to take the punishment and stay on your feet, and not be bowled over by the weight of your pack.

A lot of blokes reach the bottom of VW Valley and have the same thought: *Fuck this – it's day one of Test Week and already I'm dying.* That's why it claims so many victims.

There is another way to tackle VW Valley, and that's to handrail around it, trying to stick to the contours. By doing so you avoid a great deal of the punishing gradient, but you have to cover an extra four kilometres or so. I opt to go directly up and over and down and up again. In my book four klicks out of your way will cost too much time.

I've experimented with both options during training, and I reckon the direct route is faster, and making it within the set time limit is everything.

I reach the top of the second climb with my rifle gripped in one hand, having made my second thousand-foot ascent. I'm hyperventilating as I practically crawl onto the flatter, windswept terrain of the summit. My legs feel as if they're on fire, but I keep them moving. I grab a bottle from the side pocket of my Bergen, suck down a blast of Lucozade and keep going.

But I have to admit that by now I'm feeling seriously unsettled.

I set off last, and I expected to see a rake of blokes ahead of me. Instead, there's not another figure within sight in any direction. I question whether I made a shit call going the direct route. I wonder if it's my mind playing tricks on me.

I hit a sheep trail I remember from training and I up the pace, as I wait for the burning in my legs to fade. The path will take me around to the first checkpoint, of that I'm certain. I double it, and on the very tip of the summit I spot a couple of DS crouched in a tiny green two-man tent. It's a miracle the thing hasn't blown away in the wind.

I try to approach the checkpoint looking less fucked than I feel. I reach the entrance and go down on one knee, so my face is level with that of the DS. I pull out my map, orientate it with the compass to north and yell out my name.

'Blakeley, Staff!'

'Right, Blakeley, show me where you are.' The accent is a thick Scots one, and he's a PF bloke I don't recognise.

I place the corner of the compass at the exact point on the map where we are. 'Here, Staff.'

There's a momentary pause as the DS studies the map. He eyes me, suspiciously. 'You sure, Blakeley?'

For a moment I wonder if I've fucked up. I run my eye across the map just to make certain. 'Yes, Staff.'

There's the trace of a smile. All he was doing was fucking with my head. He glances around at the grey, leaden sky, and the wind-whipped bog grass, which is rippling like the ocean as fierce gusts tear across it.

'Nice day, isn't it, Blakeley? Lovely scenery.'

He's wasting my time, for he knows I'm against the clock. But I can't simply say 'stop being a twat and let me get on my way', for obvious reasons.

'Yes, Staff.'

He grins. But it's a crocodile smile. 'You know where you're going next, anyway, don't you, Captain Blakeley?'

'No, Staff.'

I can't admit to having learned the routes from someone else who's done selection and to having rehearsed them time and time again. There's nothing in the rule book that says you can't, but it would be taking the piss to openly admit it.

'Captain Blakeley, you're a fucking liar.'

'Yes, Staff.'

A long pause. 'Grid 967824.'

That's where the next checkpoint is. I have to point it out to him on the map.

'Get going,' he tells me.

I move off a good twenty metres and try and get my bearings, so as to choose my route. It's then that I see a figure labouring up to the checkpoint behind me. I'm shocked to see that it's Pete. He set off several places ahead of me. I wonder where the hell he's been and what can have kept him.

It turns out he tried to handrail it around VW Valley, sticking to the contours. He's looking seriously fucked, and I can tell he's regretting making that call. He's also up against it time-wise now. I like Pete and I feel for the bloke as he powers off ahead of me, trying to win himself back some vital seconds.

Today's Point-to-Point is a full circuit that takes you right back to where you started, at the Beacons Reservoir. The final section consists of a massive ridge that continues for six kilometres. By the time I reach it the weather's cleared into a crisp but sunny winter's day, and the visibility is fantastic. From up here on the roof of the world I can see for miles and miles.

I finish off by zigzagging down the last killer slope, and it's a real buzz to make it into the final checkpoint and get weighed back in. We've been allowed seven hours to do this first Test March. I've done it with a full fifty minutes to spare. I set off last, but when I climb onto the four-tonner it's empty. I'm first back in.

The rest of the lads make it okay – Al, Jez, Taff, Mark and even Pete, who manages to make up the lost time. But there are a couple of blokes who got as far as VW Valley and canned themselves. We're on a card system now. If you come in just a few minutes over time on a Test March, you get a yellow card. Two of those and you're done for. But if you VW you VW, and you're out of here.

There are two more Test Marches to go, before the big one – Endurance. Tab two is over the Black Mountains, so not far from the Brecons. It's rainy and foggy for the entire day and it's depressing. The ground is sodden underfoot and we're all of us overjoyed to get off those hills. There was more navigation required, so I've been slower, but I still make it in with forty-five minutes to spare. I'm flying.

Test March three is through the Elan Valley, so the worst is saved to last. We're split into two groups of equal numbers, half doing Elan South and half Elan North. It's so that you don't have so many blokes out on the same route that you can actually follow each other. In theory, Elan South and North are equally challenging. In practice, everyone wants Elan South anticlockwise.

I get Elan South, but I get it the other way around – clockwise. That way, there are fewer footpaths that you can motor along and you'll only make it with minutes to spare, no matter how good you are. It's mostly babies' heads all the way, and that kind of terrain is a total bitch no matter how fit and strong you are or how good your navigation might be.

We've all been trying to save one of our lives for the Elan Valley. That's also been part of the logic of me going hard early on in our first two Test Marches. I've trained on Elan South with a light pack and I only just made it in time. Now I'm carrying 50 pounds, plus food and drink. And when I trained for it I wasn't buggered from all that had gone before.

We're allowed six hours for the Elan Valley. I've dressed in thin jungle-style trousers for it, in spite of the cold. The logic is that I'll be falling into bogs the whole way, and I need to be wearing something that is light and will dry rapidly. On my upper half I've got a US Army T-shirt that wicks away the sweat, plus a windproof smock. That's all.

When I'm moving I'll be warm enough. If I stop for any length of time I'll freeze. But with all the extreme exertion I'll overheat and burn up if I wear any more layers. On my hands I've got black Army leather gloves, with the tops of the fingers cut off. That way I can still grab my map and compass easily, but they go some way to keeping my hands warm. As with my boots I've got two pairs of gloves, for one is always soaking wet after a day on the hills.

My head is bare. I've got a woolly hat in my smock pocket, which I can bang on if it gets seriously cold. But it's from your head that you lose some 80 per cent of your body heat, and I need to leave it free so I can let it burn off whatever builds up inside. I've got some oat cereal bars stuffed alongside the hat. I can bang them down me as I go, for the apricots in them make them moist enough to swallow.

To reach the first checkpoint you have to go up and over a savage feature. It's so cold with the icy winds whipping up the Valley that in places the ground is frozen solid. The chances of taking a fall when crossing one of those are pretty high. I decide to try and be clever. The lower I stay the less frozen ground I'll have to cover. I'll climb to a level where I reckon I can contour around, and that's the route I'll follow.

I get halfway up the massive flank of the mountain and my alternative path snakes off into the gloom. I move off following it, but fairly quickly the ground underfoot starts getting soft and boggy. I stumble into the first bog and I plunge downwards up to my waist in the stinking shit. I'd stood on what I'd thought was a baby's head, but instead it sank like a stone, taking me with it.

There's a moment of sheer panic when I wonder if I've truly hit the bottom, or whether I'll just keep sinking. Some of these bogs are deep and they're like quicksand: they can quite easily swallow up a bloke as big as me. I spread out my arms to either side, to act as a brake in case the mire keeps pulling me downwards. I come to a halt with the gunk up around my chest level.

Fucking nice one.

I wade forwards and somehow I manage to drag myself out. I haul myself onto solid ground, gasping from the effort, and I'm caked practically from head to toe in black, acrid, shitty muck. I take a few steps further forwards and I plunge into the next one. The trouble is I'm committed to this route now. If I turn back I won't make it in the allotted six hours.

I'm as certain of that as I have been of anything.

But if I press ahead on the route I've chosen I could sink in one of these shitty bogs, and no one might ever find my body. People have died up here before now. Still, I know I've got no option but to fight on through, or effectively I'll be binning my attempt at selection.

The bogs and the swamplands just seem to go on and on forever. I'm cursing my crass bloody stupidity. I've tried to do what Pete did on the first Test March, in spite of seeing what it cost him. By trying to be clever and cut a corner I've actually made a horrendous call. I've put myself in real danger, and I've jeopardised my chances of making it through, when I was at the head of the lot of us.

Eventually, I haul myself out of what seems to be the final quagmire. But I'm soaked to the skin from head to toe, and I look like a walking man of shit. I'm also exhausted from all of the physical effort and I'm not even at the first checkpoint yet.

I check my watch. I have five hours to make it and I'm way behind schedule. I have put myself under enormous physical pressure for the rest of the march, and I know that every second is absolutely precious now.

I force myself to up the pace to near-suicidal levels. I'm charging across fields of babies' heads, and I go tumbling flat onto my face, my rifle slamming me in the face as I fall. I force myself to get right up again, because failure is not an option. I can't afford a second's break for food, so I throw the liquid down my neck as I go.

By the time I drag myself past the final checkpoint of the day I know I'm well over the deadline. Everyone else is already in the four-tonner. There's a line of curious faces turned my way as I crawl into my space, but no one says a word. No one asks me what happened. We're all too fucked to even talk.

In any case, it's pretty obvious from the look of me that I've been through some serious shit. Pete crabs his way over with a mug of steaming tea. It tastes like pure heaven and it does bring me around a little. He lowers himself painfully like a wizened old crone, until he's laid out beside me.

'You okay?' he asks.

'Been better.'

He nods. He doesn't need to know what happened. We've all of us fucked up on one part or another of the Test Marches. I glance out of the rear of the wagon. The four-tonner's creeping through this massive valley, as sheets of dark rain slice down from the heavens. Inside the truck I feel like we're in some kind of a luxury hotel, compared to being out there.

'Only one more to go,' Pete remarks, 'then it's Test Week done.'

'Yeah. Endurance.'

'Endurance. The big one.'

The rest of the drive back is pretty much silent. After today I don't know if I'm a pass or a fail, or maybe I've just earned myself a yellow card. I've gone from the front of the pack to the very back in the space of just a few hours. If I'd recce'd that short-cut route during training, my decision might have made some sense. As it was I'd headed off blindly and just presumed it would work.

There's an old saying in the military: presumption is the mother of all fuck-ups. Never presume anything. I've forgotten all that today. But right now I'm close to past caring. At least there's plenty of room on the truck to stretch out my frozen, pulverised limbs. We're down to twelve of us by now. The Valley of the Shadow of Death has claimed another four.

Instead of crouching on a shitty wooden bench, and nodding off and waking with a jerk for the entire journey, I get horizontal and seriously comatose. I drift into a sleep of the dead. Every now and again I wake as if in a nightmare, to hear people screaming at the tops of their voices as their legs go into the agony of a cramp spasm.

A couple of times I realise that the man who is screaming is me.

*

CHAPTER SEVEN

L ife at Welbeck was extremely regimented, but in a way I didn't mind the strictures. I'd taught myself to be super-disciplined in the showjumping arena, and I found I could apply myself in the same kind of way here.

The food was utterly shit, but the strict rituals and rules associated with how you had to eat it could not be broken. You might be served bread that was mouldy, or potato that was Smash, or the so-called 'dog burgers' – burgers that seem to be made of dog food – and all of it covered in gravy that tasted like rat's piss, but you still had to eat in a highly regimented way.

There was a 'high' dining table, where only the College masters and prefects could sit. From there the tables descended in a strict pecking order, with us lot, the new boys, at the very bottom. We couldn't start to eat until we'd first done our flunky duty. We had to fill the jugs with water on all tables, clear away any used plates, and wipe down the tables.

When we did actually sit down to eat, we had to do so in a very particular way. Some of the rules were utterly pointless: we were only allowed to eat fruit if we first cut it into pieces with a knife, and it was the same with the mouldy bread. In fact, the mindless rules at Welbeck were legion: it was forbidden to put your hands in your trouser pockets, iron the creases in your trousers incorrectly, or even make your bed in the wrong way.

If you broke any of the rules and were caught you'd get punished. There were two forms of punishment. One was a 'show parade', at which you had to appear in a certain set of dress and it all had to be absolutely immaculate. You had to launder and press and iron all your kit, and as the prefects made their inspection you had to be eyes-front and remain rigid the entire time.

There were several sets of dress you could be ordered to appear in. Geed was standard dress – so blazer, black shoes, shirt and tie. College Order was a smarter set of dress for sporting and related occasions. Combat Dress was your Army combats and boots. Coveralls were your green overalls used for cleaning and other manual duties – but if you were doing a show parade in coveralls, they still had to be immaculately pressed and ironed.

Number Two dress was your smartest parade ground uniform. It consisted of a blazer and trousers made of this incredibly thick and itchy green material, and a pair of drill boots that were supposed to be polished to such perfection that you could read a book in them. You drew your drill boots from stores, and they'd have been buffed to such a degree over the years that layer upon layer of polish would have built up on them.

But College tradition had it that when you graduated you had to smash your drill boots repeatedly into the pavement, so as to bash up and craze the polish for whatever new boy would get them after you. You were only allowed to use a beeswax candle and a Sylvette cloth to polish them, and it would take days to restore them to their gleaming, mirror-like perfection.

You had to burn the beeswax and drip it into the holes and craters left by the boy before you, cementing them and rubbing them into a flawless shine. At the end you'd be so pissed off that you would vow that when it came your time to graduate, you sure as hell would smash them up for whoever was coming after you.

Punishment two was 'defaulters', and it was a classic military kind of beasting. You'd be in Combat Dress, and you'd get given an extreme physical thrashing. The Seniors would lead defaulters, and practically anything was allowed. Typically, you'd be sent on a run in full Army kit, and be forced to crawl through one hundred metres of mud, plus the tank traps – these deep concrete troughs that were invariably full of stagnant water.

Then you'd be made to squat against a wall in your soaking wet uniform in a stress position, until your knees started to shake uncontrollably and you buckled. After that, you'd be made to run up the nearest hill until you were puking up with pain. It was savage and I guess it has probably been banned in today's politically-correct times, but there was a part of me that actually enjoyed defaulters.

My lungs would be bursting and my heart pumping fit to explode, but at least defaulters made you physically tough and unbreakable. And it was nothing really compared to having to break in one of Simon Ferguson's wild Irish ponies. I preferred defaulters to a show parade any day, which was an utterly pointless and futile exercise.

I also learned a crucial lesson from defaulters. I learned that often when you think you're physically finished and your mind says you can't go on, in reality you can. Mind can triumph over matter, and you can keep your body going well over and above what you might have believed possible.

But I hated the mindless discipline of Welbeck, and especially the pointless obsession with knife-edge trouser creases and folding your bedsheets. What was it all for? How did that help you to become a better soldier? I didn't like being told what to do by those who hadn't earned my respect, either.

But at Welbeck I did have a purpose and I was truly inspired, and I told myself I could live with all that. I was surrounded by boys of my own age who were both a spur and a challenge to me. And in our military staff and instructors I had men I could really look up to and who were an absolute inspiration.

Together, that gave me a unifying purpose in life: one day I might have to go into battle and fight shoulder-to-shoulder with my compatriots, and in a life or death confrontation at war.

Geoff Rusher, the bloke who was in charge of physical education, was the one I looked up to hugely and from the very start. Rumour had it that he'd won the Queen's Gallantry Medal for saving someone's life during a covert operation in Northern Ireland. He'd been there in some sneaky-beaky, elite, plain-clothes role doing undercover surveillance missions.

He was a super-fit, ultra-hard Welshman, and he'd served in the one theatre where British soldiers were still getting whacked – across the water. The trouble was that for some reason he took an intense dislike to me right from the start. He looked genuinely disgusted with my lack of physical stamina and my low fitness levels, and he made his feelings very clear to me.

'Mr Blakeley, you're a bloody waste of a human skin!' he'd yell at me. 'Put some bloody effort in!'

I guess he could see that I was a big, athletic lad, but that I hadn't really bothered much in my teens. He was also a top rugby player, while my game was football. I was perfect second row material, but I barely knew what a second row was, let alone what they were supposed to do on the pitch.

I respected him most out of all of the staff, because he'd been on some out-there, top-secret kind of operations. He never once talked about any of these covert ops, and that only served to increase the mystique. I craved the man's respect. I vowed to win it, no matter what.

Rugby was compulsory at Welbeck, and predictably Geoff Rusher slotted me into the scrum. I forced myself to learn quickly, and to play dirty when I had to. I was big and fast and I could outpace a lot of my rivals. I learned to tackle hard and mercilessly, and with no hesitation. Rugby at Welbeck was seen as reflecting the cut of a man, and if you were fearless on the pitch you were assumed to be fearless in a fight.

My best mate was my Brummie roommate, Gareth, whom everyone knew as 'Cheeky'. He was a hilarious bloke and a master of the quick one-liners. Funny things were always happening to Cheeky, and if you were with him they'd happen to you. He had a smiley, non-threatening personality, and even when we got defaulters he seemed to keep smiling all through the torture.

We stood shoulder-to-shoulder through the worst and he and I were like blood brothers. We shared the shit food and the harsh punishments, and still we came through laughing. And that way I learned that if you had your brothers beside you, your pack, most hardships could actually become bearable, if not enjoyable.

Yet not everyone it seemed felt the same way.

We woke each morning to a freezing cold room. There was no double-glazing and the heating barely functioned. It was the north of England, it was a freezing winter, and we never got enough good food to compensate for the cold. One morning there was frost on the inside of the windowpane. I got up at the same time as Benny and Cheeky and we tried to work some warmth into our bodies.

But Matt stayed in bed. All we heard were three words from him spoken from beneath the covers: 'This ... is ... shit.'

The three of us started crying with laughter, as Matt's disgruntled face appeared above the bedsheets, like Puss in Boots in the movie *Shrek*. We got changed and went to our lessons, and we never saw Matt again – he was gone. Matt had been so keen and thrusting at first, with that Hitler-esque fanaticism, and he was the last person I'd ever thought would crack. But fanaticism alone wasn't enough to see you through a place like Welbeck.

There had been something of the Rowan Atkinson about Matt, except that he wasn't at all funny. The most amusing thing he'd ever said were those three words: *This is shit*. And even then, he hadn't intended to be funny. We laughed it off, and that made the three of us stronger. And there was a sick part of me that actually drew strength from someone else canning it. It was like in a comic book, when the evil person dies and the guy who's still alive sucks up his strength.

But either way we were down to three in our room now, and that made us easy meat in the eyes of the older cadets. Inevitably, the

Seniors raided all the Junior dorms. It sounds innocuous enough, but they truly armed themselves for war. We had these heavy feather pillows, and they'd stuff one inside another, until they were armed with the equivalent of a sack of potatoes. A serious whack with one of those from a big lad could actually knock you out.

There was a lump of a Senior called Chris Barker. With Matt gone, he started gobbing off about how we were down to three, and how his lot were going to raid us, and we were going to get battered. He was trying to spread the fear, of course, but he'd actually forewarned us. We now knew that an attack was coming.

As luck would have it my bed was by the door, and there were no locks on any of them. Our plan of defence was the age-old ploy: we'd hit the biggest bloke with maximum force, and not stop smashing him until the rest of them backed off.

We heard them coming, with the floorboards creaking under their weight. As they got to the door, I could hear them going 'shssh, shssh, shssh' to each other. I was the biggest in our dorm, and I knew I had Cheeky and Benny right behind me. I heard the door creak open and I was up on my bed, giving me a height advantage, with my double-bagged pillow held high.

As the door came open I had cover from view, whereas big Chris Barker did not. I put all my weight and force into that first blow, and it hit him like a sledgehammer in the face. He went down and out without making so much as a whimper. A second guy tried to charge inside, but he got the same treatment as Chris, and went crashing down on top of him.

At that the rest of Chris Barker's spartans turned and fled.

Cheeky turned to me and burst into laughter. 'Dave, that's the first time you've ever been of any use to us, you big, lovely bastard.'

No one tried to fuck with us again.

There was a great deal of drill at Welbeck and Cheeky and I found it all faintly ridiculous. We just couldn't see how it contributed to our soldiering skills. We were hardly about to march in ranks onto the modern battlefield to execute an attack. Or at least if we did the terrorists in Northern Ireland, or those just limbering up in the Middle East and Afghanistan, would bloody love it.

I understood the concept of weapons drill: learning to use your weapon safely. Likewise contact drills and assault drills: learning your basic fighting skills. But parade ground drill? What was the sense of that in a modern-day Army? Some regiments still spent months of every year marching to and fro. I was beginning to see how it might teach unquestioning obedience to orders, but I was also starting to sense that it wasn't my bag.

One day we were out on drill with a hundred of us arranged in strict ranks on the quad. Cheeky and I were marching along at the back, stiff arms swinging to and fro. We were bored to tears. To one side were some thick rhododendron bushes. Cheeky and I both seemed to sense the opportunity at the same moment.

'Fuck it, shall we just do one and run?' he said.

I grinned. 'Why not? Who's going to bloody notice?'

An instant later we were behind the bushes, trying not to laugh as the rest of the line thumped off ahead of us. For a while we sat there watching them drill, before we realised our problem. There was no way we could rejoin the line without being seen, and that meant we were about to get defaulters as never before. This was a whole different league from having the wrong creases in your trousers: this was disobeying orders. This was major rebellion.

I came up with a plan. I'd take Cheeky to the sanatorium – the College's sickbay – and I'd tell Matron that he was ill. I'd say he'd started to feel faint and I had to take him out of the line and escort him. That way, we could get away with not having asked permission to leave the parade, for it was a 'medical emergency'.

No one would ever dream of going against Matron, so it was absolutely crucial to bring her onside. Trouble was, she was the spitting image of Nanny McPhee. She was this massive old woman with buck teeth and hair on her upper lip, plus a huge mole on her cheek. I always had problems if ever I went to see her, for I just couldn't help staring at the mole.

Cheeky bought into the plan, for the only other option was to face the defaulters from hell. We snuck over to the sanatorium, rang the bell, and waited for Nanny to answer. All the while I was repeating to myself: *Do not stare at her mole, do not stare at her mole …*

She answered the door and took us in. I explained the story, all the while staring at the floor so as to avoid the dreaded mole. Once I was done she gave Cheeky and me a long, hard stare. She knew we were a couple of jokers, and I saw more than a flicker of doubt pass over her eyes.

I knew I needed to up the ante. We were facing hours and hours of defaulters for bunking off drill. We'd be thrashed and thrashed half to death, and probably get a year's worth of ironing duties to boot. My mind raced, as I tried to think of a solution. The food at College was abysmal and the winter was proving fierce. There was bugger all fruit and there had been several cases of scurvy.

'Look at him, Matron,' I urged. 'He's looking really grey, just like he did when he fainted on parade. He's as grey as the wall behind him. Maybe it's the scurvy.'

Cheeky was staring at me, like: *What the hell are you going on about?*

'Or maybe it's the scarlet fever,' I continued. 'Everyone's been getting it. He does look a bit blotchy, and he's been complaining of having a rash and stuff.'

'No I haven't …' Cheeky objected.

But by now Matron's mind was made up. She announced that she was taking Cheeky into the sickbay on three days' forced admittance. That meant three days' compulsory bed rest, and being force-fed appalling food by Matron with no way to refuse it.

Of course, everyone knew Cheeky and I had bunked off parade, which was about as bad a sin at Welbeck as ever you could commit. But with Matron on the case, and Cheeky locked into the sickbay, who was ever going to argue? The plan had worked, and at the end of the three days Cheeky was released, and we had a damn good laugh about it all.

Every day was a fantastic adventure with Cheeky. We'd started to earn the reputation of being renegades, but we more or less managed to offset that – Cheeky with his engaging humour, and me with my growing levels of fitness and aptitude. Still, I did get a 'gypsy's warning' – a quiet caution – from my house master to apply myself more forcefully to proper College duties.

We also got a Senior boy allocated to our dorm, to take Matt's place and to keep a watchful eye. Ryan Varney was a ginger-haired rustic lad, and a former soldier from the Royal Electrical and Mechanical Engineers (REME). He was very fit and very strong and very down to earth. He was moved in to keep some order and to lead by example. That was the theory, anyway.

The day he joined us he got his bed and his kit squared away in short order, being an experienced soldier. We were settling down to sleep, but Cheeky was still in the bathroom.

I turned to Ryan. 'When Cheeky gets back ask him if his sister's any good at dancing.'

'Why?' Ryan asked, curiously.

'He's just really proud of her dancing, that's all.'

Cheeky returned and settled down to bed, and Ryan popped the question. 'Cheeky, is your sister any good at dancing?'

'What?' said Cheeky.

'Is she any good at dancing?' he repeated.

Cheeky fixed Ryan with this uncharacteristically hard look. 'She's in a wheelchair.'

Ryan's face dissolved into sheer horror. We left him to suffer for a few long moments, but I couldn't hold it forever. Bang on cue, Cheeky and I cracked up laughing.

That line – *Is your sister any good at dancing?* – plus the riposte, came from a favourite film of ours. I knew Cheeky would pick up on the cue, and he had – perfectly. All three of us – me, Cheeky and Benny – were crying with laughter, as Ryan proceeded to give me shit. But the message had been well communicated. He may have been parachuted into our dorm to keep watch on us, but Ryan was going to have to dance to our tune a bit too.

In fact, Ryan turned out to be one cool dude. He'd brought a guitar with him, and it turned out he could listen to a song and play it pretty much by ear. We'd sit up in the evenings with Ryan playing Oasis tracks and us singing along. One night I got him to play 'Puff the Magic Dragon', and that kind of became our theme tune. It pretty much is to this day. Whenever I see Ryan these days he plays it for me – and Ryan Varney is today a veteran of the SAS.

Because Ryan had served as a rifleman he knew about infantry soldiering, so I could pick his brains. By the end of that first year at College I had a growing thirst to be a frontline soldier. I had another mate at Welbeck called Danny Matthews. His brother was in the Parachute Regiment and he was a kickboxing legend. He used to fight dressed in a PARA Reg maroon sweatshirt, with the arms cut off.

From Danny I heard stories of his brother's kickboxing exploits, plus jumping out of aircraft with his fellow PARAs, and of P Company – the Parachute Regiment's selection course. The PARAs and the Royal Marines are unique in the British military in being regular units – as opposed to Special Forces – that still require you to pass a tough selection course before you can be admitted to their number. For that reason, many see them as stepping-stones to the Special Forces.

I bought myself a book called *The Making Of A Para*. I read it from cover to cover, then started at the beginning again. This had just become my bible. I read about Arnhem, where thousands of British paratroopers had parachuted into enemy territory unsupported, and fought to the bitter end. I read about selection. I knew it would be a massive challenge getting into the PARAs, but I knew absolutely that it was what I wanted.

Cheeky, Benny, Danny and some of the others took up rowing on the College lake. We only had limited free time at Welbeck and boating wasn't for me. I had quietly decided I was going to join the Parachute Regiment, and that meant getting fit for P Company. I didn't have overly long to prepare. I had a year left at Welbeck, and then I was slated to go direct to Sandhurst for twelve months, after which I would need to try for the PARAs.

I started tabbing on my own – tabbing as described in *The Making Of A Para*. 'Tab' is actually short for Tactical Advance to Battle – in layman's terms, marching under a crushing load and carrying your weapon through whatever weather and terrain is necessary, to mount an assault against the enemy. That was what I started trying to simulate, as I marched under a loaded backpack around the forests and hills of Welbeck.

I was at a good standard of fitness, but I realised that tabbing under a heavy load required an entirely different kind of aptitude. The ergonomics were completely different, for your body got rubbed raw in unusual places and your feet blistered like hell. I realised how much I needed to harden up, if I was to have any chance of making it through P Company.

I taught myself to pack a Bergen so the weight was evenly distributed, which meant it would sit squarely on your back. I learned to lace my boots vice-tight, so my ankles didn't keep going over when moving fast under a load. I didn't have a weapon, so I acquired a length of scaffold pole to carry as a surrogate. I tabbed alone across the College estate, over hills and across country, double-timing it along the better tracks and pounding through the mud.

I started off doing an eight-miler in two hours. Over time, I got it down to an hour thirty-five. I borrowed some weights from the gym, to load on the weight in my pack. I learned water discipline: only ever to sip, and never to glug it all down before you reached the end of the march.

I was seventeen years old by now and I was alone in what I was doing. I recognised that I'd grown addicted to beasting myself and that this wasn't 'normal' behaviour. But in *The Making Of A Para* there were eighteen-year-olds who were dropped into Arnhem and had fought to the last breath and the last round. Why should it be any different now, for me?

Plus I knew I'd be going into the Parachute Regiment – if I made it – as an officer. I would be expected to command a body of warriors like no other, and that meant I couldn't prepare too rigorously for whatever might lie ahead.

My time riding horses had given me an undying love of the great outdoors and being up against the elements. I found this kind of thing infinitely preferable to being in a classroom. As soon as I was away from the College building I could get lost in the wilds where no one could see me. I found myself enjoying the loneliness and the time it gave me to myself. I focused down onto exactly what I wanted to achieve and who I wanted to be. It lifted my soul and cleared my mind, and sharpened my focus.

I knew exactly what I wanted now.

The rest of the lads at College had started to think I was a bit of a freak, all apart from Cheeky. I'd shared my dream with him, because he was my blood brother and I trusted him completely. But at the same time, it was Cheeky who reminded me that there was still time for letting my hair down and going a bit wild.

There is a Center Parcs resort about 15 miles from Welbeck. Cheeky's family took the two of us there during one of our rare weekends off. They had these old-fashioned, retro, granny-esque pushbikes on which you were supposed to cycle around the resort. Cheeky and I decided that a couple of those would be very useful at College. The grounds were huge and if you had an IT lesson it meant a good mile walk to get there.

We rode a couple of the bikes to the resort's outer boundary – a huge, twelve-foot-high barbed-wire fence. On the far side lay a cornfield thick with crop. Cheeky and I did the 'one – two – three!' and hurled the bikes over. The trouble was, one got snared on the very top of the wire. The two of us stared at it in total disbelief, then looked all around ourselves to see if we'd been spotted.

This was theft, and we knew if we got caught we'd get kicked out of College. But we couldn't help ourselves – we were crying with laughter. Because I was the biggest and seriously bulked out from all the tabbing, it was left to me to hoist Cheeky onto my shoulders. With his standing there he was just about able to reach up and knock the bike down.

We humped ourselves over the fence like characters in *The Great Escape,* and cycled off through the sunlit cornfield. We then picked up a track and made it the 15 miles back to Welbeck.

Cheeky and I started to cycle to lessons. Everyone knew there had to be some wacky story behind these weird granny-bikes, but no one could work out what it was. We used to ring the bell and laugh out loud as we wheeled past the others like Butch Cassidy and the Sundance Kid in the movie.

It couldn't last.

Some geeky cadet who was jealous of us – of the ruse; of the blatant rule breaking – worked out where they'd come from. They were absolutely unique to Center Parcs, so he didn't have to be a rocket scientist to do so. He spread the word and the rumours started to fly.

Cheeky and I learned of this and we started to flap. This could get us kicked out of College and kill all of our dreams. Late one night we tried to sink the bikes in the College lake, so as to bury the evidence, but unbelievably they floated.

'Oh shit, we're rubbish at this,' Cheeky giggled, as we hauled them out again.

We had no option but to go on a reverse mission – to return the granny-bikes. Trouble was, you had to get permission to leave the College grounds, and we were hardly likely to get it so we could return two nicked bikes to their place of origin.

Very early one morning we sneaked off on our pre-dawn mission, feeling as if we were breaking away from prison. We rode the 15 miles to Center Parcs, whereupon we promptly hurled them back over the monster fence.

With my first pistol, aged six. Little did I know that in years to come I'd be on behind-enemy-lines missions squirting a lot more than water at the enemy! My parents would take me camping every summer in north Wales – something that helped me develop a love of the outdoors from an early age.

As a young boy I was fascinated with cowboy TV shows like *Rawhide*. Clint Eastwood was my hero. This is me galloping across an African beach. I dreamed of going on epic adventures in the desert ... I would go on to do so as a Pathfinder, but I'd be riding in soft-skinned, open-topped Land Rovers, and manning a Gimpy machine gun and scanning my arcs for the enemy.

Training horses and riding for rich people became a way of life for me – until I reached sixteen, when I became too tall and heavy. I then had to look elsewhere for an outdoor way of life, as I could never see myself working in an office or a bank – unless it was with a balaclava and a shotgun. I decided to join the Army.

Following a stint at the Army's boarding school, Welbeck College, I trained at the Royal Military Academy Sandhurst and was selected to become an officer in perhaps the Army's toughest unit – The Parachute Regiment (PARAS).

Prime Minister Tony Blair sent us to Kosovo in 1999 to enforce the withdrawal of Serbian forces. Here we are about to board Chinook helicopters to fly across the border from Macedonia to face Russian forces and mechanised infantry in a race to seize the airport – an operation which risked sparking Word War III.

My view, sitting on the floor of a Chinook. The guys in my platoon were from all walks of life, but together we made an awesome fighting unit. Here we're being flown 'hot' (no prior warning) into the Kosovo capital Pristina to drive out Serbian Forces – those who had been committing mass murder, rape and torture against the locals. A humanitarian disaster had already unfolded, and we were at the tip of the spear of The Parachute Regiment (1 PARA) sent in to fix the situation quickly.

Marching into Kosovo. I am leading 1 PARA as commander of 1 Platoon, A Company. I preferred to position myself as front man because I found it easier to lead that way, but it wasn't always popular. Years later in the Pathfinders I would realise that the commander always moves behind a team who protects the command and control and essential communications systems.

Covered in dust from an active Helicopter Landing Zone. We were moved around Kosovo on various missions, hunting HVTs (High-Value Targets), war criminals, mass graves, and the Serbian killers who'd led the death squads.

'Jim', one of the Section Commanders in my platoon – a robust and dynamic operator, and a great support to me. Here he is on guard outside a Serbian Secret Police Headquarters which we stumbled into in Kosovo. Files containing details of the 'missing' – many of whom were young, pretty women – were being burnt in a makeshift furnace as the Serbs fled. We put out the fires to save the files – vital war-crimes evidence – and secured the building, prior to descending into the hell that awaited us within.

Notorious Serb warlord 'Arkan' and his so-called 'Tigers' – a murderous militia responsible for horrific crimes across the war-torn region. British forces first on to the ground like 1 PARA were tasked to hunt down such High-Value Targets, and gather the gruesome evidence of the crimes they had committed – the torture chambers, mass graves, discarded corpses.

Myself and my radio operator, 'Cloughy', in 1 PARA. We were first into Kosovo on Operation Agricola, to drive out the Serb killers and restore peace and order to the country. Shortly after this photo was taken we captured a group of hardcore Serb secret police – those who had run the death squads in Kosovo.

Inside the Secret Police Headquarters we found an underground torture chamber where locals were strapped to beds, beaten, interrogated and worse. Bloodstains covered the walls and there were chains, truncheons, metal-spiked clubs and knuckledusters. The baseball bat I am holding has 'mouth shutter' scrawled down one side of it. We would go on to find secret 'mass graves' and bodies chained to rocks at the bottom of a nearby lake. This was the first time I experienced the raw courage and fortitude of elite British soldiers when faced with the evils of this world. The pressures would take its toll on us all.

'GO PARA' – the graffiti illustrates how much the suffering locals in Kosovo appreciated our presence as a foreign force intervening in their country. We would surge the streets – putting out patrols for up to eighteen hours a day. It was exhausting work, and we were often 'drunk with fatigue', as Wilfred Owen would put it.

In May 2000 we deployed to West Africa to evacuate British, American and allied nationals as murderous RUF rebels threatened to seize the capital city, Freetown. I'd just been made Regimental Signals Officer (RSO) of 1 PARA, and my job was to run all the communications for the entire operation. Thankfully I had an amazing team supporting me! I was also the liaison officer to the SAS, plus a specialist unit called the Pathfinders – who are seen here being flown up-country to work in an isolated area. Their secretive missions and their major firefight against the rebels deep in the jungle at Lungi Loi turned the course of the war. Those inspired me to try and join them – which would mean passing the murderous Pathfinder selection course.

On patrol with 1 PARA on the dirt highways of Sierra Leone. Although we were sent in to do a NEO – a non-combatant evacuation operation – the mission soon morphed into something far more significant – to take the fight to the rebels in the jungle and finish them once and for all.

The notorious rebels in Sierra Leone – infamous for lopping off the limbs of women and children, 'short sleeves' or 'long sleeves' style – i.e. above or below the elbow. They were united by no mission other than to seize control of the country and rule by total fear, their vicious attacks fuelled by booze, drugs and voodoo. In May 2000 1 PARA were sent in to put a stop to them.

On the ground in Sierra Leone, with Joe Murray – '00 Joe' – a true legend in 1 PARA circles. Here he is at Lungi Airport as we helped evacuate people who had had their families butchered and raped by the rebels – and as their forces massed for a final push on the capital city, Freetown.

Mission accomplished.

Right after that Cheeky and I had another mission to prepare for – this one being as serious a physical challenge as a couple of seventeen-year-olds ever wished for. In spite of Cheeky's easy good nature, he was also a superlative cadet. Together, we formed a team with three others to prepare for one of the key competitions in the Welbeck calendar – the Ten Tors.

The Ten Tors is set upon Dartmoor, in Devon. It's an expanse of high moorland with its own microclimate, one that is reminiscent of the Falklands. Having read all about the Parachute Regiment's extraordinary feats during the Falklands War, this was a big deal for me. We started training for it relentlessly, for we knew we'd be up against teams from all the best private schools and military colleges in the UK.

The Ten Tors covers 55 miles, and the route touches upon the ten highest points in the area, hence the name. It takes place in the spring, which supposedly makes it easier on those competing. But this spring there were freak weather conditions, and it started to snow heavily.

We set off at 5 o'clock in the morning, with the trek slated to last forty-eight hours, and with each of us taking it in turns to navigate a section. Pretty quickly, there were lads going down with hypothermia, for the conditions were unbelievably bad. But no one in our team was suffering too much, and we pressed on.

We got to within six miles of the finish when the whole thing was called off. The snow had got so bad the organisers were worried people were going to die out there. There were a couple of lads in our team who were rejoicing that it had been cancelled – but not me. I felt frustrated and let down.

We were so close, we would definitely have made it, and we may well have been the winning team. Even if we hadn't won, just to have finished the Ten Tors in such conditions would have been a real achievement.

I thought of how the PARAs would have fared, had they called off their forced march across the Falklands due to the freezing cold and the rain. Quite possibly the war would never have been won if they had.

My dad smokes cigars. I had a Café Crème tin in my Bergen wrapped in a waterproof bag, and with a couple of cigars inside it. I had intended to smoke one when we made the finish. A Chinook heavy-lift helicopter came in to lift us out. It was only just able to make it down, the weather was so bad.

I'd never been on one of those giant, twin-rotor helos before and I decided to smoke the cigars anyway. I sat there puffing away as the Chinook pulled us out, the thud-thud-thud of the twin rotors hammering away above me.

And I thought of what it would be like to be airlifted into battle for real.

*

CHAPTER EIGHT

The Endurance March is the culmination of Test Week. It takes place over the lovely Brecon Beacons, and it's a 64-kilometre beast from end to end. But that's as the crow flies. If you take into account the savage ups-and-downs, who knows what the real distance is? The time allowed is twenty hours. At Lenny's discretion extra time could be added on if the weather turned truly bad.

No one calls me in for an interview, so I presume I've not been binned. Somehow, I must have just scraped through on the Elan Valley Test March. There are so few of us remaining now that everyone has a lower bunk, complete with a dog blanket curtain strung around it. Many of us have an extra bunk beside us on which to spread out our gear.

It's a relief just to get into the Nissen hut. It's comparatively warm and I can get out of all my piss-wet gear. I change into sweatshirt, jogging pants and trainers. It's bliss to be in warm, dry clothes. By now we've gelled as a close-knit bunch of blokes. All around me guys are helping others tape up the worst of their injuries, for there are certain parts of your body that you just can't reach on your own.

Between those of us who remain just about every sense of privacy has been forfeited. If you've had to tape up another bloke's bum crack, there isn't a lot left that you can get embarrassed over. Plus we've all resorted to peeing in our water bottles, as the hobble outside at night is proving a step too far. They double as drinking bottles during the day. It's only an issue when you forget to rinse them.

Every morning at the crack of dawn there's an obligatory parade before the Camp medic. His job is to check if there are any of us so battered and bruised that we really can't continue. It's become like a game of bluff. The trick is to cover up the worst of your injuries with zinc oxide tape, so the medic can't get a good look at them.

He's not a bad bloke. He seems happy enough to turn a blind eye and hand out the supplies of painkillers – the stronger, prescription-issue ones.

The morning of Endurance we're starting so damn early he has to see us at 0130 hours. He runs his eye over my lower legs and decides he wants to fix a stirrup to each of my ankles. They've taken such a battering as I force-marched my way across the Elan Valley, he's worried they're not going to last for another 64 kilometres.

He starts by shaving both sides of my calf muscle, and then he loops the zinc oxide tape from there under my foot and around to the other side. As a final precaution, he adds a thick strap made of the same stuff to the back of my heels.

I don't know exactly what injuries the others have suffered. Al is hobbling badly on a buggered knee, but he manages to conceal it from the medic. Pete's feet are in rags. He picked up another pair of Army-issue boots when he visited home. He jokes that with his wife's taste in designer handbags, they're all he can afford. But still his feet are damaged almost beyond repair.

As soon as you pick up an injury you start walking oddly to try to compensate, so it throws out your overall biomechanics. Other injuries are bound to follow as a result. But all that matters now is whether we can make it through today's Endurance. What follows after is a couple of weeks of downtime – Live Fire and SOP Weeks – at least when weighed against what has gone before.

Breakfast is at 0200 hours sharp. I stuff in the carbs, and run an eye over the several map sheets we'll need for today's march. It's the first time that we're actually going over the one map sheet, and we'll have to carry several with us. Scoff down, we load up the four-tonner and drive out to the Beacons Reservoir.

It's still pitch dark by the time we get there. We dismount, and again we're released individually at staggered intervals. I'm placed midway through the pack, due to my coming last on the Elan Valley. I stump off into the freezing night. It's black as a witch's tit, and there's a thin crust of frozen snow underfoot. It crunches with each footfall, the noise ringing out into the empty, echoing night.

We are forbidden from using any lights. Light-discipline is like a religion in The Pathfinders. PF operators need to feel completely at home in the night, and to make the darkness a friend. If you show barely a sliver of artificial light when you're deep behind enemy lines, it's a dead giveaway. It can easily get your mission compromised and you and your fellow soldiers captured or killed.

While I was sat in the truck I'd tried to get my eyes to adjust to the darkness. There's the barest glimmer of moon overhead, and the unearthly light bounces off the snow. But it's still well dark. The only way to map-read is by using a tiny Maglight strung around my neck on a lanyard. The end of the torch has an attachment clipped to it, so that it emits only a tiny pinprick of pale blue light.

The first stage of Endurance is a back-breaker. The route goes straight up the wide and inhospitable face of The Fan. I can just about make it out towering above me, a wall of blacker mass glowering in the dark. I push myself onwards, my head bowed against the weight on my back and my mind empty of thoughts. The rhythmic creak of my Bergen lulls me, until my mind is quite uncluttered and clear.

There is a part of me that is almost enjoying this foray into the empty night, this being swallowed by the dark and empty wilderness. All of a sudden this figure emerges from the gloom. He's ahead of me, but moving rapidly downhill. As he nears me I realise it's Taff, the ultra-marathon runner. I can't understand why he's going the wrong way – back towards the start line.

For a moment I wonder if he's somehow got his navigation messed up in the darkness. Or maybe he's taken a horrific injury? But as he nears me I can tell that that he's moving just fine. I'm about to reach out to him, to warn him that he's headed the wrong way, when I stop myself.

By the tilt of his head I know this is no mistake.

Taff, the guy who's run for the Army and is one of the fittest amongst us, is VW-ing. I haven't seen the slightest sign before now that Taff was nearing his breaking point. If anything, he seemed the least injured and fucked of any of us. He sees me at the last moment, but his eyes avoid mine. Without a word he hurries past, heading on down.

Oddly, the sight of it spurs me on. It breaks up the sheer pain and torture of scaling the massive flank of this mountain. It takes my mind away from my own suffering, and in a sense I feel pretty good now. I've recovered from my Elan Valley bog-crossing epic as best I can. My taped-up ankles feel strong enough to keep going. I figure I'm going to make it through Endurance okay.

I reach the top of the climb and the terrain flattens out into a huge patch of pinewoods. I skirt by the dark mass of the forest, and into the clear air beyond. First light is seeping over the hilltops, as I head along this ridge line with a sharp drop on either side. It's dusted with wind-sculpted snow, and the first rays of sunlight touch it off in a spark of rainbow colours.

No doubt about it, the world is beautiful. This place takes my breath away – at least what remains of it after the massive ascent. I double-time it along the ridge, climb some more and reach the first checkpoint. I report in, get my next co-ordinates, and I'm off again. It feels great to be here.

I'm flying.

I reach the quarter-way mark, so I'm 16 kilometres in. Below me I can see the vast expanse of the Beacons Reservoir nestled in the valley bottom, the water dark and distant in the dawn shadows. From here, the lake looks small and insignificant, although I know what a major stretch of water it is when you're by its side.

I start to go downhill, as I hit the first big descent. Almost without thinking I put one foot in front of the other, and in an instant I'm falling. My knee has twisted horribly, and as I hit the deck I let out this piercing, agonised scream.

'AAARRGGHHHH.'

Through the blinding fog of pain, I know instantly what's happened. I injured that knee in exactly the same way on P Company – doing my PARA Reg selection. That injury has just come back to haunt me, and – of all times – on the Endurance leg of Pathfinder selection.

It hurts like nothing ever has before. I never knew it was possible to feel such pain. I force myself to try to get to my feet, but when I put my left leg down it's total agony. I scream again and I'm cursing uncontrollably. The knee is pounding like a jackhammer, as the blood pulses through it and it begins to swell and balloon.

I try to think of something I can do, a way to deal with the injury and to keep going. I think about trying to splint it, but I know that won't get me far. It's a bloody knee injury, and knees are designed to flex and to bend. I think of trying to find a branch to make a crutch, but I know it'll slow me down so much that I'll fail Endurance.

Then I remember the medic's prescription-issue painkillers. I scrabble about in my Bergen for my medical kit, drag it out, grab the bottle and neck a handful. I don't give a toss that the medic said take two max in any four hours. I get a good rake of them down me, for I know it's going to take that and more to get me through this.

I force myself to start hobbling forwards. I hit a bit of flat, and I find I can push ahead using my right leg to take the weight. But the easier terrain ends in a steep drop that will take me down to a wide expanse of water. Normally, downhill provides a bit of relief. But right now, my knee is so totally buggered I can't see how I can bend it to enable me to descend.

I resort to crabbing my way down sideways. I get my right leg to lead so it's taking all the weight, and I find I can lift my left leg with my hands, to bring it down after it. I keep going downwards like that in little, jerky steps, but each one is torture, and that's with all the painkillers I've already got down me.

This is fucking desperate.

It takes me a full hour to make the bottom. I hobble over the road that snakes through the valley, and begin to inch my way up the climb on the far side. Somehow, the knee is better going uphill. The joint holds in place more, and doesn't keep popping and crunching about so painfully.

It's like this that I finally make it to the second checkpoint, at Fan Fawr. By now, I've had most of the others pass me. Al was first to go powering by, followed closely by Pete. Even Jez has managed to overtake me on that last uphill section. Each of them has asked the obvious question, as they've gone by me.

'You all right, Dave?'

All I can do is nod through gritted teeth and push silently onwards. The only time you're actually permitted to stop and help another bloke on selection – in other words, when you won't get binned for it – is if his life is in danger and he's in need of a casevac. I'm not at that stage yet, so none of them stops for long.

As I hobble across the level ground to the checkpoint, I keep cursing under my breath. I know that I'm finished. There's no way I'm going to make Endurance like this. But I am buggered if I'm going to VW. One of the DS is going to have to intervene and force a stop, or I'm going to push on to the bitter end.

By now I'm popping the painkillers more or less like Smarties. They seem to be having little effect on the pain, so I guess the injury has to be seriously bad. I stumble up to the checkpoint. It's that Scot of a DS again, the one I've started to really dislike. I get the sense that he's a bit of a dumb, officer-hating bastard.

He gives me the stare. 'So, what the fuck's the matter with you?'

There's no point trying to lie. It's obvious from a thousand yards away what's wrong. 'Knee's fucked, Staff.'

'Time to VW then, ain't it?'

'No, Staff.'

'Yes it fucking is, laddie.'

I grit my teeth. It's the 'laddie' bit that's really getting to me. 'No, Staff, it isn't.'

I know I'm a bit emotional right now. Who wouldn't be? If this fucker pushes it, I'm more than capable of clocking him. Punching out a DS would amount to an instant fail, but at least I wouldn't have VWd. Either way, I'm not going to give in. They can fail me. The clock can beat me. But not myself.

'Your knee is fucked. You can't go on like that. Ergo, laddie, you VW.'

I shake my head. 'No, Staff.'

For several long moments we stare each other out. I guess my pupils are maxed out with all the painkillers, and I probably do look pretty messed up. The DS is probably just trying to do his job – to ascertain if I'm fit enough in body *and mind* to continue.

The entire 64-kilometre route of Endurance only crosses two metalled roads – that's how remote it is. It's never going to be easy to send out a search party for a bloke so as to bring him off the hills. But I know the rules: a DS can only ever overrule you if you've got serious exposure, or if you're growing incoherent, which means your powers of rational judgement have gone.

Only then can they take you off.

I know that I'm neither. My leg may be buggered, but my body core remains warm and functioning and my mind is still just about clear. I hold the guy's stare. He breaks off, shrugs, and points towards a sheer drop on the far side of the checkpoint.

'There you go then, Captain. It's your funeral.'

I totter off towards the yawning precipice. The descent takes forever. I keep having to stop, so as to rest my buggered knee. I'm halfway down when I see two figures coming down the route I've just taken. One is Tricky, the other Lenny. They've got these very grim expressions on their features. I guess the Scottish wanker back at the checkpoint has reported me.

Lenny comes over to me. 'So tell me, what's up?'

I shrug. 'My knee's gone.'

'What's wrong with it exactly?'

'I don't know. I can't go downhill very easily. I have to hop.'

Lenny's expression softens fractionally. 'Dave, this is fucking desperate ...'

'Like I said at the last checkpoint, I'm happy to continue.'

Lenny stares at me hard for a few seconds, like he's seriously considering whether to overrule me. The odd thing is, I am not aware of one molecule of my being that wants him to do so. Sure, it would make all the pain stop. But for me the joy of that would be eclipsed by the crushing sense of failure.

I'm relieved when Lenny gives a shrug, and without another word sets off downhill with Tricky beside him. I watch them burn off the distance and quickly they're gone. Then I lever myself to my feet and I start my crabby, hopalong progress downwards once more.

I make the halfway mark. Here, the DS have a tea urn going and a stack of pasties. It's for them of course, to help ward off the biting chill, so I am truly shocked and surprised when one of them hands me a steaming mug of tea and a warm pasty. They don't say a word. There's no 'all right, mate, get those down you'. But I'm hugely grateful, and that simple act of kindness lifts me.

I take the pasty like some kind of beggar slumped on the pavement in Leicester Square and I wolf it down. As I eat I can see my knee shaking and juddering uncontrollably. It's so fucked it can barely hold me up. I do a time check. I'm twelve hours in and I'm only at the halfway point. It's clear I am well behind time.

It's four in the afternoon by now, and already it's starting to get dark. There is one vague upside to my present situation. I know the route from here on like the back of my hand, and there is only one bitch of a steep descent, which takes me back over VW Valley. I tell myself that maybe it's just doable.

I follow that warm pasty with a whole bunch of painkillers. The DS's unexpected act of kindness has really boosted my morale. I glance into the distance and I can see Jez labouring up the hill ahead of me, so at least I'm not that far behind the last man. To me there is no option but to carry on.

I set off in more of a hobbling rhythm. I climb this massive flank of a hill for a good mile, then start to handrail around it. I glance upwards and I can see the tiny figure of Jez going arrow-straight, and on an exact compass bearing to hit the heights of the mountain.

Lenny and Tricky overhaul me again. They're out in pairs checking that no one is shirking or cheating – like using their rifle as a walking pole – plus they'll pick up any injured or stragglers. Lenny pauses beside me. I see him scan the hillside high above us.

'Blakeley, shout to fucking Rowlands and tell the silly fucker to contour around.'

I'm glad Lenny has reverted to Blakeley, from the 'Dave' of earlier. He's gone back to formal DS speak. I figure it means he's accepted that I'm going to push on come what may, and that I'm still a part of his selection.

'JEZ!' my voice echoes around the vast expanse of the valley. 'JEZ! BLOODY ROWLANDS!'

So far on selection Jez has proved us all wrong. He's thrown down a challenge to his nickname – The Colonel – by proving himself extremely fit and robust. He's got his head well down now as he hammers up that peak and he can't seem to hear me.

I try one last time. 'FUCKING ROWLLAAAAANDDS!'

There's not the barest suggestion of a reaction from him. Lenny shakes his head. Curses under his breath. He knows it's hopeless. Either Jez makes it over that horrendous peak in the darkness and the swirling snow, or they'll be sending out a search party.

I push on. I contour around the massive flank of the mountain. I hobble through to the darkness on the far side. I know for sure that Jez is behind me now, somewhere on the blasted high ground of that mountain peak. Oddly, that knowledge alone gives me a real boost. *I'm not the last man.* It spurs me to go on.

I reach the checkpoint at the three-quarters mark by breaking down the ground before me into the shortest possible sections. It's a mental trick I taught myself on previous forced marches. You never allow your mind to think about the entire distance you still have to go. Instead, you fix your eyes on a point up ahead, maybe five hundred yards away, and you tell yourself: *just get to that.*

When you reach that point, you do it all over again. It helps you focus, and by breaking the distance into manageable chunks it doesn't seem so daunting or impossible. But it's pitch dark by now, and a freezing fog mixed with sleet has closed right in. It will make navigating the final leg extra difficult, for it's hard to see a feature to aim for or on which to take a compass bearing.

I tell myself I've walked this leg of the route dozens of times before and I know it well. There's a part of me – the part that refuses to ever give in – which is thinking I might just pull this off now. The remainder of the route is all on reasonable footpaths. I'm eighteen hours in by now, but Endurance might just be doable.

I reach the checkpoint, go down on my right knee – the only one that will hold me – and pull out my compass and my map. I show the Staff where I am. I catch the pair of them staring at me like I am completely out of my head. But it's not because I've got our position wrong. It's because I am so totally and utterly fucked.

I am so wired on painkillers my eyes are like saucers. Nothing else matters right now in my life but to get to the next grid. I'm practically foaming at the mouth from where I've necked all the pills. I'm a wild man out in the hills and the shitty night, and I have more or less completely lost the plot.

I see the DS exchange glances – like, can we really let this stupid fucker continue, or is he going to kill himself? Perhaps they can see that I'm not about to let them stop me. Maybe they can sense that there's just no telling me. I'm beyond reason. Either way, they give a barely noticeable nod and point me on my way.

I stump up a massive, featureless incline, a lone figure being swallowed by the darkness. I press onwards into the pinewoods, where the trees are dripping wet with freezing fog, which in places is turning into long, drooping icicles. I can see the route ahead in my mind's eye. The track zigzags through the wood past a series of massive boulders, before skirting the reservoir, and then you're done.

There are no overly severe gradients on any of what remains. I'd never have believed it when first I buggered my knee, but I've made it this close to home. I'm high as a kite on the painkillers, so I presume my mind can more than cope with the rest of the pain. Right now I figure an enemy could jump out of the woodlands and shoot me and I'd probably keep going.

I reach the very highest point. The black sky above me dissolves into a series of stabs of insane, crackling flame. The freezing fog is lit white from above as the lightning crashes down all around me, the hills rolling with deafening peals of thunder.

I pause for an instant and roar back at the sky: I AM STILL ALIVE!!

I grab my compass and try to check my position. In broad daylight I wouldn't even need to map-read here, I know the terrain so well. I check my bearing, get a fix on where I am, put my head down and get going. I push onwards for five hundred metres or so, and I practically stumble over a sheer drop that just shouldn't be there.

My mind is slow and sluggish. I try to press on and lower myself down the precipice. It proves impossible with a knee that's totally buggered, so I try to box around it. All that does is bring me up against more boulders and to the brink of another precipice that shouldn't by rights be there. The further I go the more it keeps happening.

'FUUUUUUUCCKKKK!'

No one can hear me scream out here, and in these kind of conditions. In any case, I've grown too tired and too out of it to care. I just presumed I knew where I was going. But in truth, I'm lost. I know it now, just as sure as I know that I've really fucked myself for Endurance this time.

I collapse against the rain-sodden flank of a boulder, and let the ice cold of it seep into me. I flail around for my map. My frozen fingers find the string and drag it out of my trouser pocket. I try to figure out just where the hell I've gone wrong, but my mind is working painfully slowly. I am frozen to the core, dehydrated and exhausted.

I'm alone on the mountain, storm-lashed, lost and injured, and I'm half out of my head on the drugs.

*

CHAPTER NINE

B y the time I was near to finishing Welbeck I was truly Army property, and they had decreed I would go straight to Sandhurst. Sandhurst's Officer Commissioning Course lasts one intensive year, and it is widely regarded as being one of the best in the world. Most who go to Sandhurst have either previously served in the Army or have completed a degree and are in the 23–29 age bracket.

I would be eighteen years of age, and I would never have done a day's proper soldiering. But to me Sandhurst was largely a stepping-stone to where I really wanted to get to – and that was the Parachute Regiment.

Shortly prior to graduation we played the ultimate rugby match at Welbeck. Our opponents were Bradford Grammar, who are renowned for having one of the UK's top teams in schools rugby. By now I was well into my position as second row. The match was nearing the ninetieth minute, with the scores more or less equal, when Bradford won a penalty right on our try line.

They decided to kick for goal. In spite of my size I was still one of the fastest in our team. The instant the referee blew the whistle for the kicker to take the penalty I sprinted forwards. I charged down the kicker, but in the process he and I collided full-on, and we both went down.

There had been a massive crack as our heads met, but oddly I hadn't felt any pain, which usually means you've done some real damage. I got up, but I couldn't see through one eye. Everyone was staring at me. It turned out I'd ripped open my forehead. The brow was hanging down my face, the wound pissing blood. I was taken to the sanatorium to see Nanny McPhee.

I was glad to see that my opposite number was in an even worse state than me. I had to have stitches, and I had a bad case of concussion, but at least I could hold my head high. We'd drawn the match, which meant honour had been satisfied. And in the eyes of Geoff Rusher, my College hero and my mentor, I had not been found wanting.

Shortly after the match I heard him handing over to a new bloke, for his time as PE instructor at Welbeck was done. I saw him nod in my direction. 'That one, he's a bloody excellent bloke. You'll get on well with him.'

I had totally reversed my reputation with Geoff. I'd gone from being the slacker and the waster to being a stalwart on the rugger field. I'd broken the College 400-metres record and I'd even run cross-country for Welbeck – which considering my initial performance at the 1.5-miler was something of a miracle.

In June of that year I did my formal attestation to the Army. If you didn't sign up for the minimum three years, your parents would have to pay back all of the money the military had invested in you at Welbeck – and that amounted to a small fortune. I had to swear the oath of allegiance on the Bible, and give my promise to be loyal to Queen and Country for as long as I served.

The Passing Out Parade took place on the Welbeck Quad, with all of us dressed in our thick and itchy green Number Twos. It reminded me of the kind of fighting dress you'd see in *Dad's Army* or *Blackadder*. My family had come down for the day, and had witnessed what was a fine spectacle. At the end of the parade we threw our forage caps in the air and shouted 'Hurrah!' – just as they do in the movie *An Officer and a Gentleman*.

Only three in my year were going direct to Sandhurst, and

neither Cheeky, Ryan, Benny nor Danny was amongst them. After the Passing Out Parade we gathered to do what was de rigueur, which was smashing up the polish on our drill boots, ready for the next guy.

My dad drove me to Sandhurst, for I didn't have a car. I'd been advised to wear a 'sports jacket', which I had presumed meant a tracksuit top. Actually, in Sandhurst speak it was a tweed jacket. I'd been given a list of clothes to buy, including grey-green trousers and white shirts. Mum had scored the lot from Marks & Spencer, for she'd decided I should have quality gear for my stint at Sandhurst.

I soon discovered that a good number of those at the Royal Military Academy Sandhurst wouldn't be seen dead in M&S. Many of the cadets at Welbeck had been from similar backgrounds to my own. By contrast, Sandhurst seemed full of those with double-barrelled surnames, who'd been to schools like Eton and Harrow.

At the state schools I'd attended, few if any pupils went on to become officers in the Army. I didn't understand as yet the stereotype that is applied to British Army officers – that they are posh, they don't tend to get their hands dirty and they drink champers in the Officers' Mess with their little fingers raised to balance the glass. I was now going to see a good deal of that with my own eyes.

There were a good number at Sandhurst who were simply buffoons. They were far more interested in the status of being an Army officer than the reality of soldiering. They liked nothing more than to play up to the posh officer stereotype. It was at Sandhurst that I first came across blokes who'd had a tailor all their lives, and had the gall to ask me who my tailor might be.

A tailor. What the fuck's a tailor? And where on earth is Savile Row?

I genuinely didn't have a clue. I felt out of my depth and pretty much all at sea. This was my stepping-stone into the ultimate military unit in my eyes – the PARAs – and I didn't have a clue about what many of these tossers were here for, not a Scooby Doo.

We gathered for our first parade as three hundred recruits – that year's intake of officer cadets. There were thirty-three blokes in my platoon, which was 27 Platoon, Amiens Company. We stood to attention before the massive, gleaming white pillars of the main building, as the colour sergeants stalked through our ranks inspecting us minutely.

The colour sergeant for 27 Platoon was CSgt Sale. He was about my height but almost twice as wide. He looked like Sylvester Stallone on steroids. He had this deep, rumbling Guardsman's voice, and he seemed to march everywhere with exaggerated, jerky Desperate Dan movements. CSgt Sale made it very clear he intended to be our daddy and mummy and trainer and torturer.

Every cadet at Sandhurst was sponsored to be there by a parent regiment. Via Welbeck I had been sponsored by both the Royal Signals and the Royal Artillery. I'd spent a few days with each during my time at Welbeck, but in truth I had zero intention of joining either. My heart was well and truly set on the PARAs, but for now at least I bided my time and kept my intentions quiet.

At first, Sandhurst was a re-run of Welbeck, only the mindless rules and discipline were even more unfathomable. There was a set order for laying out your room. Your toothbrush, flannel, bar of soap, razor blades – everyone had to wet shave – all had to be arranged in a certain way. Your flannel had to be laid out flat, open and *dry. What the hell was the point in having a dry flannel?*

Your toothbrush had to be in its cup, with the toothpaste tube laid at a regulation ninety-degree angle to it. You weren't allowed to watch TV or have a laptop, and if you had a radio you were only permitted to tune it into Radio 4. It had to be positioned on your bedside table at ninety degrees to your Gideon Bible.

Each morning I stood outside my room as CSgt Sale poked around my room, swagger stick under one arm.

I'd get the inevitable call. 'Officer Cadet Blakeley!'

'Yes, Colour Sergeant.'

'What the fuck is that?'

I'd peer where he was pointing. There on my razor was the tiniest speck of hair. I'd get a show parade for it, which was similar to those at Welbeck. I was pretty used to this by now, but we had some who most definitely were not, especially the foreign students. A good number hailed from African and Commonwealth countries. They were at Sandhurst for genuine defence reasons, and some were pretty hard and tough soldiers.

But there were others who were there simply by dint of defence diplomacy – in other words, to help British trade and overseas relations. Certain oil-rich nations in the Middle East – Bahrain and Qatar foremost amongst them – had places reserved at Sandhurst. For the sons of the stupendously wealthy Arab sheikhs, it was a rite of passage to go to Sandhurst, after which they'd get to run their fathers' military or work in their oil businesses.

Some of those cadets had massive apartments in London and drove fluorescent green Lamborghinis with diplomatic plates. Others had limos with their own driver. There was one in our platoon, called Saleem. He used to call his driver in London, order a curry, and get it driven up and delivered to his room. While the Staff had to be seen to be fair, there was something of a blind eye turned, or it would risk a diplomatic incident.

Fortunately for me, the bloke next door to me was a down-to-earth ranker called Matt Bacon. Matt had served in the First Gulf War as a corporal with the Army Air Corps. He'd come to Sandhurst from the Army Air Corps, where he'd been serving as a Corporal and been selected to go through officer training.

He was the oldest in our platoon, at 27. I was the youngest, at 18. He and I were from similar backgrounds, and we were both super fit and serious about our soldiering. On the very first day we had to do our BPFA. He came second on the 1.5-miler and I was a close third. I did better than him in the gymnasium, and when CSgt Sale put up the 'name and shame' list, he and I were equal tops.

His clothes also came from M&S, and we formed an alliance of the M&S Brothers. I confided in him my plans to join the PARAs, and he agreed it was exactly the right choice for me. He wanted to join the Army Intelligence Corps, because it was a career for life, and he wanted to be a lifer. The Corps was sponsoring his place and he was likely to get fast track promotion.

The other bloke I bonded with immediately was Dan Jarvis. Dan hailed from Nottingham, which was close to Welbeck College. He was tall and lean and he'd been first in on the 1.5-miler. He was both a mountaineer and a marathon runner, and he'd just completed a degree in international politics and strategic studies.

At the end of the 1.5-miler he had confided in me that he also wanted to join the PARAs. It made us natural buddies, and he became another of the M&S Brothers.

At Sandhurst I had to do more drill, fitness and tabbing. What was new were the lessons in war and leadership studies. These were held in one of the huge auditoria, but much of it didn't sit particularly well with me. Sandhurst taught officer cadets to lead by authority. 'You might run with the hounds, but you should never *be* a hound', was the general view. Familiarity breeds contempt, and an officer should keep himself apart.

It didn't make a lot of sense to me.

John Keegan, who was then the Head of Leadership Studies at Sandhurst, had written a book called *The Mask of Command*. It studied the lives of some of the great military leaders, including Alexander, Wellington, Grant and Hitler. In doing so, it broke command down into a scientific kind of formula, by isolating what Keegan saw as the key common factors.

But even at the age of eighteen I didn't think command was that: it was human, personal, individual and intuitive. By studying such foremost commanders and generals, Keegan had looked at those whose very positions of power meant that they would rarely, if ever, be disobeyed. They had been commanders by right, and that didn't make them *leaders*.

I was far more interested in how a corporal managed to get his men to follow him over the top, to assault the German trenches during the First World War. How did he get his men to follow him, when they knew they faced almost certain death? And how did a private soldier take over command, as had so often happened, when the senior ranks around him had all been killed?

Those were the true marks of leadership, for in those situations only via a man's moral courage, character and example could he get men to follow his lead. One of the best things I ever learned at Sandhurst came from the writings of one of the most gifted, yet under-rated generals of the Second World War. I read his works in my private hours, for he was barely on the syllabus.

Field Marshal Bill Slim had masterminded the brilliant Burma Campaign in the Second World War, turning crushing defeat by the Japanese into a stunning victory. He literally snatched victory from the very jaws of defeat. More to the point, he had done so leading a polyglot army of many races, religions and creeds. Under his leadership they were united and they had proved unbeatable.

Slim stressed that an officer should put his men first. He should put their rest, welfare and safety before his own, and lead from the front, by *example*. Only by doing so would he earn their respect and the right to lead. Slim proved modest and self-effacing, but fearless in combat, and the daring and maverick design of his missions meant they often struck deep behind enemy lines. His were some of the first unconventional Special Forces type operations, and they proved to be battle winners.

He was also universally loved by his men.

Slim wrote: 'Leadership is simple – it's just plain being you.'

Having read those words in the Sandhurst library, I would never forget them. Slim was the kind of leader I would have followed into hell itself, had he asked me to do so. And I felt certain that if I tried to adopt 'the mask of command' when I made it into the PARAs – that's if I survived selection – I wouldn't last five minutes in their number.

Due to my keenness to get out of the mind-numbing drill, I volunteered for the Sandhurst Boxing Club. I had never boxed before, and there were some seriously hard blokes on the team. There was this Czech monster who had pale white skin with a massive tattoo of a dragon down half his back and one arm. He was an animal, and I really did not want to go up against him.

Almost as fearsome was Matt 'Beast' Malone, a fellow officer cadet who was definitely not from Eton or Harrow. He hailed from a comprehensive school and his father had been a ranker in the Army. He was squat, solid and meaty, with a thick rug of hair covering his arms and his back, hence the 'Beast' nickname. He had fists like hams, and although he was slightly shorter than me he was heavier, plus he had a fine technique for he'd boxed a great deal.

The coach who took me on was Staff Sergeant McGregor, and he became the equivalent of my Geoff Rusher figure at Welbeck. He was an ex-PARA, with PARA Reg tattoos all down his massive arms. I told him I wanted to join his old regiment, and he took to me right away. Unlike CSgt Sale, who treated the officer cadets very formally, he spoke to me on the level.

One day I came back from a sparring session, and I ran into trouble. I jogged into our lines only to see our entire platoon out on parade. The Officer Commanding our platoon was a Captain Armitage. He was out front addressing the cadets. As soon as he laid eyes on me with my hands still encased in a boxer's bandages, he tore into me. Apparently, he'd called a Scale A Parade, which meant that everyone had to be there.

Normally, doing training for the Sandhurst boxing team got you out of drill. But not a Scale A. I tried explaining that I was training for a forthcoming bout, so I was going the extra mile for the Academy. Regardless, I was given five show parades on the spot, as my 'punishment'. I was fuming, but I knew if you fought against the Army system, the system would always beat you.

Captain Armitage, like all platoon commanders, had to lead our instruction on a chosen subject. His was Army Staff Writing – in other words, how to lay out loose minutes, memos, official letters and demi-official – semi-formal – communiqués. To Captain Armitage, that kind of crap seemed to be the most important stuff in the Army, and he certainly seemed to excel at it.

He set the platoon some homework in his chosen subject. You had to decide if a given task required a demi-official, official, memo … or whatever. You weren't allowed to use a computer and you had to handwrite everything. I handed it in to him on time at the start of our next lesson.

The Captain took one look at what I'd done and practically had a fit. Apparently, I had committed the heinous crime of writing in blue biro, whereas it could only ever be written in black. I was ordered to redo the entire lot, and hand it in at the start of the next class, which meant Monday morning, which in turn meant doing it over the weekend.

We had zero time off, for there were lessons on Saturday, and on Sunday a long church parade, followed by orienteering exercises, then kit polishing and ironing for the week ahead. Still, I had it ready for Monday morning, and I went to hand it in at our first lesson, which was around mid-morning.

He stared at me disdainfully, as I tried to hand him the work. 'So, are these your letters?'

'They are, sir.'

'Well, here they may be, but you were supposed to hand them in at 0800 hours this morning.'

'No, sir, I wasn't. You told me to hand them in at our next lesson.'

His face reddened to puce. 'Don't you dare answer me back. I'm putting you on a charge.'

I wanted nothing more than to smash him in the face. He was going to charge me, which meant a formal black mark would go against my record, and that might well jeopardise my chances of making it into the PARAs. But if I whacked the jumped-up little twat, then I was finished in the Army.

After lunch there was a free period. I was back in the accommodation block ironing my uniforms, when I heard the familiar ring of CSgt Sale's boots in the corridor.

'Officer Cadet Blakeley!' his voice bellowed. 'Platoon Commander's office, Service Dress, ten minutes.'

I pulled on my Service Dress, topped off by my blue Sandhurst beret. I stood to attention outside my door. CSgt Sale marched up to me, until his face was barely inches from mine. In the intense silence I could hear other cadets mooching about in their rooms, pretending they weren't listening.

'Dead – man – walking,' he hissed in my face. He stepped back a pace. 'No you're not, son.' He tilted his head. 'Hear that? They're shouting – save Mr Blakeley! Save Mr Blakeley!'

No one was shouting anything. CSgt Sale was just fucking with my head. But in a way I liked him for it. He was giving me a quiet nod that all of this was total bullshit.

'Officer Cadet Blakeley, 'shun!' he yelled, then marched me down to Captain Armitage's office.

From behind his desk the Captain read out his smug little charge sheet. 'Under Army regulation blah, blah, blah you are charged with disobeying an order and failing to hand in your work as instructed at 0800 hours. You can accept the charge or elect for trial by Court Martial. How do you choose?'

I replied with barely a pause. 'Sir, I accept the charge, sir.'

But inside I was boiling. I had a quiet suspicion as to why he was shitting on me. The rumour had got out that I was going for the PARAs, and blokes like him despised the Parachute Regiment. It represented everything that they were not, and it shamed them. And so they hated the PARAs, and those who wanted to join them.

At the end of that first term the Sandhurst boxing team had to fight Oxford University. Oxford has some 20,000 students to pick from. We had 1000. They also had a raft of fantastic athletes, not to mention the best rowing team in the world. They were understandably the odds-on favourite.

We were weighed in that afternoon. I was 84 kilos, so just into the heavyweights. Due to a last-minute injury the Oxford team was one man down, which meant that I got paired up to do a 'show fight'. Instead of fighting an Oxford University boxer, I would have to fight one of our own. And the bloke chosen to go up against me was Beast Malone.

In a way I felt relieved simply to have got a fight. I'd put all the intensive training in, so I wanted to get a bout. But on the other hand the Beast was older and heavier and far more experienced than me.

You are allowed to invite your father to a match when you are boxing for the Academy. I had done so, but he couldn't get the time off teaching, and he wouldn't bluff it and call in sick, a decision I fully respected. But the only other bloke who didn't have his father there was the Czech monster.

A couple of hours prior to the start of the fight I reported to the gym. Sergeant McGregor began to bandage up my hands and wrists, the four fingers being wrapped separately to the thumb, and bound real tight. The idea of the bandages was to give greater protection to your hands from the impact as you punched your opponent's face in. Or maybe he punched yours in.

By the time he was done bandaging me my adrenaline was pumping. I didn't want to keep burning it, for I needed to hold it back for the fight. I pulled out my Walkman so I could listen to some music. I put the Parachute Regiment's march on – 'The Ride of the Valkyries' – which has to be one of the most stirring and evocative of any military marches in the world.

I'd first heard it at a Sandhurst dinner night, when a senior PARA officer had visited. They'd played it in his honour. As soon as I heard it I was transfixed. By the end the hairs on the back of my neck were rigid. I knew the music, but only from seeing the movie *Apocalypse Now*: it's played as the US helicopter attack squadron goes in on the assault. When I realised it was the Parachute Regiment's official march, I knew the PARAs were my destiny.

As I sat there waiting for my bout, I alternated 'The Ride of the Valkyries' with Jimi Hendrix, who was himself a paratrooper, prior to becoming the world's greatest guitarist. He'd served with the 101st Airborne, an iconic unit, before being medically discharged. Apparently, he'd shown scant regard for discipline or for regulations, breaking his ankle on his 26th jump. Hendrix had been a renegade and a maverick, and his commanding officer had been glad to get shot of him.

As I walked into the gymnasium, Hendrix's 'All Along the Watchtower' was playing in my ears. In the Army you box a three-minute round, so longer than in a civvie bout. You win on a knockout or on points. As I stepped towards the ring, I could see blokes I had trained with covered in blood from their bouts. Sergeant McGregor led me through the ropes, like a gladiator into the arena.

The Academy gymnasium is gigantic. The boxing ring sat in the very centre, surrounded by the crowd. Everywhere I looked there were officers and officer cadets in their mess dress – so wearing the formal attire of each of their parent units. There were ranks of bright red jackets, black bow ties and tight black trousers. There were Royal Irish officers in their shamrock green. In short, some 2000 officers and cadets had formed a sea of colours.

The Army piper was playing the bagpipes, and I could feel the heat thrown off from the crowd. I had deliberately chosen to wear maroon – the colour of the PARAs. I knew Captain Armitage would be somewhere amongst the crowd, and I did it as a deliberate provocation. By contrast, Beast Malone was dressed in blue, which was the standard colour for a Sandhurst officer cadet.

As the younger and lighter boxer, I was out first. There were cheers for me from my mates within the crowd, Matt Bacon and Dan

Jarvis amongst them. But it was nothing compared to the deafening wall of noise that rose up as Beast Malone stepped towards the ring. The chant went on and on: 'BEAST MALONE! BEAST MALONE! BEAST MALONE!'

I guess it did have the edge over chanting 'David Blakeley!'

The Beast had the name. He also had the reputation as a boxer. Plus he sure as hell looked the part. By contrast, I was younger and there were those who reckoned I looked as if I'd just walked out of a Ken and Barbie set. Dan and Matt used to tease me rotten that I was the kind of clean-cut, square-jawed pretty boy who would be better off working as a catalogue model.

The fuckers.

The Beast lifted the rope and stepped into the ring. The referee brought us together and made us touch gloves, and then the bell rang for the start of round one. I zoned out the crowd and went forward, my moves crab-like and stiff, my chin dropped on my left shoulder. It's hard to knock someone down unless you can land a blow on his chin. By contrast the Beast was moving with light, dancing, fluid movements, ones that belied his power and his weight.

We exchanged the first blows, the Beast landing a couple of evil ones on my head. He was clearly going for point scores and playing to the judges, while I was finding it hard to find my rhythm. Towards the end of the first round my arms were feeling heavy, and the Beast was still going for the scores. Then I saw my chance.

I hammered a blow through his defences. I saw my right crunch into his face, and I followed up with a swift left hook. The first blow rattled him, and the second sent the Beast crashing to the floor. There was a gasp from the crowd, as the referee began the count, but the Beast was back up within seconds. He was wary of me now, but before we could lock horns again the bell went for the end of round one.

I went into my corner and sank into a pool of gasping sweat.

Sergeant McGregor leaned over me, towelling me down and spurting water into my mouth.

'Good on you, lad. You got him. Keep at it and keep calm. You've got him.'

I was fighting more like a judo player – waiting for my opponent to make a mistake before hammering him. I wouldn't be winning many points, that was for sure. My only option was to bring the bloke down and end it. We stepped out for round two and again the Beast landed a good few punches on me. But right at the end of the round I hit him with a second steamroller right, and it sent him reeling.

I returned to my corner, and I felt Sergeant McGregor on my shoulder. 'Right, lad, go in for the kill now.'

We rose for round three, the final round. The crowd was going wild, and again the cries of 'BEAST MALONE!' drowned out any support for me. I opened my nostrils wide to draw in extra oxygen to the brain. It was time to close now. The Beast started going for it, landing every punch he could upon my body and my shoulders. But my reach was longer, and I managed to keep him mostly at bay.

Then I saw the moment. I'd pushed him back into his corner, and I went for it. I hit him with a series of pounding upper cuts, followed by a left hook that took him off his feet and sent him down for a second time. I saw him fall in slow motion, and as he went I heard an anguished cry from the audience.

'NOOOOOOO!'

It was the Beast's father. He had his hands clutching his head, for he could tell how badly I'd whacked him. The referee began the count. It was 'eight' before the Beast managed to get to his feet. No sooner had he done so than I moved in and started to smash him, left–right–left–right–left–right … An instant later the referee had stepped between us and stopped the fight.

He lifted up my right arm. I heard the crowd around me erupt in wild cheers. The underdog had triumphed. I was pissing sweat and my head ached like hell from all the blows, but I was buzzing like never before. As I stepped out of the ring and into the crowd I saw a familiar face. It was Captain Armitage.

'Erm ... Well done, Blakeley, old boy, well done.'

What the fuck else was he supposed to say? I had just won a major triumph and an honour for his platoon. I knew at that moment he would never give me any shit again.

I went and changed into my dress uniform. After a formal boxing bout you were allowed the rare privilege of a drink in the Sergeants' Mess. No officers are allowed, except by invitation. It seemed that I was now CSgt Sale's best mate. He was lit up that a young lad in his platoon had dropped a legend like the Beast.

After a few beers I went for a piss. Over the porcelain urinals were these fantastic photos from some of the British Army's most historic moments, plus the odd cartoon and press cutting. They say the Sergeants' Mess is the heart of any battalion, and this one was no exception.

I felt a figure appear beside me. He was in full mess dress, and I noticed the red jacket with gold braid, and the pair of Parachute Regiment wings on his shoulder. More often than not, the decent officers would get invited to the Sergeants' Mess for a few beers. This bloke was obviously one of them.

He eyed me for a moment. 'Good fight.'

'Thank you, sir.'

'Good fight.' He repeated. A steely-eyed pause. 'Is this your first?'

'Yes, sir.'

'Are you going to fight any more?'

'Yes, sir, I think so.'

'If I were you, I'd stop right there.'

For a moment I was shocked. 'Why?'

'Because then you'll have a one hundred per cent unbeaten record.'

He smiled and walked away.

I realised then that was the Parachute Regiment way – while you used your muscle, you also needed to be able to use your head.

*

CHAPTER TEN

———

You use your head, not just your muscle: it's a lesson I've missed completely on this last, desperate leg of Endurance. Here, I've let my injured and exhausted body rule my fogged head. As I run my red-rimmed eyes over the map, the freezing rain and sleet lashes down heavily, splattering off the waterproof case into the thin beam of blue light thrown off by my torch.

I'm lost.

I've run out of time.

I know for sure I am going to fail.

When your brain accelerates and starts to race, that's a sure sign that you're suffering from exposure. If you allow the confusion and panic to set in, things rapidly spiral out of control. Your worried brain tells your body to start doing stupid things, like climbing down sheer cliff faces in the midst of a dark, lightning-slashed thunderstorm and with your knee gone.

The worse your body gets, the less it's able to maintain proper brain function. It's a vicious circle. One dysfunction feeds off the other, and hypothermia soon sets in. In the early stages your mind goes fuzzy, thoughts wander and you get irrational. Speech slows and slurs, as your body temperature keeps dropping. You shiver uncontrollably and start to lose all rational thought.

In the final stages, you lose all sense of yourself. You feel as if your body is burning up with heat, when actually you are freezing to death. Many who die from hypothermia are found naked, or semi-naked. In the final, messed-up moments they've ripped off all their clothing, because they think they are burning up.

I'm not there yet, not by a long chalk. But I'm on my way.

There is a technique I've learned for staying positive and focused, when you are deep in the shit. You can change the way your body and your brain operate simply by thinking positively. If you force yourself to run positive thoughts and images through your mind – happy childhood memories, thoughts of family and friends – you can turn the situation around, or at least stop it from worsening.

I do just that now. I think of nights on the piss with my mates. I think of my loving parents and my sisters. I think of the blokes I've grown close to here on PF selection. I calm my mind, and get it to focus on the map and to work out just where I am and what went wrong.

I realise pretty quickly that I've taken a wrong turn some 800 yards back in the thick of the forest. I've gone down this narrow trail and it's taken me to the verge of a massive precipice that rings the mountain top. If I'd carried on over that it would have been a good few hundred feet of vertical fall to the hard, frozen ground below.

I can't believe I've made such a basic navigational error – especially as I know this area so well. I realise now how seriously messed up I must have become, and it sobers me up instantly. I turn back and begin the long stumble uphill. I have to fight through the shittiest terrain imaginable, and all because my mind had told me to keep on going, come what may.

I reach the crest of the hill and I'm a stumbling wreck. But at least it's all downhill from here. I start the final descent. My arms are like lead weights as I crab my way ahead, lifting my right leg down each agonising step. My feet keep slipping and sliding on the slick of snow and ice underfoot. Each fall feels like a hammer blow to my injured knee.

But I reach the last checkpoint. *Finally.*

The DS have set up a tea urn for those of us who are last in. It's testimony to how appalling the weather has become that they're bending the rules like this. I take the steaming mug that's handed to me with a shaking, juddering hand. I can't even hold it still to take the first sip.

'Am in last?' I slur, my jaw hammering with the cold and the question sounding practically unintelligible.

The words have come croaking out from a throat that's bone dry with dehydration, in spite of the fact that I'm piss wet through and frozen to the core. My voice sounds like that of a stranger. I hardly sound like me any more.

The DS shakes his head. 'There's one more.'

'Jez?'

'Rowlands,' he confirms. 'He's the last.'

I turn and stumble for the truck. For the first time since I started selection the four-tonner is completely empty. It can only mean one thing: the driver's ferried everyone else back to Camp, then returned for Jez and me. I lie there, feeling lost and lonely and defeated, and convinced that as far as selection's concerned, I'm done for.

Within an instant I'm comatose.

I wake to the rhythmic rocking of the truck. I stare at the green canvas roof, then out of the open rear into the blankness of the snow-laden night. It takes me a few seconds to recollect where I am – in the back of the four-tonner, en route to Sennybridge Camp. I run my eyes around the darkened bed of the wagon, and there beside me is the rumpled form of Jez.

It's a forty-five-minute drive. I must have dropped off again. I wake once more when we pull to a final halt. This time, the driver's taken pity on the two of us. He's pulled up right next to the Nissen hut door. I fall out of the rear, shoulder my pack and manage to limp the short distance to the hut.

Inside, it's a heaped mass of snoring, steaming bodies. I glance at Taff's bunk. It's empty. He's gone.

I crawl across to my own bunk, throw back the dog blanket and clamber inside, fully clothed. An instant later, I'm utterly dead to the world.

The following morning is a Saturday, and those who've passed Test Week have got a whole weekend off. I doubt if I'm one of them. But oddly, no one's yet told me to leave. I hobble down to a late breakfast, my knee the size of a football. The cookhouse is pretty much empty, so I hoover up whatever leftovers I can find.

I'm half expecting one of the DS to ask me to head to Lenny's office after I'm done eating, which will mean that I've been binned. But I last all morning, and still there's been no word. I lie on the bunk with my leg raised on a couple of spare pillows, so as to give it some time to rest and recuperate.

I get a visit from the Camp medic, and I convince him to strap up the knee, so as to make it usable for the week that's coming. For those still on selection it's Live Firing Week, which means a lot of time on the ranges. It'll be physical, but nothing compared to what we've been through so far. With my knee strapped I should be okay – that's if I'm still in.

The medic tells me what I figure I know already – that I've dislocated my knee pretty badly. It's exactly the same injury that I suffered on P Company – PARA selection. The original injury must have weakened the joint and that's why it gave out on me. The medic tells me to keep the knee rested and elevated all weekend, and to keep an ice pack on it to take down the swelling.

During the whole of that weekend none of the DS so much as say a word to me. No one tells me if I've passed or failed Test Week. It's the same with Jez. I know Lenny can make a special dispensation if the weather comes in really bad. In effect, he's got the discretion to make a special case and allow extra time.

I figure that's what he must have done with us, for come Monday morning both Jez and I are on the roster for Live Firing.

A couple of new blokes have joined us for the next stages. The reason why is telling. On the previous Pathfinder selection only two blokes survived to the end of week two – so to where we are now. They couldn't continue with selection with just the two blokes, so they postponed the rest of their trial until winter selection came around.

Dean hails from Hereford and he's a well-respected PARA, although he's got a bit of a colourful track record. He was a corporal in the PARAs and he'd gone home to visit his girlfriend, only to find her in bed with someone. He'd proceeded to beat the living daylights out of the bloke, and got done for GBH. It was while serving time in prison that he had decided to go for PF selection.

He'd returned to the PARAs, been busted back to private, then gone for the first available slot on PF selection. He's a very cool and good-looking bloke, with tanned skin and longer, dark hair. He's got a rippling six-pack and he's bulked out with muscle. He's a smooth, sharp operator and it gives us all a boost to have him with us.

The other bloke is Smudge. He's an East End of London geezer with a bullet-shaped shaven head. He hails from 9 Squadron Royal Engineers, which is an airborne engineers unit. They're generally very physical blokes who spend their time parachuting into drop zones where they have to build bridges, dig trenches, clear war debris and generally man it about.

Smudge is incredibly capable and smart, and he could easily make it as an officer. He's not had much of a classic education, but he's intelligent and a good leader. But like Mark, our Kiwi bloke on selection, Smudge has zero interest in going there. He doesn't naturally warm to officers, and he's both suspicious of and intrigued by me. I'm a captain in the PARAs, but I'm clearly very much one of the blokes here. It's not what Smudge is used to.

Live Firing Week is a crucial part of selection. You need to be extremely capable with your weapons to make it as a Pathfinder. You need to be superlative at shooting fast and aggressively, and you need to be highly skilled on a variety of guns. You need to show you can move quickly, while shooting accurately and instinctively and not blundering into your fellow operators' arcs of fire.

Putting down a concentrated wall of lead is key to your survival, when you're operating in a small, six-man patrol. If you get bumped it will be by a far superior enemy force, and you'll have to fight your way out of there. You will have no back-up and no rescue force available, so the ability to put down fire with massive aggression and then melt away quickly is key to saving your patrol.

For Live Firing Week we head off into the Brecons to use the different ranges, each of which takes you through varying terrain. Stan Harris and Tricky kick the week off with a demo, and it's like something out of the final scenes in the movie *Heat,* when the bank robbers have to fight their way out of a seemingly inescapable trap set by US law enforcement agents.

The two of them put down a blistering barrage of fast and furious fire, moving rapidly from one position of cover to another. They kept screaming out their moves to each other as they went – 'Break left! On me! Right!' It looked like a finely-rehearsed series of battle manoeuvres, during every second of which they kept their weapons pumping out the rounds. In fact, it's instinctive and intuitive, and it's incredibly impressive.

Unlike the rest of the military they wear no helmets, for you're unlikely to wear one when in a PF patrol for real. You're also more aware of your surroundings without a helmet, and more aware of what your buddy is doing. Live firing is hugely dangerous, especially when you're doing it at this level – superfast and always on the move. Sadly, soldiers are killed each year on live firing exercises.

We unleash thousands of rounds during daylight and at night, across open fields, in closed woodland, over streams and rivers, up and over hills and down into the valleys. We are firing at very close proximity to each other. One false step and someone will end up dead. It proves hugely exhilarating, and even more so for me, as my injured knee seems to be holding up passably well.

The week culminates in an exercise where you have to operate as a six-man patrol, break contact with the 'enemy' and extract a casualty. I'm teamed up with Jez, Al, Pete, Mark and Smudge, and they make me the casualty. They do so in part because I'm the biggest unit, so I'm the biggest challenge, and they do so because they know my knee got buggered on Endurance.

While the rest of the lads put down a wall of fire, Jez has to hump up fifteen stone of me, plus weapons and ammo, and get me out of the immediate area of fire. Then they break fire, and another bloke joins Jez so they can grab me by my webbing and drag me rapidly away from the kill zone.

Too often in the regular Army you only ever do static live firing, so standing still or lying on the ranges. More often than not you do so fresh, so having done little or no exertion beforehand. In reality, you'll likely be fighting while on the move, and when you're hot, tired and thirsty from whatever has gone before.

Pathfinder selection Live Firing Week is as realistic as it's possible to make it, without being at war. People do fail it. They fail if they've only ever learned the standard Army way of going down the ranges, and their weapons skills are too formal and unsuited to such fluid, fast and unpredictable conditions.

We also do some demolitions work in Live Firing Week. We get to blow up old cars and trucks and bridges simulated from scaffolding poles, which is a great crack. But the main focus is firing the guns. Confidence with your weapon is key here, because in the PF for real it's how you react in the first seconds of a contact that will determine whether you and your comrades will live or die.

We get through Live Firing Week with no fails, and my knee seems to be holding up well. At the end of the Elan Valley Test March we were down to twelve. Then we lost Taff, when he VWd on Endurance. We've had Smudge and Dean join us, so it's pushed our number up to thirteen as we go into Standard Operating Procedure (SOP) Week, which is where we'll learn the unique Pathfinder craft.

Thirteen. We hope it's not going to prove unlucky for some ...

Special Forces normally work in four-man fire teams, with a number of those teams forming up larger Troops and Squadrons. In The Pathfinders, we learn to operate in both four- and six-man teams. Four is the minimum that would ever be deployed on ops, but you usually work in a basic team of six – the reason being that six is the number of blokes that man The Pathfinders' standard vehicle patrols.

Most normally, the Pathfinders operate in DPVs – Desert Patrol Vehicles. The DPV is an open-topped Land Rover equipped with light and heavy machine guns, and is specialised for long-range deep-penetration missions. Pathfinders also deploy on foot or via the air, but a two-vehicle patrol requires six men to operate it, which is the logic behind making six the standard base unit.

If you pass selection, you get given a PF *Tactical Doctrine Handbook,* one that lays out exactly how the unit carries out long-range communications, vehicle-borne missions and airborne insertions, the recce and marking of drop zones, calling in aircraft, deploying snipers, demolitions and more.

Your first year in the unit is spent on probation learning all of that craft, and you have to pass a number of training cadres. Right now, here in selection we're going to get given a basic grounding in all of this, while at the same time we're being tested. We'll learn only the basic bread and butter of PF operations, but it's still hugely exciting, for this is what makes the unit unique.

The first few mornings of SOP Week are classroom-based. I'm still having my knee strapped up by the medic, but the swelling's almost gone now. Live Firing Week has proved just the kind of break that it needed. In class we learn the basics of long-range high-frequency (HF) radio comms as a small patrol – so how to string up wire antennae and use them to bounce HF radio signals off the ionosphere.

Obviously, it's crucial to remain undetected when operating behind enemy lines, so you learn to use comms kit which is all but impossible to detect. You train to use top-secret comms systems – those that scramble any message into an unbreakable code. You learn how to keep changing frequencies, so an enemy has less chance of intercepting your comms or listening in.

In a six-man PF unit there are a number of key roles that have to be filled. The first is that of 'lead scout'. He's the point man on patrol, and he needs to select the route taken and so will be one of the strongest navigators. He will also very likely be first into any enemy fire, and so his weapons skills need to be especially strong. His immediate action drill is to put a double-tap into his adversary's head – two shots, which you learn to do almost at the speed of one.

He then steps out of the line of fire so he won't be targeted himself, and fires a second double-tap. The lead scout is also the person who's most likely to stumble into one of the enemy's trip flares, and especially when doing a close target recce. He therefore needs to have incredibly strong skills of detection and avoidance, so as to prevent that happening and the entire patrol getting compromised.

The patrol commander is in charge of the overall mission and the wider mission objectives, and he acts as a back-up navigator. Under him he might have any of the following: a patrol signaller, who runs the comms; a patrol medic, a sniper, a machine-gunner, a demolitions expert, or a joint terminal air controller (JTAC) for calling in the warplanes. More often than not PF operators combine several of those skills.

When out on ops Pathfinders only ever use pencils and note-pads to record intel, as pens can get wet and stop working. The only handwritten information with which they will deploy is a list that provides radio frequencies to be used for the duration of the mission.

The patrol signaller makes sure that all patrol members know where the cryptographic cards for the radios are held, so in theory one of them can grab those if the signaller gets shot and killed. Without it, the patrol will be reduced to sending comms unencoded, so via open means.

We learn all of this in the classroom, and we go out in the afternoons to practise it for real. We learn that a patrol moves with each man keeping his eyes glued to wherever his weapon is pointing. That way, you can open fire instantly and get a drop on the enemy. And we learn one of the key aspects of Pathfinder recce missions, which is how to locate, construct and remain concealed in a hide, more commonly known as an observation post (OP).

You have to find a position from which you can observe the enemy while remaining concealed yourselves. You have to move into that position covertly, remove vegetation and dig your hide without getting detected by the enemy. You use standard gardening secateurs to cut into bushes as unobtrusively as possible. You dig out earth and learn how to hide the disturbed soil.

You learn how to use chicken wire to construct a frame, upon which you replace the vegetation that you've cut away, by threading twigs, leaves, moss and the like through the loops in the wire. You fix the vegetation into the wire with matt-green gaffer tape or dark-coloured plastic ties. Once you're in your hide you can pull your chicken wire covering over you, and you'll be hidden from all but the closest of observers.

The DS take us out on the moors and show us one of the quickest ways of making an emergency hide. In thick heather you can grab your knife, slice a rough, man-sized rectangle in the earth, roll back the heather like a slab of turf, dive under it and roll it back over you. A man can lie like that and remain unseen while an enemy passes within yards of him. It's a way of making a quick and ready one-man hide, if the enemy is about to stumble upon you.

You learn to construct a skywave antenna behind your OP, hidden in woodland, so you can radio in reports on what you see to headquarters. You learn to use a range of viewing devices – from long-range binoculars to powerful thermal imaging and night vision sights – to keep watch on the enemy through all weather conditions and at all times of day and night.

You practise two men going forward from your hidden OP to carry out a close target recce (CTR). The two-man team extracts from the rear of the OP and boxes around to the enemy position, taking time and care to leave the slightest trail possible. You go lightweight, so wearing your webbing only, and you learn to probe the enemy position from many different angles, and to read enemy activity.

You learn to formulate all the information into pinpoint accurate patrol reports, complete with sketch-maps and diagrams of enemy positions, including where their heaviest weapons are positioned. You record potential lines of attack, good fire-support positions, and lines of insertion and extraction.

Because you're covered in dirt and camouflage cream and sweat and worse, you use latex gloves to write your reports, so they're legible. Those patrol reports will be passed to the Brigade Commander, or others in high command, so you can guide in a main assault force. You need to be able to communicate a lot of information very clearly and concisely to those who may have only just been airdropped onto the ground.

SOP Week ends with a two-day exercise, where we have to put all these skills to the test. As with everything that's gone before, any one of us can fail. You may have proved yourself able to survive extreme and prolonged physical abuse, but that doesn't necessarily mean you'll make a good PF operator, especially when it comes to putting into practice all the fine skills of the soldiering craft.

For the SOP Exercise, we're broken down into teams of four. Oddly, we lost another bloke at the start of SOP Week. He'd hurt himself during Endurance, but had thought it only a minor injury. Instead, it worsened until the medic felt he had to dob him in. He's been told that he's being RTU'd, but the DS have made it crystal clear they'd welcome him to try again.

We're three teams of four that set out into the wilds of the Brecons. It's 2100 hours and the night is dark. We have to move in on foot, carrying Bergens loaded with enough kit for a forty-eight-hour mission. It's a ten-kilometre infiltration to the mission objective, which for us is a remote, deserted ruin of a farm – one that right now is occupied by a very alert and hungry hunter force made up of serving Pathfinders.

I'm in a team consisting of Smudge, Jez and Al and me. We know the Pathfinders occupying that remote farmhouse are as determined to detect us lot and seriously fuck with our shit as we are to evade and avoid them. If they do, we're pretty much done for. Yet at the same time we have to get eyes on their location, and complete our set recce taskings, or we'll fail.

We tab in, taking it relatively slowly, and moving tactically as a patrol. We know that the PF hunter force is out there, roaming. They outnumber us, so they have enough blokes to man the farmhouse and scour the open countryside. Compared to how fast we moved during the Test Marches, we're creeping through the terrain. We've got our rifles front, observing our arcs and poised to open fire if the hunter force ping us.

I am on point, as lead scout, and Smudge is acting as patrol commander. We're aware that this is something of a reversal of roles, for if I do get into the PF, I'll be the 2IC of the unit. But the logic here is that you can't effectively lead what you haven't already experienced, and right now I'm getting bedded into the lead scout role.

I'm hyperalert as we press ahead, scanning my arcs of fire and sweeping the terrain all around me for any sign of the 'enemy'. We're an hour in when the weather turns. It's been pretty shitty all week, but it's largely been grey sheets of rain and sleet sweeping in off the hills. Last night the sky cleared, which has meant that the temperature has kept dropping.

The ground is frozen hard as concrete underfoot, and as we steal our way ahead the first big, heavy flakes of snow start to fall. It's so dark that the first I know of it is a crisp, icy flake settling onto my face. It melts with my body heat, but more follow. In no time we're stepping through an eerie cloud of silent, dancing grey, the snowfall muting the sounds all around us.

It deadens the noise of our footfalls, and this is great weather for avoiding the enemy. But it isn't exactly ideal for setting up a hidden OP. We're on 'hard routine' now. You always are when out on PF ops for real. It means no brewing up, no hot food, and shitting in cling film and pissing in bottles. You avoid doing anything that might lead the enemy to you or give your position away.

Brewing up in such conditions as these would create a cloud of steam, which can give you away. Even the smell of a hot meal can carry to the enemy. Plus the enemy will very likely have thermal imaging kit, which will make the heat thrown off by your stove visible from two to three miles away.

As for shit and piss, if you foul the immediate surroundings of your OP an enemy hunter force can track you to it. All it takes is for them to be using a couple of trained tracker dogs, and they'll pick up the scent from miles away. That's why sticking to hard routine is crucial to any Pathfinder operation, and why we're going to be on it for the next forty-eight hours.

By contrast, the PF hunter force can hole up in the shelter of the farmhouse until the worst blows over, and there are no such 'hard routine' strictures placed upon them. In fact, they're supposed to do all the normal things an enemy might do – including cooking scoff and using the crappers – so that we have a better chance of detecting them.

Meanwhile, we're going to be in the icy scrape of a snowbound hole gnawing on frozen Mars bars, while they'll be eating hot beans and supping brews around the fire.

It's pretty obvious that the odds are stacked against us.

*

CHAPTER ELEVEN

I had been out in the Brecons so often with the Army, it had started to feel like a second home. The very first jaunts were with Welbeck, but I was back there several times while at Sandhurst.

I was nearing the end of my year as an officer cadet when we were sent out on a six-day exercise in 'The Beacons'. It was spring, but typically it was lashing with rain and freezing cold. We were five days into the exercise, when one of the blokes in our platoon went missing. It wasn't just any old Tom. It was Saleem, our Lamborghini-driving cadet and son of the super-wealthy Arab sheikh.

It was the middle of the night, it was Saleem's stint on stag, but somehow the silly sod had vanished. We sent out a search party and it was me who found him. He was lying on the ground soaked to the skin, and in the secondary stages of hypothermia. His weapon – a loaded SA80 – was lying abandoned by his side. He was in rag state, and I was pretty surprised that he hadn't turned the gun on himself.

I liked Saleem. Sure, he got cut more slack than the rest of us, but I didn't particularly mind. He wore a thin moustache: we were forbidden from having any facial hair. He got curries chauffeured direct into the Academy from London: we rarely got a chance to go down to the chippie. But as far as I was concerned, Saleem was a good bloke – he just wasn't cut out for spending days in a freezing

South Wales rainstorm, with the odd bit of sleet thrown in for good measure.

And why should he be? Saleem had probably rarely seen snow and rain before. He certainly felt the cold worse than any of us, and right now he was frozen to the core. I picked him up, gathered his weapon and manhandled him back to our harbour.

I had to work my way through this tightly-packed thicket of young pine trees, and all the time the branches were whacking me in the face and my boots were sinking into the sodden carpet of needles. But hell – I was born and brought up to this. Who knows, if Saleem had taken me out into his native desert, perhaps the tables would have been turned.

By the time I got him back to the base camp, Saleem was like a zombie. A couple of the senior officers took him away somewhere where he could recover. Three days later we were back at Sandhurst, and there was Saleem sitting in class disassembling and cleaning his SA80. I felt pretty sorry for the poor bastard: he didn't look very happy.

Saleem absolutely *had* to complete Sandhurst – for his own honour, out of respect for his father and for his country. But that evening he was gone again. He went AWOL for three days. Eventually we found him in his room – the one next to mine, on the opposite side to Matt Bacon's – hiding under his bed. It was Ramadan, the Muslim holy festival, and the poor sod had been fasting from dawn to dusk. You can't do Ramadan and an exercise like that in the Brecons at the same time. It had almost killed him.

In spite of what had happened we welcomed him back into the platoon, and especially when he told us about Ramadan. In fact, Saleem went on to complete Sandhurst and he really did shape up. We would go on to be the Premier Platoon to be commissioned on passing out of Sandhurst – Saleem included.

However, my troubles over my choice of career – the Parachute Regiment or nothing – were only getting worse. I had been offered a commission into the PARAs, but the powers that be at Sandhurst were dead set against it. I'd also been offered a commission into the Royal Horse Artillery – 'The Gunners' – and it was that which they were determined to make me accept.

The Gunners were and are a very fine unit, but they generally stick 20 kilometres behind the front line, putting down pinpoint accurate fire from their howitzers. It is vital work, of course, but it wasn't where I wanted to be.

There was a Parachute Regiment officer at Sandhurst, a Captain Andy Harrison. He was punchy, fit and bright, and he was the kind of officer I aspired to be. One morning he called me into his office to have a private word. He had his maroon PARA beret – the one that I so longed to wear – lying on his desk.

'Dave, the fucking Gunners are trying to claim that 'cause you went to Welbeck you can't join the infantry. You have to join a corps, and the Gunners say they're permitted to take Welbecksians – so they get you.'

I was speechless. I was thinking: *The bastards – they've fucked me on a technicality.*

He fixed me with this steely-eyed look. 'But don't worry. I've gone back to the General, and we're going to get it fucking sorted.'

By 'the General' he meant Hew Pike. General Hew Pike had commanded 3 PARA in the Falklands, at the Battle of Mount Longdon. He was a hero in my eyes, and in the eyes of many in the military. If anyone could get this shit sorted, he could.

A couple of days later I ran into Andy Harrison, out for a run in his PARA Reg T-shirt. He gave me a grin. 'The General's done his stuff. We're sorted.'

The Parachute Regiment had upped their offer to a Special Regular Commission, which meant I could serve with the Regiment for sixteen years. Most officer commissions are far shorter. In that way they had trumped the rival offer and won the day. As for me, I couldn't wait to get away from all the Sandhurst bullshit, and to work alongside blokes like Andy Harrison, and under commanders like General Hew Pike.

One of my final acts at Sandhurst was to celebrate my nineteenth birthday. We'd finished training for the day and Matt Bacon, one of my M&S Brothers, asked me to go for a beer at the Sandhurst bar. We couldn't afford to drink a lot as we had no money, but I figured I deserved a pint or two on my birthday.

The bar was situated in this prefabricated accommodation block set apart in the trees. Matt was a super-popular bloke, and he'd actually sorted a surprise party for me. The bar and the anteroom were packed full to bursting. As soon as I entered I had people pouring shots down my throat. And a very well-spoken officer cadet called James Blunt pulled out his guitar and started to sing. He was bloody good, too.

I was halfway to being seriously pissed when this attractive blonde officer cadet walked into the bar. She was pretty sexy, and I couldn't understand why I hadn't noticed her before. Matt was standing next to me with a grin like a Cheshire cat on his face. She wandered over. She had her boobs pushed up a bit too much and her shirt a little too undone, but I still didn't twig.

'Officer Cadet Blakeley,' she purred, 'you've been a very naughty boy.'

For a moment I thought – *Shit, is she from the Royal Military Police or something?*

Then she started to strip. The rest of the blokes formed a doughnut ring around us, as she got me down to my boxers. She was clad in nothing but her birthday suit, and the last thing I remember was the can of whipped cream coming out – of the sprayable kind.

I woke up the next morning with the mother of all hangovers. We had a parade at 0755 hours and somehow I made it with the rest of the company, but all of us were stinking of booze. The CSgt had a face like thunder. He fumed and snorted his way up and down the line.

'Right, what the fucking hell went on last night?' he roared.

No one was answering.

Matt had smuggled the stripper into Sandhurst and somehow

he'd got hold of a female officer cadet's uniform for her to wear. This was most definitely the kind of shit that could get you kicked out. It was worse than the Center Parcs bike theft stunt that Cheeky and I had pulled off at Welbeck. Far worse.

The CSgt stopped dead in front of Matt. 'Officer Cadet Bacon, tell me – what the fuck took place last night?'

I was thinking: *Shit, he's somehow got Matt's name. Shit. Shit. This is going to snowball. We're in the crap big time.* I may have won my dream ticket into the PARAs, but not if I got kicked out of Sandhurst at the eleventh hour.

'Staff, we just had a few beers in the bar,' Matt replied. He was as cool as a cucumber. 'Just celebrating Officer Cadet Blakeley's birthday, Staff.'

'And what the fuck else went on?' the CSgt snarled.

'Nothing, Staff. A few beers. That was it.'

Matt had spent a good few years in the ranks and he knew the score. The CSgt knew he was lying through his teeth, but he had to respect that Matt was keeping stum. And so, amazingly, we got away with it.

I asked my Nan and Grandpa to my Sandhurst commissioning parade. It was a very special day for me and for them. It was Grandpa's final, big excursion before he sadly passed away. When I was a kid he used to love reading me *Charlie and the Chocolate Factory*. Charlie was kind of a role model. He was the kid from the hopelessly poor background who achieved the impossible dream – winning a tour of the secret, magical, Willy Wonka's Chocolate Factory.

In fact, by the end of the book he had achieved a great deal more than that. He was also the kid who made it by dint of his good nature and his genuine openness of spirit. I knew Grandpa would be lit up as he watched me march up the white steps and through the gates of Sandhurst in the lead platoon. I hoped he'd feel that I'd made it, Charlie-like, against the odds, and that by getting into the PARAs I had achieved my impossible dream.

That evening I got to wear Parachute Regiment dress for the first time. A tailor had measured me up for it. It consisted of light blue tight trousers with a red stripe down them; a pair of black George Boots; a black waistcoat with regimental buttons; plus a red fitted jacket with a maroon collar and regimental lapels. But I wasn't yet allowed to wear any PARA wings.

I was now what they call 'a Penguin' – a bird that couldn't fly.

A month later I arrived at Catterick Garrison, in Yorkshire, to start P Company. It was great to have Dan Jarvis, my other M&S Brother from Sandhurst, doing selection alongside me. As for Matt Bacon, he had made it through to the Army Intelligence Corps, and he and I would remain good mates for life until his tragic death on operations in Iraq, in 2004.

P Company was as tough as I had feared it would be. A lot of those who started didn't make it. We began with around a hundred blokes, and sixty-five lasted through to the end. Strangely enough, it was the aerial assault course – the trainasium – that got many of them. It includes a single plank of wood set at a height, and you have to jump from that onto another that is lower, on command.

The optical illusion resulting from how the planks are positioned makes the gap look enormous. You know it isn't, but still it looks that way. So again, it was a case of mind over matter. Several blokes were unable to make it, which meant they got binned, for the trainasium, rightly, was a simple case of pass or fail.

If you made it into the PARAs and you were stood on the back of a Hercules for real, along with forty-four other blokes, a refusal to jump would bugger up the entire airborne insertion. That was why the trainasium was a black-and-white pass or fail.

I was almost one of those who didn't pass P Company. I had no problem with the trainasium, but on the final forced march prior to Test Week I suffered the injury to my knee. We were on a ferocious downhill tab when my foot hit a patch of loose gravel, skidded forwards, and the right knee twisted horribly. It ballooned up, it hurt like hell and it wouldn't work properly.

Luckily, I had the weekend prior to Test Week in which to get some treatment. Had it happened at the start of Test Week I'd doubtless have failed. As it was the knee lasted through Test Week, which took me into the final session – the infamous 'milling'. In the milling you have to stand face to face with another bloke and for two minutes tear seven bales of shit out of each other.

Milling is designed to be a test of pure aggression. You're not allowed to use any boxing moves – so no dancing, ducking or bobbing about. You have to stand rigid, take whatever punishment the other guy is throwing at you, and give it back to him. If you go down, you have to get right back up again and keep doing so.

The morning of the milling I sat there in silence, in trainers and T-shirt. I had my name written in black marker pen on a ripped piece of pillow, which was pinned to my shirt: *Second Lieutenant Blakeley.*

The Staff came in and started to wind us up.

'Any moment now and it's going to start ...'

'Here we are then – the real man's test ...'

'Looks like some of you are shit fucking scared ...'

I tried to zone it out, so as to not be psyched out.

'So then, who wants to fight an officer?' the PARA Reg Sergeant Major announced. 'It's the only time in your career you'll get to kick the shit out of an officer and get away with it.'

Several guys put up their hands. One was a gobby bloke from the Royal Military Police (RMP). 'Me! Me!' he kept shouting. One of the others was a massive, grizzled Royal Engineer. I hoped to hell I was going to get him.

We filed into the gym and were made to sit in three ranks forming a square – the boxing ring. The Staff pulled up some gym horses, so they could sit on those and adjudicate – like kings on their thrones. There was a PARA Reg doctor present too, with a couple of medics carrying sponges and buckets of water.

The fights went in weight order, which put me pretty near the last. I saw my fellow officers go ahead of me, and most got their arses kicked. But they didn't hail from northern estates where fighting was something of a way of life.

Dan went up shortly before me. He was absolutely determined, but the bloke he was up against was a true street fighter. Each time Dan went down he got right back up again and went toe-to-toe with the bloke once more. At the end the referee grabbed both arms, and the winner was appointed. Dan had lost, but it didn't matter: he'd made a good account of himself.

There was no cheering. No applause. No fun at all. This was deadly serious, and brutal.

The RMP bloke went next, and he was paired up against a Captain Scalding, another giant from the Royal Engineers. The MP got thoroughly battered, and everyone loved it – because everyone hates RMPs. No one was allowed so much as to cheer, but there were smiles all around. Captain Scalding got cautioned for using the odd boxing move, but he'd still totally flattened the RMP.

By the time I was called to the ring the mats were spattered with blood and gore, and in spite of the medics wiping them down after each fight. I'd been paired off to fight a guy who was the spitting image of Beast Malone, only without the body hair. He had a shaven head, and his name tag identified him as a Corporal Clarkson from the Royal Engineers.

As I stepped forward I dropped my shoulders, and did my best wimpy officer act, to put him off guard. I was acutely aware that news of how I did here would quickly find its way back to the Regiment. Long before I got there, I would already have earned the reputation of being a pussy if I didn't make a good account of myself.

The bell rang. We started to trade blows. My arms were pumping left–right–left–right like pistons, as I stood stock-still and took the hits. I saw my fist strike home, and the stunned look in my adversary's eyes. I hit him again and he went down. He hit the floor hard but was on his feet almost instantly. Even so, there was a confused look in his eyes, which had started to spin.

I hit him again and again, and he went down for a second time. He was on the mats longer this time. My adrenaline was pumping like a geyser, and just as soon as he was on his feet I went for him, hammering in the blows. He was hardly up by the time he collapsed, slamming into the bloodied floor. The referee stepped forward and stopped the fight.

We were sixty seconds in and we were all done.

As I stepped out of the ring, I realised how evil my mindset had become. Those sixty seconds had turned me into a killer. I had wanted to kill that bloke. I was trying to kill him. The PARA Sergeant Major who'd been watching closely made some remark. It was something about me hitting the bloke when he'd been down.

I didn't think that I had. I'd just made sure he got no chance to get his footing, and knock the shit out of me. There was one more fight, the two heaviest blokes battling it out, and then we were finished. There was silence for a few seconds, before the Sergeant Major stepped forwards. I expected him to tell us to get ourselves cleaned up, for that was P Company done with.

'Captain Scalding, you're up again,' he announced.

I saw Scalding's head flick around in surprise, for you are never normally expected to go twice in the milling.

The Sergeant Major paused for a moment. 'And Second Lieutenant Blakeley.'

Fuck.

I knew why he was making Scalding go again: he'd been accused of using too many boxing moves. And I guess he was making me go again because he reckoned I'd hit my opponent before he was fully on his feet again. Scalding was taller than the bloke I'd just fought. He was my size, and he'd clearly done a lot of boxing in his time.

We faced up.

The bell rang.

I went in quickly with my chin down on my left shoulder, just as I'd done when I fought Beast Malone. I saw Scalding hesitate for just an instant. He was letting his head get in the way of the fighting. I struck at that moment, one massive blow that sent him reeling. He was a big bloke and he hit the floor with a massive crack, his head jerking back violently with the fall.

He clambered to his feet, but I didn't wait for him to get his bearings and come at me. I slammed my bare fists into his head, repeatedly. He went down a second time, his head twisting around horribly and his face a sickly white. He tried to get up for a third time. Somehow, he dragged his way to his feet, but his knees were gone. I hit him a final time, and the referee stepped in between us.

It was over.

We filed out of the gym into the auditorium. We sat there with our berets on and we braced-up as the OC entered. He read out a list of names.

'Corporal Clarkson – pass.'

'Second Lieutenant Jarvis – pass.'

'Captain Scalding – pass.'

'Private Horsefield – fail.'

'Sergeant Hamm – fail.'

'Second Lieutenant Blakeley – pass.'

Around 30 per cent of those who'd made it through thus far were fails. Dan Jarvis, my M&S Brother, was through. So were the two blokes I had fought. So, too, sadly was the gobby RMP bloke. I was now officially in the Parachute Regiment. My head pounded like hell from the milling plus my knee still ached like hell from the injury.

But I felt on top of the world.

I was assigned to 1 Platoon, A Company, 1 PARA, and my company commander was a Major Andy Jackson, whom everyone knew as 'Jacko'. He was a very well built, hard-as-nails commander, and the only officer to play rugby for the Battalion. Right away, I knew I was going to love serving under him.

Commanding 1 Platoon, A Company, 1 PARA, meant I was now at the very tip of the spear. Normally in a deliberate attack it was us who would get sent in first. It would be 1 PARA who would be assigned to be the Special Forces Support Group (SFSG), so in theory the Battalion could well be operating alongside the SAS and the SBS. In theory, anything was possible.

In practice, things weren't quite so rosy.

'We've just got back from NI, and we're pretty undermanned at present,' Andy Jackson told me, in my introductory briefing. 'The lads hated NI. I have to warn you – morale is pretty low at the moment. And with all the defence cuts there's even the risk of losing a battalion of the PARA Regiment.'

This was news to me. It was shocking. How could the MOD even think of cutting a battalion – that's 650 men-at-arms – of the PARAs? After Arnhem, the Falklands, and hell, even the repeated tours of Northern Ireland, surely if any body of men had proved their worth time and time again it was the PARAs.

The second-in-command of my platoon was a Corporal Tindale, for we were short of sergeants right now. He arrived to meet me wearing an old tracksuit. He explained it away by pretending he'd just been at the gym. Tindale was a massive hulk of a Yorkshireman and a fine rugby player. He was the proverbial brick shithouse and he practically dwarfed even me.

'You haven't got much of a hard act to follow,' he remarked, as he took me over to meet the men of the Platoon. 'The last officer we had was a total cock. He ended up getting into a fight with one of the lads, and the rest is history ...'

The blokes were lying around on their bunks in tracksuits and vests, and I could sense at once that I was going to have real problems here. I quickly learned that eight of those in my platoon had resigned from the Army, for they'd had more than a bellyful of Northern Ireland. They were only here to serve out the remaining few months of their time.

The last officer had been beaten up, and it was clear that I wasn't welcome. My platoon was like a rotten apple, and I wondered what on earth I could do about it. I was pissed off and hugely deflated. It was a far cry from what I had imagined over the years that I'd hungered to be a part of this Regiment, not to mention when I'd first read *The Making Of A Para*, back at Welbeck.

That evening the platoon invited me for a night on the piss. It wasn't a particularly friendly gesture: it was very much a throwing down of the gauntlet. Aldershot is a rough town, and Cheeks Nightclub – our intended destination – was about as bad as it gets. At Sandhurst, they'd taught me that an officer dressed in a blazer or a sports jacket when going out. If I did that tonight I'd get murdered.

I donned jeans and a T-shirt and headed down to Cheeks with the rest of the lads. We'd barely necked the first ale before it kicked off. Right in the midst of the floor were two of my own – Tindale, plus a killer of a bloke called Brogan – and they were ripping apart a couple of thuggish, pikey-looking civvies. They literally tore into the blokes. I knew then – if I hadn't before – that if I'd had to go up against either of these two in the milling, I'd have been annihilated.

The pikeys were in a big group but they quickly backed off. The bouncers came piling in, but when they saw it was Tindale and Brogan on the job they left them to it. Once they were done Tinners and Brogan pointed at the two blokes they'd flattened, and got the bouncers to drag them out and expel them.

According to the code of conduct that I'd been taught at Sandhurst, I should have reported them, either to the Regimental Sergeant Major or the Adjutant. But there was no way that I could say anything and keep command of my platoon. As it turned out the two pikeys did pretty much deserve it, and I used that to help justify my silence.

I figured I'd passed the Cheeks Test, but now I had to try to rebuild my platoon. I was actually the only officer in A Company commanding a platoon. They didn't even have one in 2 and 3 Platoon. Not enough officers had made it through P Company, but rightly the Regiment refused to lower standards. With a dearth of officers, the sergeants and corporals had been left in command.

I didn't have any fellow officers in A Company to lean on or talk through my problems with. But Dan Jarvis was in B Company and

I sought him out. It turned out that his experience was proving pretty similar to mine. We were both of us shocked and deeply disappointed. We'd been expecting to take charge of fully manned platoons with sky-high morale and an unbreakable *esprit de corps*.

Sandhurst certainly hadn't prepared us for anything like this.

We had A Company's Basic Physical Fitness Test (BPFA) scheduled for that week. There was a Private Ellis in the company who ran cross-country for the Army. But in the 1.5-miler I ran until I half-killed myself and I was first in. Ellis was right behind me, but the rest of my platoon were strung out towards the rear.

Jacko came up to me after the race. 'Fucking hell,' he panted. 'I can see your platoon are in for a real good time of it.'

After the BFPA was done, I got called in for my formal welcome from Lieutenant Colonel Paul Gibson, the CO of 1 PARA. He was new into the Battalion, and he made it clear he was well aware of all the problems and the challenges. He told me he wanted to put the Battalion very firmly 'back on the map'.

He wanted to breathe new life into the Battalion, and he was fighting tooth and nail to get some new recruits in, to replace the 'bad eggs' that were leaving. I told him about the sports I played, including the horse riding.

'Good,' he announced. 'I want to get you out on the local hunt wearing a PARA Reg beret. We need to do whatever we can to raise the profile of the Regiment and in whatever ways possible.'

The rest of the Army didn't particularly like us. They had a tendency to resent elite units like the PARAs, not to mention the Special Forces. With us, they argued that you'd never parachute into battle in modern warfare, so we were outdated and redundant. That pretty much defined our present struggle for survival.

But my priority right now was ensuring the survival of my platoon as a unit that was fit to fight. It wasn't about to get any easier. Corporal Tindale came up to me and announced he too was off. He had been accepted onto the Platoon Sergeant's Battle Course.

I got a Sergeant Collins as a replacement. He came to see me dressed in yet another bloody tracksuit, and announced in a broad Scottish burr that he wasn't going to be around for long, for he was shortly disappearing for selection into an elite forces unit. It was incredible. I'd fought so hard to make it into my dream unit, the PARAs, but everyone else just seemed to want out.

Two weeks later there was a promotion board in Battalion, and I got allocated a new guy. Sergeant Douggie Muirhead turned up to meet me in immaculate Parachute Regiment uniform, making him more or less the first soldier in my experience to do so. He looked fit, hard and capable. I sensed a change in my fortunes here, and in Douggie I wasn't to be disappointed.

He was shorter than me but stockier, from all the years spent tabbing. He had slightly dark skin, dark hair, and a refreshingly upbeat attitude. He'd come across from C Company, and it was clear that he was very well respected by all the blokes. I was hugely relieved. I knew I was going to struggle on my own, but with Douggie at my side I had a real chance to reshape 1 Platoon as I wanted it.

We started doing regular, ten-mile tabs in the Aldershot Training Area, an expanse of woodland, hills and sandy tracks. We did the tabs buddy-buddy style – teamed up with one other so you could help each other and get water out of each other's packs.

We halted on one of the first of those tabs for a water stop. I'd been allocated a new section commander, who'd replaced one of those who had resigned. His name was Jim Pugh and he was my 'buddy' for the tab. I turned to him and reached for the straps on his pack to remove his water bottle.

He held out a hand to stop me. 'No need. Water is for poofs.'

I let him get my water out and I took a good long pull. We set off again, practically running under our loads. By the second water stop Jim was practically dying of thirst. When I offered him his water bottle he snatched at it grumpily, and necked it without a word.

Once we were back at base I asked Douggie what was the problem with him.

'Jim's a slick operator, boss,' Douggie told me. 'It's just that he's pissed a few people off and he hasn't got his promotion to sergeant. He's thinking of leaving. But he's a first-class soldier, so don't write him off.'

My platoon had three fighting sections of eight blokes. On operations I'd keep one in reserve, and send two forward to take on the enemy. Douggie would be the driving force as sergeant, with me sitting beside him in command. Jim was my point section commander, so he was right at the tip of my spear. I'd heard what Douggie had said about him, but we needed to be tight or we'd fuck up.

We were sent to the US for a six-week training exercise. Jim, Douggie and I had to work very closely now, whether we liked it or not. One of the first things we had to do was plan a platoon ambush. The enemy force would come down a track with a ninety-degree turn at the end of it. The plan that I came up with was to hit them after they had made the turn, which is how it was done on all the courses I'd attended and in the manuals.

It was Jim who pointed out another way. We needed a cut-off group set to one flank, so as to ensure maximum attrition of the enemy – in other words, so we annihilated them. He suggested we place it so that both forces were aware of their arcs of fire, so there was no risk of a 'blue-on-blue' (friendly fire).

It was a fine suggestion, so I adjusted the plan accordingly. We executed the ambush firing blanks, and smashed up the 'enemy'. An Army general was flying overhead observing the exercise. Afterwards, I was called in by Jacko, and he passed me the General's congratulations on a finely-planned and well-executed attack.

'Thanks, sir, but it was largely Corporal Pugh's idea,' I told him.

In my book you gave credit where credit was due.

Douggie was with me, and he let Jim know what I had said. Jim suddenly started to feel valued, and from then on he would prove an incredible support to me. He hated the fact that officers always got the credit when things went well, but it was often the blokes who'd put together the plan. With me around, he sensed things were different now.

With Douggie backing me and Jim coming onside, we started to pull the platoon around. It was only just in time. I'd joined Battalion in May 1998. In June, we – the hated 1 PARA, the authors of the notorious Bloody Sunday killings – were slated to return to Northern Ireland. It was only for a short stint policing the marching season around Drumcree, but even so it was going to be my first deployment on operations for real.

As things turned out, my policy of letting the blokes lead the platoon with me didn't win universal approval. We were doing rehearsals for the riots that Drumcree would inevitably bring, when I was called in to see Lieutenant Colonel Gibson. I was about to get my own gypsy's warning.

Gibson had with him John Georing, this monster of a bloke who was the 1 PARA RSM. He was a massive, gravel-voiced Welshman, and he was on a level with Tinners or Brogan in terms of being a hard case. As Gibson proceeded to upbraid me, I could feel Georing's ice-blue eyes boring into me.

'I'm not happy with your platoon's performance, David,' Gibson told me, icily. 'I don't give a fuck what the blokes are saying or what their issues are. You need to grip your platoon, as you are the point platoon of Battalion.'

'Yes, sir. Understood, sir.'

I knew exactly what he was driving at. The blokes were being sent back to the most hated theatre of all and they were not happy. We were undermanned, morale was far from being tops, and we were going back to NI. The CO's warning left me between a rock and a hard place. I decided to listen to my head-shed still – to Douggie and Jim – but to take more of an aggressive, forceful lead.

But I was worried. 1 PARA were forever associated with Bloody Sunday, and whenever we went back across the water the IRA thirsted for revenge. If it all went tits-up I could easily get thrown out of the Regiment. I was the youngest officer in Battalion, but if they thought I wasn't strong enough to lead they'd dump me, for it made me a dangerous liability.

Yet it was hard to get the balance right. If I took too strong a lead I'd lose the blokes and have a mutiny on my hands. I was only nineteen years old and I was commanding the toughest soldiers in the regular British Army, with my platoon being at the cutting edge of our operations. The only thing that might have been harder was to command an SF unit.

None of this had been in the book that I had read – *The Making Of A Para*. It only mentioned the glory and the honour. It only described the incredible ferocity and achievements of the Regiment in the Falklands, and elsewhere in battle.

Right now, the reality was far from what I had dreamed it would be.

*

CHAPTER TWELVE

B y the time we reach our destination – the remote farmhouse where the PF hunter force is holed up – it's snowing heavily. Our mission is to report on 'enemy activity', and recommend how a battalion of PARAs can move in and attack. But right now, Al, Jez, Smudge and I can barely see the hands in front of our faces, let alone get eyes on the enemy base.

But there's no way the DS are going to call it off just because of a bit of snow. I know from my study of the maps that there's a wooded ridge that sits above the farmhouse. We skirt around and move into the woodline. It provides cover from view in case anyone from the hunter force has got their thermal imaging kit out, and is scanning the terrain. It also provides a bit of cover from the weather.

It's pitch black and eerily silent in amongst the rows of pine trees. We push in deeper and it's all but dry. There's barely a dusting of snow underfoot, the umbrella of pine needles is so thick above us. It's tempting to site the OP right here in the woods, but the problem is the trees would shield the target from view, plus we'd never be able to dig through the mass of tree roots.

Leaving Jez and Al in the lee of the wood, Smudge and me move forward to scout out possibilities closer to the target. We decide the best place to site the OP is just behind the lip of a small hill some 500 yards distant from the farmhouse. The enemy will be on the far side of the hill, in the sunken dip of the valley. As long as the weather clears, we'll have a good view of the place from up there, but the lie of the land should keep us hidden.

Smudge and I move back to the woods. We approach Jez and Al with our rifles in one hand and our other hand held out to the side, so as to form a crucifix shape. That's the signal that it's a friendly force coming back and not an enemy patrol. In such shitty conditions as these it would be easy enough to mistake your own for the bad guys, and open fire on them.

A voice rings out from the woodline, muffled by the snowfall. 'Halt! Advance one and be recognised!'

Smudge and I move forward, so our forms become more visible.

'Halt! Three,' announces the voice in the trees.

'Four,' we respond.

Our chosen security code number for tonight is seven, and three plus four equals seven. We gather as a four and share our information. Al and Jez have seen bugger all movement from their vantage point, so we have to presume the enemy are waiting out the storm in comfort, which means there's no time to lose to get down to our chosen position and get digging.

But first things first, we're all going to have a crap in the shelter of the woods. It's good to get it done before we move into the cramped confines of the OP, but even here we're going to bag it and take it with us. I go first, dropping my trousers in the icy blast, and poor old Smudge has to hold the cling film for me. I bet he never imagined doing that for an officer!

Once I'm done Smudge hands me the steaming wrap of crap. This is deadly serious, the SOP Test, so no one's pissing about here. I bag the unsavoury offering, seal it into a sandwich box and stuff that into the top pocket of my Bergen. That way, I won't keep pulling out old wraps of my own shit whenever I want to get some scoff or drink or extra ammo out of my pack.

Then I roll out the cling film for Smudge to have a go.

That done, we move into the OP position. We get there, go firm for five minutes in good cover, and silently observe our arcs. There is absolutely nothing moving out there apart from tree branches swaying in the wind, and thick flurries of snow. Once we're done with the watch, and we're certain the enemy aren't about, we drop our packs and haul out the shovel.

This is no fold-up mini-shovel. With conditions such as these and the ground frozen solid, a mini-shovel would be about as much use as an ashtray on a motorcycle. This is a full-sized job, one that I've had strapped down the side of my Bergen. I've got it wrapped in a hessian sandbag, so that the metal doesn't clang against anything, or reflect any moonlight or man-made light.

I volunteer to start. Two of the others move a good distance away, in order to provide a protective screen. One goes forward, so as to keep watch on the target. Another positions himself to our rear, which should stop the enemy sneaking up on us from behind. The third guy, Smudge, sticks close to me to help with the digging.

We're hyper alert as I start to scrape away the worst of the snow. We're going to make a lot of noise as we do this, and it might draw out the enemy. I bend and start to dig for real. The shovel lets out a hollow, steely thud, as it impacts with the rock-hard earth, the shock of it sending a harsh, jarring impact up my wrist bones.

It is horrendous going. I have to cut my way through the frozen surface, which is a good six inches deep. Within minutes I'm burning hot, and I have to peel off the layers. If I don't and I allow myself to sweat heavily into what I'm wearing, I will very likely freeze to death in the OP. Rather than evaporating, the sweat will cool and pool around my body, eventually turning my sweat-soaked clothes into sheets of ice.

I rip off my softie jacket and smock, so I'm dressed in just a T-shirt and long-sleeved HH vest. I tear the black woolly hat off my head, but I keep the gloves on. I'm wearing proper Gore-Tex winter mountaineering gloves, and I'm determined to keep my hands from freezing up. With frozen fingers you can't operate a weapon, which could prove fatal if the enemy ping us.

I break through the frozen crust, excavating a coffin-shaped depression some eight feet long and four feet wide. I've got it cleared down to six inches by the time I let Smudge take over. He's spread a waterproof poncho on the ground next to the grave-shaped hole that we're digging, and I've been piling the semi-frozen clumps of soil onto that.

With Smudge having taken over the excavation, I lug the poncho over to the woodland and proceed to scatter the earth where it won't disturb the snow cover. A pile of fresh black soil against white snow is a dead giveaway. In this way, with Smudge digging and me ferrying away the spoil, we fashion a scrape that is no more than four feet deep along its entire length.

It's just large enough for four blokes to crouch in side by side, and with the lip of earth before us hiding the tops of our bodies from view. All we have to do is lever ourselves up a foot or so, and we can see right down into the enemy's domain – that's if the weather clears. We pull in branches and undergrowth all around us, and by first light we're more or less invisible to anyone who might be passing.

We set up a rota system. One bloke will rest in the midst of the grave-like depression, though there's no room to lie down. Another will have eyes-front on the enemy. A third guy will be up at the woodline, manning a rear sentry position and watching our backs. A fourth guy will be recording anything of interest in his notebook, and preparing briefings to radio through to HQ.

We've been told to pay particular attention to enemy numbers and movements, to any heavy weapon positions at the farmhouse and to any kind of vehicles they may have.

Come sunrise the temperature rises slightly, and the snow starts to turn to sleet. But if anything, it's worse. We pull on our Gore-Tex overtrousers and jackets – but crouched in a freezing hole like this it is sheer bloody misery.

Sleet and slush pools around our feet and our arses, where we're crouched in our self-dug grave. The camo cream that I've caked my hands and face with starts to run into my eyeballs. I hate it when it

After months of intensive solo training over the Brecon Beacons – during which I had no option but to sleep in my car between tabs – I began the brutal selection course to join the elite Pathfinders. It is widely seen as rivalling that of the SAS – making it the hardest in the British Army. I wanted to be the best of the best and to work in small teams of highly capable men who are hand-picked from volunteers from any unit across the whole of the Armed Forces. I would nearly die of exposure in the unforgiving winter in the Welsh mountains and eventually need knee and shoulder surgery.

Shattered beyond imagination: the mental and physical exertion on Pathfinder selection has been known to break many a good man – plus soldiers have died on elite forces selection out on the hills in brutal weather.

Very quickly during selection you start to suffer severe blisters on feet and backs, as well as burns on thighs and shoulders from crushing packs. Medics become gods in our eyes and help us push our bodies beyond whatever seemed possible. Painkillers became 'Smarties': I ended up necking them to keep going when badly injured on the final, 64-kilometre murder march – known as 'Endurance'.

Micro-navigation and the ability to contribute and lead is key to being a Pathfinder and elite soldier.

Pathfinders are taught to penetrate deep behind enemy lines using covert means of insertion – either by parachute drop, in small teams driving 4x4 vehicles or on foot. They need to be able to operate for long periods in remote enemy areas undetected, and fend for themselves. Whilst resupply by parachute or helicopter may be possible, often they are forced to live off the land – eating whatever they can scavenge, hunt or steal.

The wolf pack. I am second right of photo, with a team of guys from a mixture of elite units – Pathfinders, SAS, plus South African Task Force troopers. We're armed with AK47s – so 'local' weaponry – and we've parachuted into the African bush along the border with Zimbabwe, at the start of an epic tab under massive loads through the savanna of east and southern Africa.

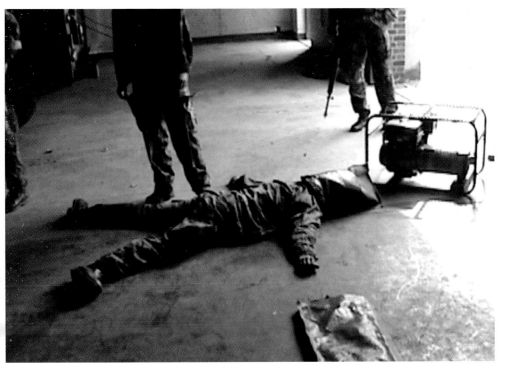

The grand finale of the Pathfinder Selection Course is 'Resistance to Interrogation Training' and 'Combat Survival' – where you are put through a highly realistic and convincing simulation of being captured, beaten, tortured, and interrogated by the enemy, which lasts several days. You do this to prepare yourself for capture for real – and to learn to hold out for long enough so as not to give your fellow patrol members away, or reveal the nature of your mission, when you're on operations behind enemy lines.

My team. After Pathfinder selection you go on to train in all elite parachute-borne methods to insert into enemy territory covertly and unseen. The highlight of this is the HALO (High Altitude Low Opening) jump, whereby you leave the aircraft at extreme high altitude, plummet earthwards in a massive freefall, and only open your parachute at the last minute. HALO enables a very fast, low-profile and secretive insertion into enemy terrain, and is a specialism of the Pathfinders.

About to take the leap of faith. We conduct freefall descents from such extreme high altitude that we have to use oxygen-breathing systems to keep us alive. It is so cold that we're dressed in specialist survival suits to keep us from freezing to death as we hurtle through the air.

The moment of truth. Jumping from the rear ramp of a Hercules C130 on the roof of the world is the biggest adrenaline rush you can ever experience. It's the most alive you can ever feel, and when you're in the company of fellow Pathfinders you know you're with the best in the world.

HALO-ing 'James Bond' style. Even among elite units very few soldiers ever get to do these kind of jumps that every Pathfinder specialises in. HALO is our bread and butter. We progress from daytime jumps to doing them in small teams at night, so as to insert behind enemy lines undetected.

does that. I have a change of socks in my pack and I'm tempted to use them. I can feel the cold and damp seeping through my leather boots, which is dangerous.

If your hands freeze you can't fight. If your feet freeze you can't walk, or bug out if the enemy stumbles upon your OP. Either could prove fatal on a real life op, and could fail me on my SOP Test. I risk a sock change. I warn the others what I'm doing, then remove one boot and make the change before starting on the other. That way, I've only ever got one boot off at a time.

My socks done, I lean back on my Bergen, and shift around the tiny strip of roll-mat that I've got cushioning my arse. The earth beneath me is a frozen slick of slush, but it's my turn to rest now, and somehow I've got to try to get some shuteye. We've got to last forty-eight hours of this, and sleep is going to be a vital part of remaining alert, completing the mission task and staying alive.

I realise that I need a piss before I can sleep. No point drifting off only to have to wake up a few minutes later to use the john. I grab a plastic Coke bottle, one that I've taped up with black gaffer tape so it doesn't crackle or reverberate when I snake into it, or reflect the sunlight off the bare plastic. We are squeezed in right on top of one another, and when at first I try to pee it goes everywhere.

I'm acutely aware how annoying this must be for the blokes to either side of me, who've got spattered. When you're this confined and unable to move – not to mention frozen to the core – anyone who is lazy or inconsiderate or downright stupid really gets on your nerves. Pretty quickly, you'll end up wanting to kill him. I have to experiment with different ways of leaning over until I can finally get the piss going fully into the bottle, and let rip.

By last light the weather has cleared enough for us to risk a close target recce (CTR). We've not gleaned a lot of information yet on the enemy, and we need more. If we fail to achieve the mission objectives, we could fail SOP Week. Even though the conditions are utterly inhuman, we still have to bring home the goods. You can't stop a war just because the weather's turned bad.

Smudge and Jez head out on the CTR, leaving Al and me in the OP. They'll use micro-navigation tactics to find their way closer to the farmhouse. They'll count their steps as they walk, using that, a compass and the maps to work out more or less exactly where they are to the nearest few yards. When they're close they'll resort to crawling, and they'll belly-crawl the final few dozen yards.

You can't afford to use a GPS when on a mission such as this. You need to learn to do it all without one, because GPSs can and do fail. They can seize up. They can run out of batteries. You can fall in a river and destroy one that way. Plus they throw off a faint glow from the screen and even that can be enough to give your position away. It's a big no-no, as far as light-discipline goes.

Smudge and Jez are gone for hours. The weather is growing colder and colder, and the night is awash with thick snow. This is coldness like I have never felt, and it's made a hundred times worse by the fact that we're sitting in a frozen grave with no shelter, and we're unable to move. We can't even brew up a hot drink, or heat up some food to warm us, for that would be a fail.

We've been here a day and approaching two nights now. It occurs to me that in a regular unit this would have been called off long ago. The wind gets up, and the wind-chill factor makes it colder still. It's practically blowing a blizzard all around us. I feel my head start to go. I can't think straight. My words slur. I know I'm starting to go down with hypothermia. I can tell that Al is too.

Heaven only knows how Jez and Smudge are faring, out there somewhere in the darkness. We expected them back hours ago. The night is deadly, deadly cold. You can't wear Gore-Tex over-trousers when doing a CTR, because the material rustles noisily as you walk or crawl, and could give your position away.

Jez and Smudge are very likely soaking wet through from the waist down, and with the damp and cold seeping into their boots. It always does from a wet pair of trousers. Or maybe they've been captured. Either way, this exercise could well end up killing them, or us. No doubt about it, this has gone from being an exercise on PF selection to being a full-on survival tasking.

Without an intelligible word being said between us, Al and I decide we have no option but to cuddle up like a couple of lovers. We do so to share the body heat. Al is this big, hard, roughly-spoken PARA, but right now we're clutching each other like our lives depend upon it, which they very possibly do.

We can't brew up, for that would mean breaking hard routine. We could make the call that we're at risk of dying here and so we have to, but the DS might argue differently and fail us completely. If you wrap an OP mission simply because you're cold and wet, or brew up because you're freezing, you bugger the mission. And if you do so on an op for real it'll very likely get you killed.

For a moment I think back over the Bravo Two Zero mission of the First Gulf War. Eight SAS blokes were airlifted into Iraq and forced to go on the run, whereupon the weather turned abysmal. In the midst of the Iraqi desert it started to sleet and snow. Those without adequate cold weather gear quickly went down with hypothermia.

The weather proved to be the one enemy they couldn't defeat. They shared body heat and broke hard routine to brew up, but even so the cold proved a killer. Three men died, four were captured and only one escaped. The long shadow of Bravo Two Zero hangs over Special Forces soldiering, and it's no wonder my mind drifts back to that fateful patrol now.

Al and I squeeze together like a couple of limpets. But neither of us has moved for hours, and we're stone cold to the core. Eventually, after what feels like a lifetime, Smudge and Jez return. They're cold and shaky and jittering, but in a way they're in better shape than us. At least they've been on the move, which means they've generated some body heat to warm themselves.

They can see immediately that Al and me are hypothermic. They lower themselves into the grave-scrape and get their bodies close to ours, to share warmth. With their free hands they start to rub us down vigorously, so as to work some warmth into us.

They concentrate on our backs and the back of our arms, which is the direction from which the bitter, driving wind has been hitting us.

The very presence of the two of them lifts our morale. Smudge talks us through what he's seen of the enemy, as they massage the life back into our bones. He tells us we're all going to take a walk to the woods to get our circulation going again. Our minds have become so sluggish that we haven't even considered doing this.

We stumble up to the woodline, Smudge and Jez helping us as we go, for our legs are frozen solid. It's not good tradecraft that we've all abandoned the OP, but this is life and death stuff we're dealing with here. Al and me move like a pair of crippled and very old men. The woods are sheltered and snow-free, and it's noticeably warmer in there.

It's sheer bliss to get into their cover.

We spend an age massaging the life back into our limbs.

Smudge and Jez give the nod that we've recovered enough to risk a return to the OP. But it's been a close call. Another hour or so, and Smudge figures either one or both of us could have gone into a coma, we were that bad. And the ultimate irony is that we had been worried sick for the two of *them*. That's how messed up your head becomes when you're into the secondary stages of hypothermia.

As the first hints of dawn flicker across the dark, stormy skies to the east, we tell ourselves we've only got another twelve hours to last. No doubt about it, the night was touch and go. But surely, come daybreak the worst will be over. We've survived the death-shift – the night watch in this frozen grave of ours, one that's now inches deep in icy slush – and crucially, we've done nothing to break with Pathfinder SOPs.

We've also done nothing that we know of to alert the hunter force to our whereabouts. It was the night that threw the worst at us, and come daybreak we'll be sorted. The temperature should lift a little, the snow and the wind could lay off for a while, and maybe the thin winter sun will break through the grey-white clouds scudding overhead.

We live in hope, as always.

*

CHAPTER THIRTEEN

As it happened, Drumcree with 1 PARA proved far less of a drama than I had feared. We duly got petrol bombed and stoned and spat at, but no one on either side was shot or killed. We fired off a few baton rounds, but that's about as heavy as it got. It was viewed largely as a success, because the IRA failed to maim or to murder, and we prevented the two sides of hatred from tearing each other apart.

Drumcree was only ten days, but it worked wonders for my confidence. We'd kept the marches largely peaceful, and it meant that I'd now commanded my patrol on operations for real. I'd learned a lot from the blokes and I'd stood shoulder-to-shoulder with my men while in command. We'd had no Bloody Sunday re-run. No major incidents to speak of. We'd done well.

We returned to Aldershot to get just what we needed in my platoon – six guys fresh into the Regiment. One was a black dude called Baz Butler, a super-fit guy who'd sprinted for England. He was incredibly capable and keen to get ahead and to learn. He was just the kind of bloke I needed to keep the platoon moving in the direction it was headed, as were the others.

My section commanders were all in it for the long term now. None was about to leave. In fact, my head-shed was about as good as it could get. Jim Pugh was well and truly firing on all cylinders, after his initial 'water is for poofs' attitude. He was a real platoon sergeant in the making.

Jim hailed from the south of England, and with his black hair and dark eyes he was a handsome lad – at least when his face wasn't screwed up in anger. He didn't go to the gym, but he was always out on a run or putting rounds down the ranges. He was still grumpy and brutally sarcastic with the lads in his section, but Douggie was right: Jim was a great soldier when the shit went down.

Corporal 'Sandy' Sanderson was my second section commander. He had a shaven head and a thick Mancunian accent, and he was super fit and hyperactive. His catch phrase was – 'I'll flip you for a ...' Sandy was always trying to get the lads to flip a coin for just about anything. He'd flip for a brew, for a 'slave for the day' – so whoever won had to polish the other's boots and generally slave about. He'd flip for who got the bacon sandwiches from the NAAFI, who did the laundry, or whatever. He was great with his men, a demon on the weapons, and one of the funniest blokes in the entire platoon.

Corporal 'Johno' Johnson ran the third section. He was a Kent lad and was a calmer, more mellow kind of a bloke. Like Sandy, he had a shaven head, but he complemented it with a long, droopy moustache. Johno wore the same kind of kit the PARAs had done at Arnhem, give or take a smattering of Gore-Tex: a PARA smock, with a scrim scarf (a knitted camouflaged scarf) knotted around his neck. In short, he was your archetypal PARA.

We were supported in the head-shed by Lance Corporal 'Cloughy' Clough, my signaller. Cloughy was a tall, East End of London lad who'd had no classic education but was exceptionally bright. He could read me like a book, and he sat on the radio net scanning the chat, acting as an invaluable filter and support to me.

My runner was Lance Corporal Powell, who hailed from the Yorkshire Dales. He had a pale, sandy complexion, and his heart and soul was in the Parachute Regiment. He was loyal to a fault, and his role was to pass verbal messages around the platoon whenever we were out on operations.

None of those guys had any intention of leaving the PARAs any time soon, and so it was that we turned my platoon around. By October 1998 we'd won the accolade of being Top Platoon in A Company. I'd been with the PARAs for six months now and this was some result.

We spent our time mounting up the Chinooks, heading out on exercises, digging trenches, tabbing and parachuting into yet more exercises. The CO, Lieutenant Colonel Gibson, kept pushing us, for he wanted us to be the best. But we were still totally up against it in terms of what kind of ops we were likely to get.

All we really had to look forward to was more Northern Ireland, for that was all there seemed to be on the cards right now. And there were many within the British Army who argued that the future lay in heavy armour – not lightly-armed airborne forces – and that a regiment such as ours was largely history. But in fact, they were about to be proved very wrong.

One lunchtime a rumour started circulating in the Officers' Mess. 1 PARA were the Spearhead Battalion right now, so we were ready to move at a moment's notice. Word was we were heading for Kosovo. The conflict there was complicated – as always seemed to be the case in the Balkans – but it boiled down to a bunch of Serbs forcing hundreds of thousands of ethnic Albanians out of Kosovo, with reports of mass graves and possible genocide.

The Balkans seemed to be defined by a centuries-old culture of ethnic hatred, and it had erupted now in Kosovo. The whole situation was complicated by the fact that the Serbs were a foremost ally of the Russians, and by the fact that we had no one on the ground to be our eyes and ears. And that, it seemed, was reason enough to send us in – to establish some basic ground truth.

The prospect of Kosovo was hugely exciting. It wasn't Northern Ireland, where we were hated and loathed. There was also the sense that we might be on the side of the angels this time, and that in Kosovo we could be a force for good. I had a slick, tight platoon under me. We were chomping at the bit to get used. And whatever we were being sent into in Kosovo, we would be first in.

Colonel Gibson called the entire Battalion onto parade, to address us on the coming mission. 'We're going to Kosovo, on a peace-enforcement operation, but that doesn't mean you won't be getting into any scraps. The Serb police and army are hardcore, and there are those amongst them who are mass murderers. They've refused to withdraw from Kosovo, which they see as part of Serbia, so there are plenty of chances of firefights. This will put 1 PARA back on the map.'

Colonel Gibson hadn't been the most popular of COs, for he was seen as being forceful and pushy and not too personable with the blokes. But these were strong, fighting words. And over the months I'd seen how he'd fought tooth and nail to turn the Regiment's fortunes around. He wasn't treating his command as a popularity contest – and why should he?

We moved into the auditorium for a briefing by the intel guys. I knew from the news that the Serbs had been up to some bad shit in Kosovo. The then Prime Minister Tony Blair had been out to visit a concentration camp on the Kosovo border, and it was all over the TV. I was more interested to learn whom we were going up against and what kind of arms they might bring to bear.

Being such close allies of the Russians, the Serbs were equipped with just about everything the Soviets had – so main battle tanks, armoured personnel carriers, anti-aircraft missiles, the works. To make matters worse, Kosovo was awash with paramilitary forces like the notorious Arkan Tigers – brutal Serb supremacists, whose leader carried a baby tiger cub on operations.

We – NATO – had air superiority, but only for so long as the Russians stayed out of the conflict. General Sir Mike Jackson, one of the Army's most respected commanders, was tasked with putting together an ad hoc NATO force for Kosovo. Being an ex-PARA of incredibly high repute, he'd decided that we should be at the forefront of any action. But his Kosovo Force – KFOR for short – would somehow have to include the Russians, if they were to be kept onside.

It was left to men like General Jackson to finesse the details, as we at 1 PARA prepared to deploy. We flew out in battalion strength – so some 500 PARAs and support elements – from RAF Lyneham, in the British military's fleet of ageing Tristars. My platoon was shovelled onto one in which you actually sat facing backwards, which was a horrendous way to fly.

We arrived in Skopje, in neighbouring Macedonia, and the old faithful four-tonner trucks took us into the forested mountains on Macedonia's border with Kosovo. It was mid-May by now and already the country was roasting hot. We got well into the shelter of the woods, and the first thing we did was construct our bashas – rough sleeping platforms with a waterproof poncho strung between two trunks to provide shelter from the sun and the rain.

The atmosphere in the camp was sparkling. Here we were at the absolute leading edge of the British military effort, and we weren't in Northern Ireland. It felt fantastic, whatever the mission might bring. We got our kit shipped in: ammo, rations, bottled water. We broke it down, piled it into our Bergens and distributed it around our webbing, until we were dripping with ammo and grenades.

We were issued with maps for the area and then began our briefings. Kosovo being a land-locked country, the only route in from Macedonia was to punch through the Kacanik Defile – a narrow, precipitous ravine through which snakes the only main road. The problem was if we sent the entire British military force through that way it would be hugely vulnerable to attack. Mountains rose to dizzy heights on either side, so it was an ideal place for an ambush.

General Jackson's plan was for 1 PARA to be airlifted into the Kacanik Defile, to secure its entire length. British armour would then pass through us, and punch onwards towards Pristina, the Kosovan capital. We'd be airlifted forward again, to leapfrog the armour. The capital would then be ours, the Serb forces would be driven out and we could start stabilising the situation.

Jacko, my company commander, briefed me on this, and I in turn briefed my men. We were in total isolation in our wooded camp – so we had no mobile phones, no access to the media or other links to the outside world. We put in a makeshift range, and began live firing to get our weapons zeroed in, plus we started pushing out foot patrols onto the high ground, to get a sense of the lie of the land.

We'd been there a couple of days when I was unexpectedly woken at 0600 hours by Cloughy, my signaller. Apparently Jacko needed me over at his basha right away. Under his poncho shelter Jacko had a map of Kosovo pinned to a tree, with various markers on it identifying key points of interest. I gathered with the commanders of 2 and 3 Platoons to hear what he had to say.

He fixed us with a burning gleam in his eye. 'Situation has changed. The Russians, although supposedly part of KFOR, have decided to go it alone. US satellites have picked them up crossing the border into Kosovo in an armoured column, and they're steaming ahead for Pristina. Their aim is to seize the airport, so they can control all access into and out of the country.'

He paused. 'General Wesley Clark, Supreme Allied Commander Europe, is sat back in Washington and he's fuming. He's ordered us into Kosovo to seize the APOD – the Air Point of Disembarkation – in other words Pristina Airport, and to deny it to the Russians.'

Jacko sat back, as he let his words sink in. I felt the hairs go up on the back of my neck. *Fucking hell – we were getting sent in to go up against the Russians, and we were supposed to be on the same side.* 'Deny' is a typical British exercise in understatement. It's used a lot by the Army. What it actually meant when used in this context was: *You are to use all necessary measures to stop the Russians.*

There was a chorus of muttered 'Fuck me's' from the blokes.

'A and B Company will lead the heli-borne assault onto Pristina APOD, in the first wave of Chinooks,' Jacko continued. He was speaking remarkably matter-of-factly, considering what we were about to do. 'Land south of APOD and seize the eastern side; the remainder of Battalion will come in as second and third waves. Be ready to leave on standby for take-off ...'

Fuck me, this was actually happening and it was happening right now.

As we turned to leave, Jacko added one more thing: 'CO's orders are to wear berets, as opposed to helmets. The world's media is going to be watching this one. He wants them to see and know it's the PARAs going in.'

The red Parachute Regiment beret is hugely distinctive. We'd carry helmets in our Bergens, so we could pull them on if it did kick off big time. But we liked the CO's way of thinking here. It sent a powerful message: we're the PARAs, and we're back. We loved the CO's mindset, but still it was a ballsy move, and it surprised us.

But not as much as the news that we were about to go to war with the Russians.

Douggie had been with me at the briefing. As we stepped away he gave a long, low whistle of amazement. 'Fuck me, this is going to be interesting.'

I laughed. 'No shit, Sherlock.'

Talk about being the master of understatement. In reality, this had all the makings of the start of the Third World War.

As we walked back to our part of Camp I had a barrage of thoughts racing through my head. This was an outrageous turn of events: from a peace-enforcement op, we were now going head-to-head with the old enemy – the Russians. It might turn out to be a stand-off only, but I didn't think that very likely.

The Russian military had a massively hierarchical, top-heavy command structure, and mostly their troops were conscripts. They'd be working to a pretty inflexible set of orders: *to seize Pristina Airport at all costs*. Ground commanders were likely to have zero room to manoeuvre if the situation changed dramatically on the ground – like 1 PARA flying in to get to the airport ahead of them.

I wondered whom exactly we were up against. They were sure to be sending in a very capable unit, if they were aiming to take the airport from under the noses of the British and Americans. They might even be the Spetsnaz, the Russian Special Forces. They were moving ahead in armour, so they'd likely have APCs at the very least – armoured personnel carriers. The best we could mount against APCs was a light anti-tank weapon (LAW), a foldable, 94 mm one-use shoulder-launched missile.

We'd have the MILAN Platoon coming in on the back of us – MILAN being a superb armour-killing missile – plus we'd have a mortar and a machine gun platoon. But still, I didn't exactly relish the thought of going head-to-head with any Russian armour. Our orders as A Company were to hold the eastern side of the airport, and that just happened to be the direction from which the Russians would be steaming in.

Nice.

We'd have fast air flying over Kosovan airspace, but the Russians had their own warplanes massing on the Serb side of the border. If we called in the British Tornadoes and Harriers, plus the American F15s to smash the Russian armour, that was going to be the route to the Third World War.

Douggie rushed off to stores, to get extra water, ammo and rations issued. We had no idea how long we were going in for, and we figured you couldn't have too much ammo if you were going up against the Russians. I double-checked the maps and worked out a series of actions relating to how the platoon would respond to a specific set of threats on the ground.

I got Powell, my runner, to go around the section commanders and pull them in. Jim, Sandy and Johno hurried over and I gave it to them straight.

'Change of plan. We're getting sent in to deny Pristina Airport to the Russians, who are en route from Serbia to get there before us, with heavy armour and the works. Warn the blokes: make ready. Orders in 20 mins.'

Sandy, who was always laughing and flipping for a brew, had his eyes practically popping out of their sockets. 'You what? ... Fucking hell!'

Johno had bent to light a ciggie. He was kind of frozen with the lighter halfway to his lips. There was a look in his eyes like this cannot be for real. Then I saw him spark the ciggie, take a deep drag and smile. As to grumpy Jim, I'd never seen a bloke so rapidly transformed into such a picture of pure happiness.

We'd just recently come away from six weeks battle simulation training in the US. We'd spent the time crawling under wire, through ditches and over obstacles with live tracer pounding over our heads. Prior to that we'd parachuted into Poland on a simulated assault so as to seize an airfield. We couldn't be better prepared for a mission such as this one, and we knew it.

The blokes gathered to form three sides of a square, facing the maps I'd taped to various trees. Cloughy, my signaller, had managed to rustle up a schematic of the airport itself, showing roughly where our platoon fitted in.

'Right, to the south-west of Pristina lies Pristina Airport,' I began. 'Russian units who are supposedly part of KFOR have decided to steam ahead and seize it. No orders have been given for them to go in. I repeat: General Jackson, Commander of KFOR, has issued no such orders. As far as NATO is concerned this is a renegade force and we are being airlifted in to stop them.

'On the lead helo for 1 PARA will be 1 Platoon,' I continued, 'so we will be first in. We will mount up the helo in reverse order, so 3 Section first, followed by 2 and 1. First off will be 1 Section, followed by HQ, then 2 and 3. Once off the aircraft 1 Section takes the 12 o'clock to 4 o'clock arc; 2 Section the 4 to 8 o'clock; 3 Section the 8 to 12 o'clock. Go firm for five minutes and observe arcs. Then 1 Section will lead off to take up positions, here and here.'

I prodded a stick at the eastern perimeter of the airport. 'Half of 2 Platoon will also be on our helo, so they'll mount up before us. We go in in fighting-order only, so full webbing, plus day sack with spare ammo, water and food. Your Bergens will follow at some stage when they can get them in.

'We're going in with weapons made ready and a round in the chamber,' I added. 'Right: actions-on. One, and the key one, as we're going up against the Russians.' I allowed myself just the barest hint of a smile. 'Don't fire unless fired upon.'

There was a ripple of nervous laughter.

'The Serbs and Russians do have SAMs, so if the helo gets shot down we stay together as teams wherever possible and move back to an ERV. That's it.' I paused. 'Get a meal on and a brew, for we don't know when we'll be getting our next.'

The briefing broke up. I got Powell to rustle me up a boil-in-the-bag pasta meal, and dose it heavily with Tabasco sauce and garlic salt. As I ate, I studied the maps some more and ran over the plans one last time. This had been rushed, but it was a simple enough kind of an op. We were making it up as we went along, but what did we expect when going in against the Russians?

We tabbed the one kilometre down to the open fields that fringed the woods. As we did so we heard the thwooping beat of a fleet of Chinooks thrashing the air, as the airborne armada came thundering in. I emerged from the treeline to see the largest gathering of helos I'd ever laid eyes on. There were fifteen Chinooks, plus a half-dozen Pumas, and Lynx gunships in support.

We'd put the mortar and machine gun teams in the Pumas, plus the MILAN Platoon. That way, they could fly in on the flanks of the Chinooks, and set up fire-bases to either side of the main force. We moved into the open cornfields where the air armada was gathered. There was stiff, golden stubble underfoot – all that remained after the recent harvest – and the smell of avgas (aviation fuel) heavy in the air.

An RAF air adjutant directed us to our aircraft. We gathered at our allotted Chinook. The sun was burning bright above us, and Douggie was doing the rounds with extra bottled water, to make sure we all stayed hydrated, which was vital this close to going in.

As I looked around me, I could barely believe this was happening. The most I'd ever seen before was a company airlift, on exercises. The fact that such a massive number of airframes had been made available just went to show how serious this shit was.

As Douggie fussed around the blokes, I went forward to have a word with the aircrew. The forward aircraft were all from the Special Forces Aviation Squadron. Sandy was already having a good natter with the door-gunners, who manned the six-barrelled miniguns. I figured he was dying to have a pop with one of the Gatling-type door-guns. Knowing him, he was more than likely bagsying a weapon, in case a door-gunner got whacked.

I got around to the front and I could see the pilots in the cockpit of the giant helo, the side windows of which were thrown back to give them some air.

'I'm David, platoon commander, 1 Platoon,' I called up to them. 'Can you show me the route of the flight path?'

'Yeah, sure,' came the easy reply. 'See you at the ramp.'

We met at the helo's rear. The pilot extended a hand to me. 'I'm George. Good to be flying you.'

I spread my map out on the open tail ramp, while we ran over the flight plan in detail.

'So, we'll fly from here around here, making a wide, looping eastwards approach to the airfield,' George explained. 'There are suspected KLA camps here, and the UCK – a variant of the KLA – are here. Don't want to overfly them. In theory, they're the good guys, but they may assume we're Serbs or even Russians, so we'll route around them. Plus there are Serbian forces all over the shop, and they do have SAMs.'

The KLA was the Kosovo Liberation Army, the Albanian resistance that was fighting the Serbs. SAM was the acronym for surface-to-air-missile – basically any form of guided missile capable of shooting down a warplane.

'NATO has had aircraft shot down,' the pilot continued, 'so we'll be flying tactically, at low-level, nap-of-the-earth kind of stuff. Our aircraft will be leading the way. There's an AWACS E3D aircraft, and it'll be the control platform for the air package. Plus there's CAPs on call, in a racetrack position, as required.'

An AWACS aircraft would be something like a Nimrod, with the eavesdropping, monitoring, early warning and communications capabilities to oversee the entire airborne operation. CAPs were basically Combat Air Patrols, so flights of fast jets capable of mounting air strikes on our behalf.

'So, we're good to go?' I asked.

The pilot nodded. 'Yep. Should be wheels-up in ten. Which reminds me, I need to get the blades turning.'

The pilot was so calm and collected you'd think he was about to fly some exercise on Salisbury Plain. I returned to the blokes and gave them the sketch. As I did so, I heard the whine of the starter motors as the turbines fired and the Chinook's twin rotors began to spool up to speed. The note of the turbines kept rising and rising, until it had built into a deafening, high-pitched scream, the downwash of the rotors hammering into us.

We whipped our berets off and stuffed them into a side pocket of our smocks, lest the rotor-wash rip them off our heads. We rose up on one knee, and bunched together to mount up. I kept my eyes on the loadmaster on the helo's open ramp, waiting for the signal to pile aboard. Douggie was at my side, and for a moment I felt him tense. He turned to the blokes behind us.

'Right, men,' he yelled, above the noise, 'get off that helo, go down on one knee in fire positions, make ready, fix bayonets and fix berets rouge! Hold the ground, stay switched on, and await orders.'

By now there were fifteen Chinooks turning and burning, and I could barely hear the last of Douggie's words. My pulse was pounding away as the adrenaline started pumping, the sweat pouring off me. I saw the loadie give us the signal and we were pounding up the open ramp and into the Chinook's hold.

After the blinding sunlight of the open cornfield, it was dark as the grave in there. It took a few moments for my eyes to adjust to the gloom. I could see the yellow glare of the corn stubble out of the rear of the aircraft – the terrain that we were leaving behind us – and felt the giant helo shifting and juddering about as it strained to get airborne.

This was it – we were going in for real. We were poised to fly across the border into another country, and seize their main airport in direct defiance of the armoured might of the Russians.

If ever there was a mission to die for, this was the one.

*

CHAPTER FOURTEEN

——————

As the blades turned ever faster I could feel the powerful blasts of hot air hitting my face, the downdraught roaring in through the open ramp. I couldn't hear a thing any more, for the noise was overpowering. To either side of us, row upon row of blokes from 1 PARA were surging into their own aircraft, as we prepared to get some 600 crack fighting men airborne.

But all of a sudden I noticed a change in the pitch of the turbines, as the pilot started to ease off the power. I wondered if the Chinook had suffered a last-minute fault, and whether we'd have to cross-deck into another airframe. Gradually, the rotors came to a thwooping stop. It was then that I could hear that all around us other aircraft were also powering down.

I locked eyes with Douggie. Neither of us had a clue what was going on, and there was no way I could make radio contact with Jacko from where we were cooped up in the helo's interior. Presumably we must have been delayed for some reason, or worse still the mission was getting stood down.

I unbuckled my safety and hurried across to the open ramp. Douggie and I stared out into the sunlit glare. The last of the helos were shutting down, their rotors decelerating from a whirling blur and the individual blades slowly becoming visible.

We jumped down from the ramp. Douggie sparked up a ciggie and offered me a drag. I didn't smoke much as a rule, but I did when on operations. At moments of high tension it helped to calm the nerves, and I sure as hell needed it now.

As I sucked in a blast of nicotine, I saw a figure hurrying across towards us. It was Jacko's runner.

'We're getting stood down,' he yelled, just as soon as he was within shouting distance. 'Get your men and head back to the harbour area.'

I felt an immediate sense of deflation, as if someone had just popped my bubble and all the adrenaline was gone. That was all the runner had for us, and he moved off directly to the next aircraft. I had no idea why we'd been stood down. Had the mission been postponed, or had it been canned? I very much suspected the latter. With the Russians racing for the airport, if we weren't going now we very likely weren't going at all.

We trekked back to the woodland and settled down to have a brew. I was supping my tea and wondering what exactly had happened, when a buzz went around that was almost as shocking as a mission such as this getting called off at the last minute.

Cloughy had picked it up on the radio. 'Fuck me, boss, did you hear? Private Woods refused to get on the helo. The blades were turning and he just wouldn't get on ...'

'Jesus. You're shitting me.'

'No, boss, not Jesus: Private Woods.'

That was a typical Cloughy wisecrack. 'Ha, ha. Seriously: *Woodsy refused to get on?*'

'That's what I'm hearing, boss ...'

The news hit me like a bucket of cold water in the face.

Private Woods was in another Company, but still it was inconceivable that he'd have refused to mount up the helo. It was about the last thing I'd ever have dreamed of happening, and it slammed home to me the deadly serious nature of the mission we'd been about to undertake. For a PARA to refuse to go on a mission was incomprehensible. You'd rather have a bloke die on you than have that happen. The PARA Reg prided itself above all else on courage, and this was about as bad as it could get.

The word went around like wildfire, and I could see the shock and incomprehension in the eyes of my men. They were stunned. In a way, this had eclipsed what had happened with the mission getting stood down. We always knew that could happen. It was the same with any op: it was never a 'go' until you left the aircraft and had your boots firmly on the ground.

But this – this was beyond comprehension, and it struck right at the heart of who we were and what we prided ourselves on. We may have been about to fly into the teeth of Russian armour and possibly Armageddon – but heaven forbid that any one of our number would refuse to execute the mission as ordered. It was beyond impossible – or at least so we had thought.

It wasn't long before Cloughy had more news. The rumour mill was flying now, and this concerned why we had been stood down. Word was that General Jackson, the KFOR Commander, had called Tony Blair direct and told him that the mission needed to be called off – for there was every chance it would trigger the Third World War.

Apparently, General Jackson had been liaising directly with Blair, and he'd spoken to General Wesley Clark, the Supreme NATO Commander, and told him he wasn't prepared to carry out a mission that would trigger the next world war. While it was totally alien to us to disobey an order, we knew General Jackson to be a superlative commander who was not afraid of a fight.

We had to presume he'd made the right call.

General Jackson was known to us as 'The Prince of Darkness'. He was a fantastic leader of men, one with the fortunes of the Parachute Regiment at heart. He must have figured that taking Pristina Airport in the face of the Russians wasn't exactly going to further the cause of peace in Kosovo. If it had kicked off with the Russians, the Serbs would have seen that as a clarion call to arms, and we'd likely have had the shitfight from hell on our hands.

Still, I'd burned a lot of adrenaline in the last few hours, as had my men, and this was a huge comedown. By mid-afternoon we had it confirmed that the Russians had taken Pristina Airport. I sat around with Douggie and my section commanders, shooting the shit.

'Fucking Gen Jackson – big bollocks, eh?' Douggie remarked.

I nodded my agreement. 'Yeah. I guess that's why they call him The Prince of Darkness.'

'I heard he was an awesome CO when he was in charge of 1 PARA,' Sandy added.

Jim snorted, grumpily. 'Still fucking shit to get stood down.'

Johno shrugged. 'Never mind, eh. Still got our moment of glory to come.'

By that he meant the mission to secure the Kacanik Defile, which as far as we knew was still one hundred per cent happening.

At 2100 hours I went in for a briefing with Jacko. Apparently, Downing Street and KFOR were still trying to get some sense out of the Russians. They wanted to know why they'd gone in and taken the airport against orders, and risked a Third World War. Of course, we all knew why: it was so they could control who flew in and out of Kosovo. But a formal explanation from the Russians would have been something of a conciliatory gesture.

Apparently, General Jackson's position was that KFOR's mission was to secure the withdrawal of Serb forces, and to enforce peace thereafter. Triggering a major conflict that could have flared across the region and with massive global ramifications wouldn't have furthered that aim. It was a fair one.

Still, I lay awake that night with my mind a whirl of thoughts. I had wanted to go in and do the op as ordered, but in retrospect it had to have been the right decision to stand the mission down. Still, I felt a bittersweet mixture of relief and disappointment.

But mostly, the last few hours had brought me two major shockers in quick succession. As far as I knew General Jackson had denied General Clark's direct order. I presumed Blair must have supported him in that, but still it struck me as setting a dangerous precedent.

All my training to date had been that you never, ever disobeyed a direct order, and that made this hugely unsettling.

If you were ordered to jump off a cliff, you might point out the deficiencies in the order, but you wouldn't disobey it. If you were empowered to choose what orders to obey then the whole system of command would break down. Arguably, everything you did in war was dangerous, so when did it become too dangerous for orders to be obeyed? I'd never heard of this happening before, and I had never even considered it an option to not obey an order.

It crossed my mind that my men would very likely be entertaining the same thoughts and doubts right now, and that meant that potentially my own command had been undermined. But at the same time I sensed that General Jackson's was the right call. It was still my first experience of someone disobeying an order, and I was struggling to understand what it might mean and where it left us.

As I lay awake mulling all of this over, I began to reach a clearer sense of understanding. The American military hadn't trained for peacekeeping, and they had little experience of such operations. By contrast, we'd had decades of such experience in Northern Ireland, the Balkans and elsewhere. Sure, we were a bayonet, but we couldn't just be stabbed in willy-nilly.

And for certain, General Jackson's call had been the right one.

Very early the next morning we prepared to move out and secure the Kacanik Defile. As A Company were going to be first in – that put my platoon at the very tip of NATO's conventional forces as they went in on the ground in Kosovo.

I say conventional forces, because we knew there were Special Forces elements in ahead of us. In fact, the Kacanik Defile had been recce'd by a tiny, elite unit called The Pathfinders, and right now they were positioned high in the forested mountains. A specialist elite recce outfit, they'd have eyes on the road running through the Defile as we were airlifted in, so they could warn us of any hostile forces that might be preparing to hit us.

I knew of The Pathfinders already. I'd been on exercises where they were involved, and I'd seen them HALOing into targets. I'd been hugely impressed by the men who made up their number, but I hadn't really considered yet whether I might want to try to join them. I was a 21-year-old captain in 1 PARA commanding a crack platoon at the forefront of operations. This was as good as it got.

It was 0330 hours when we started to move through the silent and darkened woods. As we mounted up the CH-47s, I felt damn certain this mission wasn't about to get stood down. The Chinook lifted off, and we crossed over the Kosovo border as the sun clawed over the massive peaks to the east of us. The pilots were keeping lower than a snake's belly, and to either side of us thick woodland flashed past the porthole-like windows.

I was trying to keep track of where we were on the map, but at this altitude it was pretty bloody hopeless. After a twenty-minute rollercoaster of a flight, we put down on the main highway – the only flat piece of terrain that was large enough to land a Chinook. We burst out of the rear ramp, and spun into all-around defence, for we had no idea what we were moving into here.

Moments later the Chinook was airborne again, the downdraught throwing sand and gravel into our exposed faces. Once it was gone, we fixed berets rouge. There was a deep and heavy silence, broken only by the distinctive, thudding beat of the CH-47 as it faded into the distance. We took cover on the roadside and set up a mortar team to provide supporting fire, as further flights came in with more men.

Suddenly, the silence was torn apart by this thunderous roar as a massive missile went tearing past right over our heads. In the quick flash of its flight above us, I could see that it was some kind of cruise missile, and it was being guided towards a target. It went powering onwards into the mountains, and a few seconds later there was an almighty great explosion.

Cloughy was on the radio, and he came off with news for me. 'Boss! Boss! The PF are in contact over to the east of us.'

Apparently, the Pathfinders (PF) had been ambushed by a renegade Serb outfit, and they were engaged in a fierce firefight to drive them out of a series of buildings. It was they who had called in the cruise missile. As for us, we had a massive drop falling away to one side of us, and a near-vertical wall of rock on the other, so there was no way in which we could go to the PF's aid.

In any case, our mission was to hold the road and allow British armour through. As we went firm in our positions, more news came in via Cloughy. The Pathfinders had moved in to take the Serb position, and apparently they'd stumbled upon their first mass grave. The Kacanik Defile was beginning to take on a really sinister feel, as we got just a taste of the kind of horrors that had taken place here.

Mordor, without the Elves.

Cloughy called me over to the radio. Jacko was on the air to speak with me. I took the handset.

'Charlie Charlie One, Zero Alpha, prepare to move figures five, pushing further north.'

'Figures five' was Jacko's way of saying in five minutes time, and Charlie Charlie One was standard radio speak for all commanders on this net.

No sooner had Jacko spoken than I heard the clatter of tank tracks from behind, and the first of the British Challenger main battle tanks lumbered around a bend in the road. The heavy armour was escorted by smaller Scimitar armoured fighting vehicles. A dozen came through and then there was a short gap before the next squadron roared past.

The armour having moved through us, Jacko put out the shout for his platoon commanders to come in. He was positioned at the centre of the Company, a good hundred yards up the road. I dashed over, and there he was with his map out and barking orders.

'We're going into Pristina now!' he announced, stabbing a finger at a patch of open terrain just to the north-west of the city.

'What's our task when we get there?' someone asked.

'No time for that now,' Jacko answered. 'Get on the Chinooks. When you land surge the city, then wait my orders.'

I ran back to my blokes and yelled out the orders, such as they were. The lead Chinook came down in a cloud of choking dust, and we hammered up the rear ramp. No sooner were we on board than we were airborne again. This was all about keeping up the momentum now, and surging forward to keep one step ahead of the armour.

The pilot dropped the Chinook's nose, piled on the power and we thundered eastwards through the Defile. Below us the narrow chasm opened out into a wide plain, with here and there the odd farmer, and what I presumed had to be rebel gunmen gathered at the junctions of tracks, plus the remains of what appeared to be burned-out villages.

Then the Chinook was over the city itself and searching for somewhere to put down. The pilot chose a likely field, and seconds later the wheels were down in the long grass. We piled off the open ramp into all-around defence. A few hundred yards away I could see a series of massive, Soviet-style apartment blocks, with crowds of people surging out of them to watch our arrival.

I grabbed my map and compass as Sandy crouched down beside me with his GPS. He read me our grid, I plotted it on the map and orientated it to north. At least now we knew where we were. Behind us and to the west other helos touched down, and further platoons of PARAs rushed off the rear.

Jacko called us over again. 'Right, 1 PARA are surging Pristina. This is A Company area, here. 1 Company lead off and take this road into the middle of the city.'

'Any boundaries?' I asked. In other words, were there any areas we shouldn't go, either because other friendly forces were there, or maybe the Russians.

'None. Just surge the area. No fucking about – get going!'

I raced back to my platoon. 'We're surging the city! Jim – 1 Section leads, followed by 2 and 3. Go!'

We spread out into marching order, and moved down a track into the outskirts of the city. Before us a massive crowd awaited. It was like walking down a stretch of the London Marathon with men, women and kids five to ten deep on either side of us. They were crying tears of joy and throwing roses onto the road before us, as we pushed ahead into the shadows of the first buildings.

We couldn't take the flowers they offered us, for we were both hands on our weapons. I had to presume that every one of those present here had had a relative or loved one killed in the bitter conflict that had consumed this city. An old woman with a battered and wrinkled face framed with a black gypsy shawl stepped forward and tried to offer me a tiny cup of coffee. She grabbed at me, her face a mass of tearful, toothless smiles.

I'd never known anything like this before. It was surreal. We hadn't so much as fired a shot yet, but still we were being treated as heroes and saviours. We pushed a good kilometre through the crowd and still it showed no sign of thinning out. It seemed as if the entire Albanian population of the city had flocked to this area, for we represented safety and security.

We knew there were Serbs in the city, and they were intent on doing one last round of killings and torture, so it made sense for all these people to have come. But when and where were we going to come face to face with the killers?

Jim pushed ahead leading 1 Section, with 2 and 3 flanking him. All of a sudden, we emerged from the crowds and the streets were totally empty. It was spooky. Weird. The atmosphere was suddenly quite different. It was darker and quite sinister. I could sense it: I guessed the others could too. I caught the fleeting glimpse of the odd figure down the end of an alleyway or a road, but they certainly weren't hanging around to welcome us, or to throw any flowers.

Then: *Bang! Bang! Bang!*

The first bursts of gunfire were answered an instant later by the bark of an SA80 firing, and I knew my blokes were in a contact.

Cloughy's yell confirmed it: 'Contact. Wait out!'

We hard-targeted it, sprinting forward and zigzagging to make a difficult target of ourselves. We'd developed the skill in Northern Ireland, where the IRA nearly always worked in ones or pairs. You needed to move forward as fast as possible, while still trying not to get shot, to have a chance of catching the gunmen, for they often did a 'shoot-'n'-scoot' – in other words, they'd fire then run away.

If you wanted to catch the fuckers you had to run towards those who were shooting at you, as your flanking teams pushed around the edges and tried to encircle them. I did just this, moving forward with my weapon in the aim, as Cloughy and Powell covered me. I reached the end of a narrow alley, with my back against the wall, and I could hear shouting from my right. It sounded like it was 2 Platoon in action, for I recognised some of their voices.

I ran across the road, with Cloughy and Powell on my heels. There lying face down on the tarmac was a figure surrounded by a spreading pool of blood. He had on blue trousers and a matching jacket, which we knew was the uniform of the Serb police. His jacket was undone, showing a grubby white T-shirt beneath it, which now was flecked with blood. His hair was a greasy mop and his chin was thick with days-old stubble.

One of the young lads on 2 Platoon still had his rifle in the aim. He looked as white as a sheet, and it was obvious he'd just shot the Serb dead. I shouted across to 2 Platoon's commander.

'Nick, we're securing this side of the road!'

He shouted back confirmation. I got Jim, Sandy and Johno to spread out down our side of the street, in case any more of the fuckers tried to have a pop at us. The other side of the street was covered by 2 Platoon. Via Cloughy on the radio I gleaned the first snippets of what had just happened.

The Serb policeman had been drinking with a bunch of others. He'd seen the 2 Platoon lads moving down towards him, drawn his pistol and loosed off a load of rounds like it was the Wild West. Private Lamont, one of the newest in the platoon, had been the first to see him. He'd levelled his rifle and shot him dead. The rest of the Serb coppers had turned and fled.

Jacko turned up to check things out, and after a quick heads-up he sent us on. We patrolled further into the city. A pattern started to emerge. We'd hit large sections where the population flooded out to greet us, showering us with tears, flowers and more coffee. Then we'd reach an area that felt eerily hostile and deserted.

Finally, a woman in her early forties with crooked, broken teeth wouldn't let me pass. She seemed to be either mad or desperate or both. She grabbed me in an iron grip and kept trying to hustle me towards a building in the distance.

'There! Over there!' she kept yelling, in broken English. 'Serb police live there!'

I gathered the blokes. 'Right, she seems to think that's some kind of Serb police outpost. So, we're going to move in and clear it.'

We approached it from the side and booted in the door, but the place was deserted. I opened a cabinet on the ground floor, and hey presto there were four AK47s and a case full of grenades. Sandy led his section upstairs, and found a whole load of pistols, and some Claymore anti-personnel mines. From the outside it looked like any other house. Inside, it was a bloody war in a box.

Clearly, if this was what we could find in one unremarkable house in the midst of an unremarkable estate, the city had to be crawling with weapons. And for sure, there were a number of people here right now who didn't view us as their saviours exactly. The two together could prove a fairly lethal combination.

Sandy slung the AKs over his shoulder, and we packed the rest of the war-in-a-box into our daypacks. It was time to move on. Before leaving, Sandy showed the rest of the guys how to unload and make safe an AK. It was non-NATO weaponry, so few of us had seen them before. We headed into a patrol base that Jacko had set up in a deserted school, and dumped all the Serb weaponry. It joined a growing pile of such kit that the others were finding.

'Get around all the buildings where the Serb police and army were,' Jacko told us. 'Get the weapons off the streets, and start to build the intel picture. Work in multiples from now on – one on patrol and one off, resting.'

A multiple is half a platoon. It was how we patrolled in Northern Ireland. You didn't need a full platoon to control or occupy a street, and working in multiples you could cover more ground. I told Douggie I'd take the first patrol out. He could get some rest, and take his out just as soon as we got in.

Our patrol lasted into the evening and the first hours of darkness. Our main problem became one of communicating with the locals. People kept trying to drag us here and there to investigate something, but we couldn't make ourselves understood. We had a card with a few phrases in Serbo-Croat on one side and Albanian on the other. But in truth it was next to useless.

We got back to base having found a load more weaponry. I told Jacko that our number one priority had to be to get some interpreters. We dossed down on the floor of the school. No one had any proper sleeping gear, for we'd come in with only our day sacks. So we bedded down on the hard concrete, with most of us having just a thin, survival blanket to toss over our bodies and our webbing for a pillow.

Before going to sleep, I got the low-down on what had taken place at Pristina Airport. The Commander of 5 Airborne Brigade, Brigadier Adrian Freer, had apparently marched up to the Russian commander on the Pristina Airport apron. Brigadier Freer was a short, ginger-haired PARA who was hugely respected by the blokes, and widely considered to be barking mad. He was utterly eccentric in that classic English way, and routinely wore a scrim scarf over a Spetsnaz T-shirt.

'What the fuck are you lot doing here?' he'd demanded of the Russians.

They hadn't known quite what to say, and thus the confrontation at the airport had been defused. I went to sleep laughing at the thought of it and feeling on top of the world.

The next morning I woke up, got some scoff down me and went and sought out Jacko. Overnight he'd somehow rustled up a terp. Our guy was a sandy-haired, bearded and gangly Pristina University undergraduate. He was studying chemical engineering, and his skin was so pale that it looked as if it had never seen the sun. It promptly earned him the nickname 'The Moth'.

He was effusively friendly and he did speak great English, although he did so in an annoyingly high-pitched squeak. Still, it was way better than messing around with the phrase cards.

We set out on patrol with Moth sticking to my heels. Within ten minutes we spotted this column of thick, dark smoke rising into the dawn sky. It looked ominous and we decided to investigate. As we neared the source of the smoke, it turned out to be this enormous, squat, stark concrete edifice some four floors high. There was a courtyard at the front fenced all around and with massive steel gates.

It looked like some Soviet-era prison, and it dwarfed the buildings all around it. Somehow, the place exuded a dark menace and a brooding evil.

Sandy turned his bald head towards me. 'Boss, I bet that's a cop shop.'

He had an uncanny instinct for sniffing out the enemy.

'Right, off we go then,' I confirmed.

We reached the building and Sandy turned to me again. 'Boss, people have left here just minutes ago.'

How the fuck did he know this? I was about to ask him, when I noticed the expression on the face of our terp. He had gone white as a sheet and his skin looked deathly cold.

'Moth, what's up?' I asked him. 'What the fuck is this place?'

'This is MUP Police Station,' he muttered. 'Many bad things happen here.'

'What's the MUP?'

'Serb secret police – like KGB, only no rules ...'

He makes it clear he did not want to go in. Just the sight

of this place has clearly put the fear of God into him.

'What's the matter?' I asked.

'Those who go in never come out.'

'Well we're going in, and we sure as hell are fucking coming out again.'

We pushed through the gates, which were half hanging off their hinges. Inside, there was shit absolutely everywhere: overturned office furniture mixed with empty AK47 magazines, garbage and even human faeces. It looked as if a tornado had ripped through the place. The fire to the rear of the building was growing ever higher, suggesting that it had only recently been lit.

'Sandy, go stamp that fucking thing out,' I told him.

At the heart of the fire was a rusty old oil barrel stuffed full of papers. Sandy took a flying karate kick and booted the thing over, then stamped out the worst of the flames. As he did so, I realised the fire was made up of tonnes and tonnes of official-looking documents, many of which Sandy had just saved. I helped him put out the last of the flames, then bent to pick one of them up.

A face stared up at me. It was a black-and-white passport-sized photo of a young and very beautiful woman. She looked to be around Moth's age, no older. The photo was stapled to the left-hand side of the paper, which was full of a typed Cyrillic script – so written in the Russian alphabet. It looks nothing like our own and I couldn't make out a word.

One thing was clear though: as I flicked through a few of the pictures they all shared the same hopeless expression, as if they knew at the moment the photographs were taken that their lives were pretty much over.

I turned to our terp, and waved the paper at him. 'Moth, what the fuck is all this? Who is she?'

He wouldn't answer. He wouldn't even step any closer to the barrel. I grabbed his arm and manoeuvred him nearer.

'What is this? Who is she?' I tried again.

He glanced at the top sheet of paper, fearfully, as if it could somehow leap up at him and strangle him. 'Melina Berashi,' he mumbled. He glanced at me, his eyes glazed and unfocused. 'Melina Berashi. That is her name.'

I fanned out a load more of the papers. 'And these? Who are they? What does it mean?'

'These are ... These are all the people they have taken.'

'What d'you mean?' I asked, sharply.

'These are the missing. The disappeared.'

*

CHAPTER FIFTEEN

W e doused the fire until there was just the odd fleck of ash spiralling skywards. Jim's section led the way into the building's interior. He'd been in there barely a minute, when I heard a voice echoing up from somewhere below.

'Boss! Boss!' he yelled. 'Down here!'

I headed through the building, which was a mass of overturned furniture and debris. A flight of concrete steps led off to one side. Jim's cry had come from there. I moved down the steps. No windows opened up onto the ill-lit stairwell, and it led into some kind of a basement.

The steps opened into a narrow corridor, lit by a single bare bulb. To one side I could see a row of bars of what had to be cells. One cell was far larger than the rest, and it was from there that Jim had called me. I hadn't managed to wash for a good few days, as you don't when you're out on ops. I knew I had to smell. But down here, there was this overpowering, sickening stench – one of piss and shit and stale sweat and terror.

I turned into the room. There was Jim, along with the lads from his section. They were staring around, their faces masks of shock. In the stunned silence, Jim nodded towards one of the walls. It was filthy dirty, or at least I took it to be dirt. Then I realised that it was red. For a moment I thought there had to be some old red paint spattered on the walls and the floor.

It was then that I realised it was dried blood.

I focused on what else was in the room. There was a row of old, iron bedsteads with no mattresses. Each had a leather belt tied to its head and its foot. On a table to one side was a range of particularly savage-looking knuckledusters. One was of solid steel construction, with huge spikes welded to the front – the part that would make contact with someone's body or head.

I noticed a massive wooden baseball bat. It looked abnormally bulky, and then I realised that it had some twenty or more nails driven through it, so as to form a spiked club. Scrawled across the handle in black marker pen were the words: MOUTH SHUTTER.

There were assorted knives and machetes scattered around the place, most with a crust of dried blood still adhering to their cutting edges. There was even a bloodied hacksaw blade. I shuddered to think what had gone on down here. Piled up in the far corner was a heap of discarded clothes. I guessed they'd stripped their victims – both men and women – before starting work on them.

This place was fucking evil. It was a medieval torture chamber transported into the modern day. This MUP secret police lot had done little or nothing to clear up the evidence of their evil deeds. They'd left the tools of their trade lying everywhere, plus the blood drying on the walls.

As I ran my eye around the place it came to rest upon one of the modern-day innovations that the MUP had seen fit to add to their medieval dungeon. Next to one of the beds was a low table. It was piled with bundles of cotton wool, and what had to be bottles of medicines or drugs, plus hypodermic needles.

I picked up one of the bottles. 'Atropine' the label announced. Atropine is used as a muscle relaxant for those with heart conditions, but it can also be used as a tool to aid interrogation, and has been by some of the more evil and lawless of the world's regimes. Clearly, this MUP lot were fully paid-up members of their club.

Sandy walked in. He stopped dead. He gazed in shock at the blood-spattered walls and the torture equipment, before his eyes came to rest on the iron bedsteads complete with their straps.

He shook his head, like he couldn't believe what he was seeing. 'Fuck me.'

Sandy was always the joker, no matter what the situation. I'd never once seen him lost for words, or a fitting wisecrack. He was now.

A couple of Jim's blokes called from another room. 'Boss! Boss!'

I stepped through into what was obviously the MUPs' locker room. There were rows of uniforms, some of which were camouflage gear and looked distinctly military. There were batons, helmets and stacks and stacks of pornographic magazines and videos. It was porn of the most horrific kind. It was bloodsucking, vampirish, evil garbage and the presence of it here made it doubly sickening.

I went back upstairs. I found Cloughy and put a call through to Jacko. 'Hello Zero, this is Alpha One Sunray, fetch Sunray – over.'

He came up on the net almost instantly.

'We're at some kind of an MUP base,' I told him. 'They've left a stack load of documents, which they were trying to burn. Plus there's a load of other stuff you need to come and see.'

Jacko didn't ask why or query me. 'Roger. I'm on my way. Out.'

That's what made Jacko such a great commander – he never questioned his blokes. He knew I wouldn't be calling him down here unless he needed to come.

Jacko pitched up together with his sergeant major, a hardened veteran of the Falklands Campaign. Both were visibly ashen-faced once I'd shown them around.

''Right, Dave, secure the building,' Jacko told me, gruffly. 'I'm going to let Battalion know.'

I got a cordon thrown around the place – a ring of blokes with strict instructions to let no one through. That done, we began a more methodical search. On the first floor we stumbled upon piles of condoms scattered around everywhere, plus loads of empty vodka bottles. The combination of the condoms, plus the alcohol and the bare wire mattresses with the straps made me want to vomit.

No one had to think very hard to work out what it all had to mean.

There were also stacks of Claymore mines and grenades, plus who knew what other stray ordnance lying all over the floor.

I gave the order. 'Right, stop the search! This place could be booby-trapped. We need EOD.'

EOD stands for Explosive Ordnance Disposal – the bomb detection guys. Cloughy sent out the call to get an EOD team over pronto. I went outside to get some much-needed air. I felt dirty and dark just from having spent a few minutes in that place. I glanced around. I couldn't see a sign of Moth, our terp, anywhere. I guessed it must all have proved too much for the poor bastard.

One of my blokes called me over to the cordon. Apparently, a BBC TV reporter had pitched up and was mooching around outside. The lads kept feeding him the set line: 'Step away, sir, there's nothing to see here.' But he wasn't buying it. He'd seen the red beret of the PARAs all over the front pages of the British newspapers, and he knew that wherever we went there was bound to be a story.

I went to have a word with him. He seemed to know already that this was an MUP base, and that bad things had gone on here. I guessed some of the young lads on the cordon had been talking, and I couldn't say that I blamed them. We were all of us in shock, and it was far from easy to keep a thing such as this quiet. I told him I'd let him in to film just as soon as I got clearance to do so.

I left him pacing back and forth in front of his vehicle, from where I could hear him rehearsing his lines. 'It's hard to see how crimes like this have anything remotely to do with any kind of policing ...'

Next thing the CO, Colonel Gibson, pitched up. 'Right, Dave, what's the brief?' he asked me, brisk and businesslike as usual.

I told him about what we'd found and about the BBC guy outside. He told me to keep the place secured and that they were going to bring down a whole entourage of reporters. The Battalion press officer was on the case, and he'd walk them through the building and the story. The BBC reporter waiting outside could join them.

This place had just become the biggest story in all Kosovo, the CO explained. It was the 'smoking gun' everyone had been looking for. Here was proof of what the Serbs had been doing in Pristina, for this was where they had 'processed' thousands into the mass graves that were only just starting to be discovered.

The media arrived. Cameramen flooded the building. Film cameras whirred and flashguns popped and sputtered as the photojournalists secured their close-up shots of the horror. As the commander of the patrol who found the place, it was left to me to show the journalists around the worst parts.

The BBC reporter asked me if I could be in his shots? Better still, would I be willing to say a few words about what we'd found here?

'You're okay with that, Dave, are you?' our media liaison bloke asked me.

I told him I was. I agreed to go with it, because I knew the CO wanted to put the Parachute Regiment back on the map. But I also agreed to go with it because I was shocked and disgusted by what we'd stumbled into here.

'We are paratroopers and it takes a lot to shock us,' I told the reporters, 'but this is terrible. I am not being dramatic: this is truly evil. We feel very angry that those who did this could get away with it.'

Word spread like wildfire about the MUP base and more and more press arrived. It had become a media circus by now and I just wanted to get myself and my blokes out of there. A second multiple was sent out to relieve us, and we started the tab back to our school base.

En route, Sandy kept asking our terp if he was all right.

'Yes. It is just very difficult for me,' Moth replied, quietly.

'Yeah, fucking evil bastards, eh?' said Sandy, with real emotion.

Already, we were starting to feel a burning hatred for those who had done this and had seemingly got away with it scot-free.

'Boss, who're Reuters?' Cloughy asked me. 'Some bloke kept saying he was from Reuters.'

'Only the biggest press agency in the world. Whenever you see a press story anywhere in the world, it's often from them.'

'So, does that mean we're going to be all over the newspapers?'

'Yeah, probably. But not you, Cloughy. You're too ugly.'

It was important to keep the humour and the banter going, for it was that as much as anything that would keep us human in the midst of all this shit.

'If those people on the photos are the "missing" where did they all end up?' a voice asked.

It was Powell, my runner. I knew what he was driving at: *Where are all the bodies?* We all looked at our terp.

He held his hands up in a gesture of helplessness. 'There is a lake outside Pristina. People say a lot of them have been taken there.'

We got back to our base, and a bundle of British newspapers had been delivered. There were photos of PARAs with flowers being thrown in their path, and there was even one of a mass grave with a sergeant major from 1 PARA standing guard over it.

In another front-page photo I recognised one of my fellow officer cadets from Sandhurst. Vicky Wentworth was a strikingly beautiful brunette, with gorgeous hazel-green eyes. She'd gone on to join the Royal Logistics Corps. The 'loggies' had come in on the back of our operation, and Vicky was pictured bent over a mass grave, in floods of tears.

As I flicked through the newspapers, one thing became clear to me. The CO's idea of going in with berets on had proved to be a mark of pure genius. As a symbol of the liberation of Kosovo, it had captured the imagination of the British public, if not of the wider world. Other British Army units were here too, but we had been first in and we'd captivated the media and the public alike.

But I was aware of something else too. My platoon had just stumbled into a torture chamber, a place of mass horror, of rape and vampire-porn. Some of my blokes were eighteen years old. I was only twenty. This kind of stuff was far from easy. In fact, it was the stuff of nightmares. Ever since we'd been sent into Pristina, morale had been sky high, but the darkness was starting to come home now.

We'd had zero preparation for this. No one had ever run the let's-go-find-a-torture-chamber exercise. I'd always imagined myself parachuting into war, tabbing ten miles with legs burning and under a crushing load, fixing bayonets and closing with the enemy. That was the kind of stuff that I'd read about in *The Making Of A Para*.

But not this. This shit was seriously dark.

Some of the mugshots in that MUP station hadn't looked a lot different from our brothers and sisters back home. Hell, I had two beautiful sisters ... This MUP lot had kept doing this, on and on and on, until thousands had been raped, mutilated, dehumanised and exterminated. I felt as if I had looked over the precipice and into the very pit of evil.

This was real *Lord of the Flies* stuff, and the Serbs had clearly become addicted to the dark side. I guessed it was there in all of us. I wondered if any of the blokes in my platoon would have been capable of such horror, given the right combination of unlimited power over life, drugs, drink and peer pressure. I wondered – *would I*?

I figured maybe some of the other lads were having similar thoughts right now. It was deeply unsettling. I knew I had to keep a lid on all of this. If any of this came out into the open, it would unnerve the younger blokes particularly. I knew that I needed to show a strong and unruffled lead, one that they could comfortably follow.

But the flip side was this: for how long could we keep compartmentalising such stuff? For how long could we leave it all buried? Either way, I was feeling exhausted. I hadn't slept properly for days. The pace of ops was hardly likely to drop any time soon. I needed rest.

I drifted off into sleep, aware of a burning desire within me for some payback. We needed to get the fuckers who had done this, and who knew how many of them were left in this benighted city? All the MUP lot had needed to do was remove their uniforms and blend in with the local civvies. If we could track some of them down, that at least would be some form of catharsis.

We kept pushing out patrols to scour the streets, and we kept getting tip-offs from the locals. One led to a university campus where once again we had to step into evil. The smell hit us even before we'd entered the bare concrete stairwell. It was the scent of death, death on a mass scale, and death that was several days old.

If you have never smelled it, you can't imagine what it is like. There aren't the words to describe such a smell. Those of us with scarves pulled them up around the lower half of our faces, to try to filter out the stench. Then we descended into the basement.

The buzz of the flies lay over everything, like a low and ceaseless murmur. The bodies were lined up in two rows. They were stiff with rigor mortis, and some were in the advanced stages of decomposition. Even more than the sight of it, the smell made me want to bolt back into the open air and chuck my guts up.

But I knew I couldn't do that. It wouldn't set the right example.

'Why're they so stiff?' one of my blokes asked.

'Rigor mortis,' Sandy replied, trying to sound strong and confident. 'The blood stops flowing and some kind of a process sets in which makes the limbs go stiff. Rigor mortis.'

'Look at the size of that bloke's head,' another of my young blokes said.

I looked where he was pointing. There was a corpse whose head had swollen to twice the size of your average basketball. It was horrifying. Like stepping into a sick horror movie. I tried to think of something to say, but when faced with this what could I say that wouldn't sound crass or stupid?

'Yeah, the head does swell up sometimes once the body has died.' It was the best I could manage, but it sounded so bland and inconsequential.

'Same size head as Powell, that's all.' It was Cloughy, and the black humour was just what we needed. As long as we could keep the humour going it meant we weren't cracking up, or at least not quite yet we weren't.

Fighting down the gag reflex, I forced myself to do a closer inspection of the corpses. Most were males aged somewhere between their late teens and their early forties. In military parlance, these were 'men-of-fighting-age'. Most had been savagely beaten. Their bodies betrayed the signs of their injuries. Mostly, they had been finished off with a single shot to the head.

On some of the more recent victims I could see the cordite burn marks, which meant that the executioner had done his work at close range – most likely with the muzzle of his pistol held right against the condemned man's forehead. As far as I could tell the victims had been stripped of their identities – so they carried no papers, wallets or anything of that nature.

This it seemed was a dumping ground for nameless, faceless corpses – one of the final links in a chain of mass murder that had taken people off the streets of Pristina, through places like the MUP base, and to here, and then onwards to the mass graves. It was like a corpse clearing house, a temporary dumping ground for the bodies.

The lighting was almost non-existent, as was the ventilation. If I tried to describe the smell of human death in that place, it was a warm, sickly-sweet, putrid stench that you felt would never leave your nostrils.

One of my blokes stopped by a corpse. 'This guy's moving!' he cried out. 'Oh shit! Oh fuck, no! It's fucking alive with maggots ...'

We got out of there into the open air. The dead in that basement were the young men of Pristina – those who might have offered resistance to the Serbs' savage rule. The fact that they had been segregated suggested there had been a cold efficiency and order to the slaughter. Slowly, piece by piece, the bigger picture behind the mass-killing was starting to emerge.

We handed over the location to 2 Platoon, for I needed to get my blokes out of there. Seeing death was a part of war, but rarely did a soldier get as up close and personal to it as we had done. More to the point, it was one thing seeing the body of your adversary – an enemy soldier killed in the cut and thrust of battle. It was quite another seeing a mass of defenceless victims who had been executed in cold blood.

On the way out of the university we passed by what had to be a science laboratory. I glanced up to see a load of foetuses bottled in formaldehyde. There was even a pair of Siamese twins pickled in one jar. They looked alien-like. Worse still, at the rear of the lab some kind of mad university professor bloke was trying to give a lecture to a smattering of students.

How could you carry on teaching, when your basements were stuffed full of rotting corpses? How could you? Every hour we were in this city we seemed to stumble across more and more extreme and bizarre shit and horror. This was fucking beyond weird. I needed a break. I guessed we all did.

We were out the following evening doing a night patrol. Jacko had briefed us to try to get involved with the locals, as a way of gathering intel and getting weapons off the streets. While the Serbs had been armed by the Russians, the Kosovo Albanians had been armed by neighbouring Albania, which was another country awash with guns.

The city centre sports hall had became the dumping ground for whatever we confiscated, and it was filling up fast. Being the biggest in my multiple, it was often left to me to boot in the doors of the buildings we were searching. I'd smash the first door in with my Lowes, and we'd often clear thirty buildings on a single patrol.

This evening we were out clearing a street when an ancient-looking tractor started to putter towards us. Sat up front was a wizened old man, and he was towing a trailer that was piled high with vegetables. An old crone was sat in the trailer, her wrinkled legs dangling over the end, her face a mass of toothless smiles.

'Stop that couple,' I heard Sandy order some of his blokes.

Why on earth did he want to stop a couple of old pensioners, I wondered. But again, I wasn't going to be the one to question Sandy's unerring sixth sense. The tractor ground to a spluttering halt. The trailer was piled high with these gorgeous-looking green peppers, apples and baskets of bright red tomatoes. Sandy stepped forward and stuck his hand into one of the baskets of tomatoes. It came out gripping a grenade, and he found more beneath the apples.

He moved on to the green peppers, and started pulling out brand-new looking AK47s. The old woman kept smiling and put her hands in the air, as if to say – *it wasn't me*. The old bloke just stayed where he was gazing rigidly up the street ahead of us. We confiscated all of the weaponry, then let them go on their way.

If we tried to arrest everyone we came across with weapons we'd have detained half the city by now. In any case, we weren't a police force. We were soldiers. In fact, there was no police force in Pristina right now. There was no fire brigade or ambulance service, either. Right now, there was only us, and there was clearly just about no one in this place who was above suspicion.

You couldn't even trust a couple of wrinkled old pensioners driving an apple cart.

*

CHAPTER SIXTEEN

We were a week in when another old woman accosted us. She kept crying and tearing at her hair and dragging us towards a stairwell that led up into some high-rise. We'd given Moth, our terp, a day off, for it looked as if he was about to buckle under the relentless pressure. As a result we couldn't understand the old woman, but still we let her drag us inside.

She took us up to the sixth floor. I went first into her apartment, with Sandy on my shoulder. The place stank. As I ran my eye around it I realised she had to be the world's biggest hoarder. She seemed to have kept every can of tuna or rice pudding or jar of pickled gherkins that she'd ever eaten. It was the weirdest thing that I had ever seen and it was all but impossible to move.

She dragged me through the heaps of junk and garbage to a single bed. It was filthy dirty, and on one side was the body of a man who looked about the same age as her. I guessed it had to be her husband. Over his lower half was spread a sheet, and it was horribly soiled and festering. This was proper gag and vomit stuff.

The old man had obviously been dead for several days, but the old woman just kept grabbing at us, as if she somehow wanted us to waken him. I glanced at Sandy. I could see that even he was on the verge of puking.

I turned to speak to Cloughy. 'Get on to Jacko. Tell him we've got a body. Looks like he died from old age. Request someone to remove the corpse.'

Cloughy relayed the message, then came back with this. 'Jacko says there isn't anyone. He says we'll have to do it.'

A few minutes later the Company Sergeant Major arrived driving one of our wagons, and with a body bag. We had no gloves, so Sandy and I were forced to hoik the corpse into the body bag barehanded. As we tried to slide the cold and clammy body in feet-first, the old woman was crying uncontrollably. She was hysterical. She just didn't seem able to accept that he was dead.

With Cloughy and Powell helping, we carried him down the stairs and drove him over to the official corpse dumping ground – which by now had become the university basement that we'd discovered earlier. With no police force and no morgues, where else were we supposed to put them?

I got back to base and was trying to find the appetite to eat, when Jacko came to have words.

'We keep finding bodies,' he said, 'and we're going to have to keep dealing with them. But somewhere in the Army regs it says if you have to deal with dead bodies you're entitled to extra pay. I think it's a one-off payment of twenty-five quid per bloke, so I need a list of all the blokes in your platoon who've had to handle a corpse ...'

'Twenty-five quid? Sir, that's a bloody joke. But I guess we may as well put down all of our names ...'

Everyone started cracking the jokes now. It was along the lines of – *Me too, me too – I want to handle a corpse!* But I could tell that the drip-drip-drip of the horror, plus the dark surrealism was really starting to get to some of my men.

A couple of days later we were out on a foot patrol near where we'd had to remove the old man's corpse. Moth was back with us again, though his day off didn't seem to have done much to lift his spirits. We were passing a similar apartment block to the old woman's when a group of very distinctive-looking figures emerged.

We were a multiple – so twelve blokes. They were six.

I sensed it was payback time.

All six were dressed in three-quarter-length black leather coats, so like your archetypal Mafia figure. This I knew was the uniform of the MUP when they were out and about in 'plain clothes'. More to the point, I could see that one of them was trying to conceal a pistol and another had an AK47 'hidden' under his coat.

'KFOR!' I yelled, pinning the blokes in my SA80's sight. 'HALT OR I FIRE!'

Three of them stopped dead in their tracks. Three ducked back into the building. Sandy's section thundered forward and took down the three who'd stopped, slamming them face down onto the ground, I led the charge through the doorway and up the stairs. They were twenty paces ahead of us as me, Cloughy and Powell went pounding up the steps three at a time.

We cornered them on the top of the stairwell. They turned to face us, the biggest of the blokes thrusting out a chin thick with stubble.

'De? De? De?' he started going, aggressively. *What? What? What?*

In an instant I'd kicked away the fucker's legs, and wrestled him down onto the hard concrete of the stairwell. He kept trying to wriggle about and free himself as he shouted and yelled, but the bloke was going nowhere. Cloughy and Powell were giving the other two exactly the same kind of treatment, and grinding their piggy faces into the hard edge of the stairs just for good measure.

We got their weapons off them and wrestled them down the stairs, while all the time they kept yelling objections and trying to break free. There was no doubt about it: this lot had once been some of the overlords of a chaotic and murderous Pristina, and their word had been law.

But not any more.

We hustled them outside, and I was pleased to see that Sandy had the others ground into the earth, with a boot pressed hard into the small of their backs. There was a good deal of gobbing off and yelling as we wrestled ours down, but eventually we had them where we wanted them – six blokes lined up in a row and well covered by our guns.

The bloke that I'd tackled seemed to be the leader. He was dark-skinned and dark-haired and very Italian Mafia. I glanced around for Moth, and found him cowering behind a vehicle a good distance away. He was scared shitless and he was clearly doing his best to hide. I called him over. By my tone, he knew he had to come.

'Ask them who they are, and what the fuck they're doing wandering around with weapons,' I told him.

Before Moth could translate, I heard the leader of the six snarl something. Moth was frozen with fear. I got a hold of him and shoved him right in front of the bloke.

'Right, I want to know what the fuck he's saying.'

'He says they weren't doing anything. He says they were doing nothing.'

I knew this was a lie. I knew the leader had been threatening Moth. But I could see that our terp was absolutely petrified, so there was no point pushing him any further. I searched the six some more and got their IDs. I got Cloughy to call their names in to Jacko, to see if we had anything on them. We didn't, but that didn't mean a thing. We had fuck all intel on just about all of the bad guys in Pristina.

I got on the radio myself and asked if Jacko wanted them brought in.

'Take their weapons and get rid of them,' Jacko told me. 'There's no prison facility. We've got nowhere to hold them.'

By now, I was shaking with pent-up aggression and fury. I could see murder in the eyes of a lot of my blokes, and I guessed I had the same look in mine. We knew who these guys were. They were six of the worst killers and thugs that had ever walked these streets, and I didn't doubt for one moment they were MUP. And doubtless, they'd had their 'fun' in the MUPs' chamber of horrors.

If we couldn't detain them I wanted nothing more than to take them around the rear of the apartment block and slot them. But that I figured would make us no better than they were, in addition to which it would earn me a Court Martial on charges of murder. I was burning up with frustration, yet we had no choice but to let them go.

En route back to base Moth was barely able to hold it together. No sooner had we got there than he went straight to see Jacko and resigned. Whoever those blokes were, they'd put the very fear of God into him.

I asked Jacko for a replacement terp, and he promised to get me one. 'With a bit of luck you might even get a hot chick,' he added.

'What d'you mean? There aren't any chicks who're terps.' I hadn't seen any, anyway.

Jacko laughed. 'Dave, you need to get up to Battalion HQ. They got first dibs. It's crawling with these smoking-hot babes.'

Strangely enough, sex seemed to have become an indelible part of the weird reality that was going on down here. Recently I'd been warned by Douggie that there were shagging couples everywhere on the streets of the city. Apparently, people were flooding back into Pristina, and they seemed to be celebrating the liberation of their city by getting it on.

I'd taken my patrol out that night, only to find a car parked in a darkened corner of some waste ground. There was something suspicious about it, so we'd stalked up to it and surrounded it, guns drawn. I moved right up to the front window, weapon in the aim, only to see it was a young couple having it away in the rear of the car.

A little later that night we'd heard a couple of girls leaning out of their window and hollering: 'Soldier! Soldier!' They didn't sound as if they were in any great degree of distress, but we figured we should go and investigate. We went up to their apartment, and it was chock-full of hot girls playing music and partying.

They offered us some slivovitz, the local brew, so we each had a small glass and a natter. We were there for a good ten minutes before we said our reluctant goodbyes and got the patrol under way again.

We continued for an hour or so, but the streets were largely deserted. Then we came across another high-rise apartment with windows thrown open onto a balcony and music blaring. We figured it had to be another party. The whole city seemed to be at it – parties in war zones.

I glanced upwards, and then I saw it: there was a guy silhouetted on the balcony with some form of assault rifle. For an instant I saw him crouch down and sight along the length of the weapon's barrel, and then he slipped back inside.

I led my multiple forward in a hard-target dash for the building. We made the entrance without being fired upon. Leaving Sandy's team to secure the block, I led the charge upstairs with Jim directly on my heels. We approached the door silently, and I could see it was open a crack, so I didn't even need to kick it in. I hoped to fuck it was those leather-coated MUP blokes in there.

I shoulder-barged the door, my weapon in the aim and my finger tight on the trigger. The door crashed open, I went through it and did an instant sweep of the room. Pretty much immediately I found myself face to face with Johno and his team. Johno's eyes were spinning out of control as he stared down the gaping barrel of a weapon being wielded by his own platoon commander.

'Johno! Fuck! Fuck! Fuck!' I cursed. 'FUUUCKKK!'

I lowered my weapon, but my heart was pumping like a machine gun. I knew how close I'd just come to slotting one of my own blokes.

'Johno, what the fuck're you doing still out? And fucking here!'

Johno's section was part of Douggie's multiple, and they'd been out patrolling directly before us. But Douggie had said to me at our handover that all his blokes were back in.

'Douggie said you were fucking all in! We nearly slotted you when we saw you on the balcony with your longs. This is our AO.

We were told you were back at base. *Johno, we almost fucking shot you!'*

AO stands for Area of Operations. In our allotted AO there shouldn't have been any other armed forces operating, and if we found any they were by default the bad guys. Johno knew what a fuck-up this was. He was basically lost for words.

'Sorry, boss,' was about all he could manage.

'Who the fuck's just left their weapon unattended on the balcony?' I demanded.

Johno looked around at his blokes. No one owned up. I was shaking with anger by now. We had so very nearly killed some of our own. The rules of engagement were that if someone pointed a weapon at you, you had the right to shoot them.

There were local girls in there and they looked scared as fuck. It was clear as day that the party was very much over. I saw the music get flicked off and the drinks get put down.

'Pack your shit and let's get going,' Johno told his men.

I took the whole lot of us directly back to base. So far, everything had been working so well on this operation, but one momentary slip like this and we'd been that close to disaster. I went direct to find Douggie. I shook him awake.

'Douggie, we nearly shot Johno's team.'

He rubbed the sleep from his eyes. 'What?'

'They were still out. Johno's fucking team. You said they were back in.'

'He said he was five minutes behind us. You mean he was still fucking out?'

'That's what I'm telling you. We saw the fuckers on some balcony with their weapons, and damn near slotted them.'

Douggie glanced at his watch. 'Boss, Johno's completely in the wrong here. No way should he have stayed out two fucking hours after he'd said he was in.'

'Don't I fucking know it. Honestly, Douggie, we were about to pull the trigger and kill those guys. My finger was on the trigger and the safety was off. Everyone's tired and we all make mistakes – but it was that close to a total fucking disaster.'

I was still shaking with nervous anger as I tried to get some sleep. Having a quick drink and doing some hearts and minds stuff was all good, but not if you extended your patrol for two hours and without telling anyone. In theory we could have blundered into them on the streets. We would have seen the weapons, thought they were a Serb death squad and mown down the lot of them.

I wrestled with it all night. I kept waking up and wondering what the hell I should do about it. It was made all the more difficult because Johno had been one of the Staff when I did P Company, so we had a special bond. Eventually, I decided there was only one option. Plain and simple I'd go and brief Jacko on all that had happened. Jacko was a fair bloke and I had every confidence he'd make the right decision.

I went and told him in the morning.

'Okay, Dave, leave it with me,' he said.

Jacko removed Johno from his post as section commander, and swopped him with a guy from stores. I'd rather have had Johno any day, for he was a vital part of what had become a well-oiled machine. He'd been a role model for me during P Company, and we'd gelled. But after what had happened something had to give.

Johno seemed to take it all in his stride. He didn't seem resentful that I'd raised it up the chain. All credit to him, he seemed to be cracking on.

But a little later I got called in to see Jacko myself. 'Dave, I've been given a picture of you and your multiple in an apartment drinking with some local girls. Care to explain?'

'We were in that apartment for no more than ten minutes. Yeah, we chatted to some girls and we had a shot of slivovitz each. You've told us to interact with the locals. Then we cracked on with the patrol. What we didn't do was stay there drinking for two hours, abandon our weapons and overstay our patrol without telling anyone, and almost cause a blue-on-blue.'

Jacko nodded. 'That's what I thought.'

Just as soon as Johno had been removed from post I'd noticed a couple of the blokes take against me. They must have passed the photo to Jacko. This Kosovo mission was stretching us as never before, and it was starting to break us apart. It was dividing us amongst ourselves, and divided we would fall. But I knew that Jacko had made the right decision, as it seemed did Douggie.

'You did the right thing, boss,' he told me. 'We've drawn a line in the sand, so let's just crack on. We're over it. There's loads of shit still to do.'

A couple of days later I got a rare and much-needed day off. There was a lake on the outskirts of Pristina, which the British Army had been taking squaddies to as a kind of a makeshift resort. It was a chance to get some sun and a swim and to wind down a little. A couple of the blokes fancied going so we headed out there in some of the vehicles.

For a country that had seen so much horror and suffering, Kosovo could be stunningly beautiful. The lake was no exception. It was a vast stretch of water, with dense green pine forests sweeping down from dramatic hills right to the water's edge. The sun was burning hot and the lake looked irresistible. I joined the others who were already there, stripped to my boxers and dived in.

The water was clear, crisp and bracing. I'm a good swimmer and I powered out a couple of hundred yards, with each stroke feeling as if the lake was somehow cleansing me. I was washing off all the darkness and evil in which I'd been immersed for the past few weeks in its purifying waters.

I kicked out some more, rolled over and floated, gazing up at the clear blue sky. Perhaps humanity wasn't so evil and doomed to tear itself apart after all. These past few days I'd started to feel like we were so many rats in a cage. I'd started to feel that the future held only darkness. But maybe there was a God, after all.

My thoughts were interrupted by a frantic yelling from the lakeside. For a moment I figured one of the lads in the water had to be in trouble. Then I realised it was a bloke in full uniform standing at the water's edge, and he was yelling at the lot of us and waving his arms about like a madman.

'GET OUT OF THE FUCKING WATER! GET OUT OF THE WATER! NOW!'

Suddenly, instinctively, I knew what was wrong. With a jolt of horror that hit me like a bolt of lighting, I began to strike out for the shore. I swam desperately, like I had a great white shark snapping at my heels. But in fact it was worse than that – for this was where they had hidden the bodies.

This was the lake – or one of the lakes – where the MUP and their ilk had dumped the 'disappeared'. They had weighed down the corpses with rocks roped to their bodies and flung them into the depths. It had only just reached the attention of the British high command that this was a lake full of corpses, at which moment they had raised the alarm.

I knew now that I really needed out of this place. I knew that a lot of my blokes did too. We were approaching six weeks in, and if we didn't get relieved soon I knew that someone in my platoon was going to crack, and maybe even me.

It wasn't just us that were suffering. Every day there seemed to be violent shouting matches and worse between Serbs who had remained in the city and returning Kosovo Albanians. Mostly it was over property. When the Albanians had fled, the Serbs had moved in and claimed their houses as their own. Now the Albanians were flooding back and trying to reclaim their homes.

It was ugly, bitter and explosive.

We had started to question what we were doing here, especially after having to let those six leather-coated MUP thugs go. And now I'd had my dip in the lake of bodies. Yet still we had to get out on the streets in an effort to dampen down the tensions between the two sides of this divided, hate-filled city. And with Moth gone and no replacement terp, we couldn't even understand what they were trying to say to us.

It was dusk and we were out on patrol when a pretty Albanian-looking woman came running up to us. She was shouting and screaming and pointing towards a house a few dozen yards away. We couldn't understand everything, but the gist was there was bad shit going down in that building.

We hard-targeted it over, and Powell was just ahead of me as we went through the door. He booted it in, and we came face to face with a massive, beefy Serb standing there in his vest and boxers, his hairy gut hanging out. Sprawled on the floor was a young and very beautiful Albanian girl, and whatever he was about to do had made her quite hysterical.

In a flash Powell had grabbed the bloke and dragged him outside. As he went by me, I could tell that the Serb was out of his head on drink or drugs, and he stank of stale sweat and worse. The bloke was minging.

I checked the girl over, with Cloughy by my side. She kept screaming and crying, and her shoulders shook uncontrollably as she sobbed out these words to us, but I couldn't understand anything of what she was saying.

Then I heard the screaming from outside. What drew my attention more than anything was the fact that the words were being yelled in English, and in a thick Yorkshire accent.

'YOU FUCKING CUNT! YOU FUCKING PEOPLE! WHAT THE FUCK WERE YOU DOING IN THERE?'

I dashed outside. It was Powell – Powell my runner, the guy I'd always thought of as the quiet one in my platoon. He had his weapon at his side, and the monster Serb gripped by the throat. He had him pinned up against the wall, and the guy's eyes were bulging like Powell was going to strangle him.

I heard the Serb croaking out some words in broken English. 'What? What? What? Nothing! I do nothing.'

'TELL ME WHAT YOU WERE FUCKING DOING, YOU FAT, GREASY FUCK.'

The Serb was a lot bigger than Powell, but he seemed to be

possessed of a superhuman strength right now. He lifted the bloke up by his neck and began to shuffle him along the wall, all the while screaming abuse into his face.

I knew that I had to intervene. 'All right! Powell! Drop him!'

There wasn't the hint of an acknowledgement. The red mist had well and truly come down, and he looked as if he was going to kill that Serb with his bare hands. I grabbed hold of Powell and physically dragged him off the guy and away.

'YOU!' I yelled in the big guy's face. 'Best you fuck off out of here while you still can!'

He didn't need a second urging. He turned on his big, fat, cowardly, bullyboy legs and stumbled off as fast as they could carry him. I turned back to Powell. He'd gone as white as snow, and he was shaking with pent-up aggression mixed with raw adrenaline. Right now I figured he was my main concern.

'FUUUUUUUCK!' I heard him scream. 'I've fucking had enough of these fucking cunts. FUUUCKKK!'

He turned and slammed his fist into the hard brick of the wall. I could understand exactly how he was feeling. I was pretty close to where he was at myself. A few more encounters like this one, and one of us lot was going to end up slotting one of them.

I got Cloughy to sit outside with Powell and have a ciggie or two. I checked the girl was all right. By now a friend had turned up to sit with her and comfort her. And just as soon as I could I got the patrol turned around and back into base.

It was clear we were long past our sell-by date. This was real Vietnam crack-up and burn shit. We needed to get ourselves gone. If we didn't I was going to start losing guys. I'd been that close to losing Powell today. He was about to unload big time on the bad guy. We risked one of us lot ending up being tried in a court of law – and not the authors of these brutal war crimes.

I went and told Jacko that my patrol was at the point of meltdown. He told me we were due to get rotated out of there anyway. Not a moment too soon we packed our bags and moved down to the main admin building, sited in the sports stadium where we'd been piling up the mountain of confiscated weaponry.

From there we were airlifted out by helicopter, rotated via Skopje and flown back to the UK, whereupon the biggest piss-up ever ensued. The lads needed to let their hair down and 'decompress' as never before. So did I. And that's exactly what we did.

Kosovo had changed everything. After Bloody Sunday, 1 PARA was arguably the most notorious unit in the British Army. But now we had been transformed. Overnight almost, we'd become the highest profile British military unit, and in a wholly positive way after all the media coverage. We were also now one of the most operationally experienced, after all our Pristina adventures.

After Kosovo, we figured bigger and better things were coming our way. General Sir Mike Jackson was now Chief of the General Staff, and we knew he was angling to get his regiment, the PARAs, a load more work.

And as it happened, we were just about to land another mission into the bloody heart of darkness.

*

CHAPTER SEVENTEEN

A month after Kosovo, Johno was back as my section commander and we could even have a laugh about Kosovo, and about when I'd damn near shot him. It was the November of that year when the CO, Colonel Gibson, called me in for a private word. I wondered if I was in trouble. After all, this was the bloke who'd once given me a gypsy's warning about not gripping my platoon.

'Dave, I've got good news,' he announced. 'You're going to be my next RSO.'

RSO stands for Regimental Signals Officer – basically the bloke who ran all communications for the entire Regiment. This was the last thing that I'd ever expected or wanted. RSO was a senior captain's job. I had only just turned twenty-one and I was still a lieutenant.

'Technically, the Army system doesn't recognise you as old enough to be a captain,' Colonel Gibson continued. 'But I'll write to get you special dispensation, because I will be making you my next RSO.'

'But sir, I thought you had to be twenty-three or twenty-four to make captain?'

'I don't give a shit about the rules. After Kosovo, 1 PARA will be getting more ops and I want you in my GB planning cell running comms.'

Colonel Gibson was the man who'd transformed the Parachute

Regiment from being threatened with swingeing cuts, to being the most high-profile and experienced regiment in the Army. A lot of blokes didn't particularly like him, but I reckoned he had real balls, and I respected him a great deal.

The trouble was RSO was something of a poisoned chalice. Most RSOs didn't last a matter of months. The Signals Platoon was forty-five strong, with a full sergeant major and four sergeants forming its head-shed. On exercises or operations, most other platoon commanders could hide their failings, and look as if they were doing their job. Not the RSO.

The RSO had all those eagle eyes upon him. Comms were either up and running or they were a disaster. Moreover, like any unit in the British Army, we worked over long distances with shit communications equipment. As Colonel Gibson's RSO, I might not last very long.

'There's one other thing,' Colonel Gibson added. 'We've got a very important infantry test exercise coming up February, so I can't afford to send you on the Signals Officer's Course. You'll need to get Signals Platoon to teach you on the job, then run it all for me. I take it you're good with that?'

'Yes, sir. Absolutely.'

With a man like Colonel Gibson, what the fuck else was I supposed to say? I had a week in which to hand over my platoon to Douggie, who would take command while they got a replacement officer.

I went and told him the news. 'Mate, I'm off. They're making me RSO.'

For a moment Douggie looked totally gobsmacked, and then he burst out laughing. 'RSO. Fucking everyone gets fired from that job! Still, at least we get to keep you in Battalion.'

We shook hands. 'Thanks for all the support, mate, especially in the early days.'

'No worries. It's been good.'

I'd grown tight with my blokes. How did you part with such brothers? We had drinks in the NAAFI that Thursday night, and

I got given a bronze statue of a paratrooper. I thanked the section commanders personally – grumpy Jim, sixth-sense Sandy, and Johno whom I'd almost slotted. Then I said a few words to them all.

'Thanks for a great two years. I'm only going next door anyway, so we'll see each other around. And Kosovo was awesome ...'

As RSO I fell under the influence of 00-Joe, or 'Double-Oh Joe' as we pronounced it. 00-Joe was one of the biggest blokes in the entire Regiment. He had hands like shovels and an enormous droopy moustache. He hailed from Glasgow, was the hardest bloke around, and did zero fitness 'because he didn't need to'. Some said he'd been nicknamed 00-Joe because he thought he was James Bond.

Either way, 00-Joe was a real man-mountain and his reputation went before him. Word was that he'd been up and down the ranks already. On one occasion he'd got busted for some misdemeanour, and had been called into a former CO's office. He was told he was getting demoted from sergeant to corporal. He proceeded to drop onto all fours and crawl around under the CO's desk. The RSM was going apoplectic, screaming at 00-Joe to explain himself.

00-Joe glanced up: 'I'm searching for Justice.'

He was the biggest character in the Battalion, and I knew that if he didn't take to me I was finished. He'd make my life hell and make sure I got fired. 00-Joe loved the sound of his own voice. He never stopped talking. In fact, I had a strong suspicion Colonel Gibson had appointed me as RSO so I could act as a sound barrier between him and 00-Joe. It was some challenge.

Luckily, 00-Joe decided to check me out, and the bloke he spoke to was Douggie. He got a fairly glowing report, and so he concluded I was all right. Mostly, he seemed intrigued by the CO's crazy plan to make a 21-year-old lieutenant with zero Signals qualifications his new RSO, not to mention the idea of training me on the fly.

00-Joe and his team of sergeants started the bizarre process of training their 'boss' in the communications skills and procedures I was already supposed to know, so I could in turn command them. They did so brilliantly and with real panache. It was just as well, for 1 PARA was about to get a truly peachy mission dropped into its lap.

In early May 2000 I was pulled into the CO's office, along with Lenny, the 1 PARA Ops Officer. Until recently Lenny had been 2IC of The Pathfinders, and he was hoping to go back to command the unit. We hadn't served together for long but we'd become good mates, and Lenny had told me several stories of derring-do with the PF.

As a result I'd flirted with the idea of maybe trying to join their number, but right now the CO was about to drop the mission to die for on us, and very much as 1 PARA's baby. It was 0830 hours, so bright and early, and several other officers gathered to hear what the CO had for us.

He started off in his usual, poker-faced style. 'We're going to Sierra Leone. Today.'

Just like that. No warning, not even the hint that anything was brewing prior to that moment. He loved a bit of theatre, and he was in his element right now, especially as neither I nor Lenny nor any of the others had the faintest idea where Sierra Leone was.

'We're going in at Battalion strength to execute an NEO.'

None of us knew what an NEO was, either, but we weren't about to own up to it. Thankfully, the CO's intel officer was there, and perhaps sensing our growing consternation he pulled out a map and began to explain.

'*As you know*, Sierra Leone is a small country on the coast of West Africa. There's a civil war, and rebels are poised to take the capital city, Freetown. A large number of British and allied expats are holed up in the capital, and they need evacuating. That's our NEO tasking – a *Non-combatant Evacuation Operation*. We're going in to secure the airfield and get them out of a very nasty little war.'

'I know we're not Spearhead Lead Element right now,' the CO took over. 'We're not supposed to be on twenty-four hours notice to move. PWRR have it right now. But I've told PJHQ we don't need twenty-four hours. We can go quicker: we can go today.'

PWRR was the Prince of Wales Royal Regiment, a regular infantry unit, and PJHQ was Permanent Joint Headquarters, the central planning cell for all British military operations. And between PJHQ and the CO, they'd somehow cooked up this crazy scheme that we were going to deploy to a war in Africa *today*.

My mind jumped to my laundry. I'd just dumped a full load in the wash as I came over to see the CO. The Army washing machine took forever. It wasn't like a civvie machine. It took two hours or more. I wouldn't even have any dry clothes with which to deploy.

'That's it,' the CO continued. 'No bone questions, 'cause I'm not in the mood. If you start banging off, then you're off the mission.'

Lenny and I glanced at each other. Sheer chaos and madness was about to ensue. 'Sir, you do know A Company are away on Exercise Red Stripe ...?' Lenny tried.

Exercise Red Stripe was a live firing exercise in Jamaica.

The CO waved a hand to silence him. 'I know. That's why I've rung the CO of 2 PARA, and they're lending a company to come with us.'

We were utterly lost for words. Everyone.

'Oh, and be prepared to move out at 1100 hours,' the CO continued. *Shit, I really wasn't going to have any dry kit.*

The Motor Transport Officer was in the briefing. I saw his face drop like a stone. 'Erm, sir ...' he tried.

The CO cut him off. 'Just make it happen. Everyone.'

There was a chorus of 'yes, sirs' and we turned as one and practically bolted for the door.

I heard a voice call after me: 'RSO.'

'Sir.' I turned around.

The CO paused for an instant. 'I need a laptop. That's an RSO's kind of job. I need one so I can speak to the UK while we're en route.'

'Sir. Shall I speak to Brigade?'

'There's no time to speak to Brigade. Speak to the Admin Officer, tell him I need a laptop, and get some cash.'

'Cash?'

'So you can drive into Guildford and buy me one.'

'Sir.'

I practically sprinted down the hall to the Admin Officer's cubbyhole. 'John, the CO needs a laptop, I need to buy it and I need some cash.'

'Uh ... okay.' For a moment I saw it cross his mind that he couldn't actually get his hands on enough cash, but then he realised that the CO would fire him if he didn't. He opened the safe, drew out a bundle of readies, then spoke to his assistant, who ran off to fetch some more.

I grabbed the cash they'd gathered and hurried down to my office. It was already a hive of frenzied activity, for word had well and truly gone around by now.

'I've got to drive into fucking Guildford and buy the CO a laptop,' I practically yelled at 00-Joe. He burst into peals of laughter. 'Don't let the fucking transport go without me. Oh, and can you get my weapon? Oh, and my kit.'

'Boss, just go get the fookin' laptop,' 00-Joe boomed. 'I'll send one of the blokes to your room and stuff all your kit into yer Bergen. Now, off ye go.'

By the time I'd jumped in my clapped-out maroon Ford Escort it was 0900 hours and I had two hours before the transport would leave. I ragged it out of Camp, and was breaking the speed limit by the time I passed the RMP station. I hammered it into Guildford, did a couple of laps before I found a Curry's, grabbed a member of staff and got my hands on some computer kit.

The CO wanted an insecure, civvie means of comms back to HQ, because it was often more reliable and versatile than our own. A laptop, plus modem and webcam should do it. I queued, paid the cash, and drove back at top speed. I got back to base at 1045 hours and rang 00-Joe on his mobile.

'Stop flapping,' he told me. 'Last vehicle knows you're on it. Got yer Bergen, weapon, webbing but not yer daysack.'

Daysack. Daysack. It was in the bloody laundry, being washed. I sprinted for the laundry, grabbed the sack, stuffed it full of a pile of wet washing and legged it for the last of the coaches, which were just preparing to leave.

En route between the base and RAF Lyneham the CO briefed us on the mission. We were going to fly out to Senegal, a country friendly to the UK and a little further up the coast from Sierra Leone. From there we'd mount up a flight of Special Forces C130 Hercules transport aircraft, and do a TALO onto Lungi Loi Airport, on the outskirts of Sierra Leone's capital, Freetown.

TALO stands for Tactical Air Landing Operation. Basically, you use a TALO when flying into an unsecured airstrip in the teeth of an enemy force – which was exactly what we were doing now. The C130s would fly in tight together and at treetop level, put down at high speed, slam on the brakes, and we would pile off the open ramps. They'd be airborne again before they'd even stopped moving.

If you saw a TALO taking place at London Heathrow you'd think the aircraft were about to crash – into each other, or the runway. But it was the perfect way to get a load of PARAs onto the ground in the midst of a civil war, when the time or the assets weren't available for us to parachute in. We trained for TALOs relentlessly, and those elite forces pilots were the best in the world at what they did.

The elite forces Hercules carries additional armaments, plus extra high-tech defensive measures. It was reassuring to know that it did, for right now we had just about zero intel on the whereabouts or exact strength of the enemy, or how they were armed. And for sure, the rebels in Sierra Leone were not to be taken lightly.

For over a decade Sierra Leone had been racked by a bitter and bloody civil war, one defined only by senseless brutality and bloodshed. The Revolutionary United Front (RUF) rebels numbered in their tens of thousands, and they seemed to espouse no concrete political or other ideology. Indeed, their sole aim appeared to be to

'Under canopy' – the parachute. After a monster HALO freefall the chute is triggered at low altitude. Flying techniques are practised and practised relentlessly, so we can land undetected together as a tight stick, and then gather up our kit, set off on foot to carry out our kill, capture, surveillance or sabotage mission.

Having passed Pathfinder selection, I headed to Africa to train with Kenyan Masai warriors – the masters at bush survival and navigation. 9/11 had just taken place – Al-Qaeda flying airliners into the Twin Towers in New York – and we knew we were about to get very busy. Shortly after this photo was taken I would be rushed back to the UK to join the Pathfinders preparing to depart for a secret Special Forces base in the Middle East, and from there into Afghanistan.

On the ground in Afghanistan. Unusually for a Captain I am working as rear-gunner on the Pinkie, and I'm under orders from a Pathfinder Corporal, who commands the vehicle. Leadership in the Pathfinders relies upon experience and capability, regardless of rank. I've just joined the unit, and I'm here to learn the ropes. Once I've 'served my time' and proved myself, only then would I be given command of a patrol. This is the ethos of elite forces, one we share with the SAS, SBS and a handful of other units.

On an intelligence-gathering mission inside a fortress run by notorious Afghan warlords, we were surrounded and I had a gun held to my head. The Afghan gunman – high on hashish – had grabbed my assault rifle and threatened to put a bullet in my head. So I grabbed his RPG7 rocket launcher, levelled it at him, and threatened to blow his head clean off his shoulders in return. It was a stalemate – and hence myself and fellow Pathfinders made it out of there alive.

View from a mountain in Afghanistan. Me and seasoned Pathfinder 'Ginge' on a mission working with Afghan warlords.

Pathfinder patrol about to drive aboard a Chinook helicopter and be flown covertly to a discreet Landing Zone where they will then infiltrate by vehicle to the enemy target.

After operations in Afghanistan I had passed my probationary period and was given command of a Pathfinder patrol of six men – in my view, the ultimate soldiers, and the kind of blokes I'd always dreamed of soldiering alongside. We deployed behind enemy lines in the Iraqi desert on a mission that helped change the course of that war – a story told in my first book, *Pathfinder*.

Clearing my head on operations in the desert. The billiard-table flat terrain of the Iraqi desert made for a nightmare when trying to penetrate deep behind enemy lines: there was no cover to hide in, or to fight from if pinged by the enemy.

Yours truly.

spread anarchy and terror across the nation, and to rule simply by dint of fear.

They were renowned for mounting attacks with names like 'Operation Kill All Your Family' and 'Operation Kill Every Living Thing'. They'd surround a village and shoot it up, rape the women, and round up the boys and girls who were of 'suitable' age to make into child soldiers. They'd force the boys so 'recruited' to rape their own mothers, kill their fathers, and then 'join' the rebel ranks.

Child soldiers recruited in this fashion – and they made up the hardcore of the rebel forces – had nothing left to live for. Having killed and brutalised their own parents, their only 'family' was the RUF. After laying waste to a village, the rebels would lop off the hands or legs of those still alive, as a means of spreading total fear.

Those women and children about to have their hands chopped off were asked if they wanted 'short sleeves' or 'long sleeves' style. Short sleeves meant amputation above the elbow. Long sleeves meant below.

In terms of senseless, mindless brutality and horror, Sierra Leone made Kosovo look like a tea party. To make matters worse, some 17,000 United Nations peacekeepers had been sent into the country, but they had proved hopelessly ineffective. There were several problems. One: there was no peace to keep. What Sierra Leone needed wasn't peacekeepers: it was a war-termination force.

Secondly, the Kenyans, Jordanians, Indians and other soldiers who made up the UN force – then the largest such United Nations operation in the world – were hopelessly ill-equipped and ill-motivated. Many of the UN 'peacekeepers' possessed no radios, nor even Army boots. It was hardly surprising that they'd proved so utterly incapable of standing against the rebels.

In fact, in recent days the UN peacekeepers had been kidnapped in their hundreds, and their white UN armoured personnel carriers had been seized by the RUF so as to help them prosecute their war of terror more effectively.

Incredibly, the RUF had been highly successful in their aim of taking the capital, Freetown, and seizing control of the country. Twice they had done so, bringing sheer anarchy and chaos to that benighted city. Their rule had only faltered when the rebels had decided that with no one left to go to war against they would start fighting amongst themselves.

Twice the rebels had been forced out of Freetown and back into the jungles, but they had never completely gone away. And with the UN 'peacekeepers' now in-country, there was no one with the strength of will, the right equipment or the *esprit de corps* to stand against them.

Right now, the RUF were marching on Freetown, and they were once more poised to descend upon the capital like a swarm of locusts. As we flew onwards towards West Africa, our largely unspoken remit was not only to rescue our own and allied citizens: it was to put a stop to the rebel advance.

The only forces we had in-country right now were a handful of SAS blokes, so we were likely to be first in to the action, just as we had been in Kosovo. As we flew onwards towards Senegal in the trusty RAF Tristars, an idea came to me. If we had an SAS team with eyes on the airport, why couldn't we simply fly direct into Sierra Leone in the Tristars, and land?

I put the suggestion to the CO. 'Sir, if there are SAS on the ground already, is the airport in theory secure? And if it is, why can't we Tristar into the airport right now, which gets us in quicker?'

The CO fixed me with this calm, level gaze. 'That, David, is a good idea. Go speak to the pilot, then get PJHQ on the net.'

I went forward to the cockpit and explained to the RAF pilot just what we were thinking. He had an expression on his face like he'd just shit himself. He didn't say as much, but it was clear that the last thing he wanted to do was to jet into a war zone. But he was an officer in the RAF, and if he was ordered to he'd have to go.

With 00-Joe's help I managed to patch a call into PJHQ, and got the key people there on the net. I passed the radio handset across to the CO.

He spoke into it. 'This is Paul. Do you want me to go to the first location, or am I able to go direct to the second location?'

He was being a bit guarded in what he said, for this was insecure means. There was a short pause, while those at PJHQ had a conflab over the CO's suggestion, and then a voice came back in reply.

'Paul, there's a group of 500 rebels getting much closer to the airfield. It's not secure. Go to the first location, and proceed as planned.'

We landed in Dakar, the capital of Senegal, and set up a temporary planning cell in an empty hangar. C Company would lead the TALO into the airfield, because A were away on Exercise Red Stripe. The Battalion HQ element would go in with C Company on the first aircraft, and that included me. Happy days.

There was one further development we were briefed on, and this made the mission hugely personal for us all, but especially so for me. Major Andy Harrison of the Parachute Regiment had just been kidnapped by the rebels, while on a liaison mission with a group of UN peacekeepers.

Andy Harrison was one of our own. He was also none other than the person who had mentored me through Sandhurst, making it his personal mission to ensure that those who had wanted to force me into The Gunners didn't get their way. To my way of thinking, I owed Andy Harrison big time, for without him I'd never have made it into the PARAs – this shit-hot, iconic unit.

In fact, Andy Harrison's kidnapping was part of a bigger picture scenario that was only just starting to emerge, one that ratcheted up the stakes still further. The RUF had surrounded and laid siege to some 500 Indian peacekeepers in their UN base, at Kailahun. Andy Harrison had been captured as a result of that siege, along with fourteen other UN troops.

But that was only one in a wave of such kidnappings, all of which were targeted at seizing British soldiers.

In Makeni, some 120 miles to the west, the RUF had surrounded and laid siege to another base, this one staffed by seventy Kenyan peacekeepers. Inside the base was another PARA major, Phil Ashby, as well as Lieutenant-Commander Paul Rowland of the Royal Navy and Major Andy Samsonoff of the Light Infantry, and it was the three Brits that the rebels were seeking to get their hands on.

Major Dave Lingard, a signals officer from the New Zealand Army, was also with them, and as the RUF were unable to distinguish between a Kiwi and a Brit, he was seen as being an equally worthy target for the rebels, who had vowed to spill British blood.

As of yet, no British soldiers had been killed, but Andy Harrison had fallen directly into their hands. He had been beaten and threatened with execution, and several other British soldiers were also facing clear and present danger.

The rebel leadership had put the word out to 'get the Brits'. In fact, this was the start of the RUF's 'Operation Kill British', the overall aim of which was to make Sierra Leone into the 'next Somalia', as far as the British military were concerned.

In October 1993, in Mogadishu, Somalia, the US military's elite Rangers, SEALs and Delta Force had taken a hammering from Somalian rebels – so much so that their peacekeeping operations in that country had been brought to a premature end. In May 2000, in Sierra Leone, the RUF rebels planned to do the same to the British forces – in Operation Kill British.

It was 0200 hours – so not even eighteen hours after the CO had first warned us we were deploying – when the 180 men of C Company loaded up the two C130 Hercules aircraft. As we took off into the darkness, we were further briefed that two Royal Navy ships, HMS *Argyll* and HMS *Illustrious*, were being diverted to West Africa, so they could sit off the coast and put down naval gunfire support. We also got warned that the 500-strong rebel force was making direct for the airport, and were barely a few kilometres out. It was going to be a race to see who could get there first.

All 180 blokes on those first two Hercules aircraft were going in self-sufficient for a good week or more of operations. That meant that we were laden down with massive Bergens stuffed full of all the obvious. As we approached the airport – the Hercs flitting across the darkened jungle like giant moths, and showing not the faintest glimmer of light – we were ordered to our feet.

Using the red cargo netting lashed to the C130's side I levered myself up. You do TALO standing, so your legs can help take the impact of the landing, and so you're ready to pile off the ramp immediately you touch down. But the Bergens were fucking heavy, so each of us was clutching onto the cargo netting, and trying to help the bloke in front stand, as the pilots brought us in low and fast.

We hit the ground, there was a sickening, juddering impact, and the sharp screech of brakes and of wheels locking up on wet tarmac. As the loadies signalled the first guys to go down the ramp, I could see the smoke thrown up by the C130's tyres billowing into the hold. As far as I knew, no one had done a TALO for decades, and whatever might happen as a result of this one we were sure making military history.

As I prepared to sprint down the open ramp I made my weapon ready, putting a round up the spout. You'd never do so in-flight, for the impact of the landing could trigger your weapon accidentally. It was first light by now, and as I thundered out of the C130's dark hold there was the barest fringe of a ragged sunrise above the jungle to the east of us.

I hit the tarmac, and fanned out with the rest of the lads, my weapon in the aim and scanning my arcs. Ahead of us the C130 rumbled onwards, and within seconds the roar of the turbines rose to a fever pitch again, as the aircraft went to full throttle and got airborne.

As the Herc clawed skywards, I dropped my Bergen, so I could move more quickly if we came under fire. The pair of aircraft disappeared over the near horizon, kissing the treetops as they kept as low as possible. The noise of their engines faded quickly on the still air, and was replaced by a sweaty and clammy silence.

It was barely 0530 hours but already it felt hot and humid as hell, like stepping into a sauna. I kept scanning the wall of jungle to my front, but not a soul could I see anywhere.

With the roar of the aircraft gone, the jungle wildlife decided to strike up a rhythm again. The cicadas began a chorus of breeep-breeep-breeeping, and from out of the thick jungle came a series of sharp screeches and cries, as a flock of what looked like brightly-coloured parrots went skitting through the trees.

TIA, I told myself.

This is Africa.

The previous morning I'd been doing my laundry back at base, in Catterick. Now we were here, in the midst of a crazed African civil war. I could hardly believe it. Outside of this airport runway, we didn't have a clue what was going on. We were in a country I'd never even heard of before, one ruled by no rules at all. By the law of the jungle.

I glanced westwards, and there was the barest glimmer of light on water – the sea. I looked north, and spotted the first figures I'd seen, other than my fellow PARAs. A group of maybe a dozen or so of what had to be airport staff had wandered out of the terminal building and were stood there, staring right at us.

C Company went forward, one platoon moving to take the terminal, the other two to secure either side of the runway. That way, we'd hollow out a secure area within which we could start to operate. Colonel Gibson and his HQ element went firm just outside the terminal building, so they could co-ordinate the rest of the Battalion coming in.

Gibson began barking orders, the first directed at yours truly. 'RSO, get me a location! RSM, I want to know what aircraft are coming in when and where. Get sparking.'

We had 180 of us on the ground now, and we needed more in as soon as, for there were 500 rebels bearing down on us and we were expecting to get hit at any moment.

My immediate priority was to find the CO somewhere we could set up Signals, plus a makeshift HQ. I made a beeline for the terminal building, which was an off-white, saggy shed of a place about three stories high. I had never in my life seen such a run-down piece of shit of an airport, and it was made all the more *Apocalypse Now*-like due to the dense jungle that bent over everything.

As I stepped towards the building it crossed my mind that the motley crew of airport officials wouldn't have the faintest clue as to who we were. The SAS lads had known we were coming. That was it. As far as this lot were concerned, some foreign force had just flown in from out of the blue and seized their national airport.

I had 00-Joe with me as we approached the terminal. A handful of locals in these crappy, mismatched uniforms were staring at us as if we were Martians or something. A skinny bloke tried to block our path.

'All right, big man?' 00-Joe boomed, in his thick Glaswegian accent, and the skinny bloke stepped rapidly to one side. 'Hey, don't run away. I need a good location for the CO's headquarters. Any suggestions?'

The guy stared at 00-Joe in total consternation. English is the second national language of Sierra Leone, but this bloke obviously couldn't understand a word of what 00-Joe was saying. 'Errmmm ...'

'I'll take that as a "no",' said 00-Joe, cutting him off.

Joe got the guy by the arm and led him off to one side of the terminal building. I grabbed another bloke and did the same on my side. There was a door with a sign hanging at a crazy angle. 'FIRST CLASS LOUNGE' it announced. I poked my head inside. It was a disaster.

I guessed in Economy you sat on the floor. In First Class you got to sit on some plastic chairs. There was an aircon unit juddering away in one corner, but there was no noticeable difference in the air temperature inside or out. Still, it was perfect as the Battalion Ops Room. There was some kind of security official in there, and he was staring at me as if I'd just stepped off Planet Zog.

'Right, this'll do nicely,' I announced. 'We'll be using this as our main base of operations ...'

The security bloke came and waved a hand in front of my face. 'No, no, no, no, no ...'

I knew that there wasn't a rat's chance in hell of any civilian aircraft going in or out of this airport for days now, so it wasn't as if the First Class Lounge was going to be in demand.

'Won't be long,' I told him. I delved in my Bergen and pulled out a British Army ration pack. 'Here, have this as compensation.'

That seemed to silence him.

I showed the room to 00-Joe, and that was it – we'd staked our claim. As we got comms up and running, the rest of the Battle Group started to get flown in. By mid-afternoon we had 800 PARAs on the ground, and we had a ring of steel thrown around the airport.

By evening the lads were well dug-in, and we felt ready for whatever the rebels might throw at us.

*

CHAPTER EIGHTEEN

That night 00-Joe and I dossed down on the one luggage conveyor belt. It didn't work, and hadn't done for years, so there was hardly any chance of it starting up in the middle of the night with the two of us asleep on it. As an added bonus, it lay at the entrance to the Ops Room, which was now fully up and running in the First Class Lounge.

Signals was a 24/7 operation at the best of times, and we'd been having serious problems establishing good, secure comms with all parties. All night long blokes kept waking me with yet another issue that needed sorting. Each time I found I was lying in a pool of water, which turned out to be my own sweat.

The following morning we gathered as the head-shed for an Orders Group. Our mission codename was Operation Palliser, and we now needed to focus down onto the mission's first objective – the NEO. People were getting kidnapped and butchered all over the country, so it was an absolute priority to get British civilians out, plus any other Europeans, Americans or similar expats.

The simplest way to do so was to get them to the airport and fly them out on a bunch of Tristars. Trouble was, between the airport and the capital was a large expanse of water – the Freetown Estuary. In fact the airport lay in an isolated area of jungle due west of the city, which presented us with another major problem.

If the rebels tried to take Freetown, they'd advance from the jungles to the north. In short, they could move directly on the capital itself, rather than taking us on here. If they did that they could embark upon the orgy of rape, pillage and murder they no doubt had in mind, and there was little we could do to stop them.

'Right, this is the plan,' the CO announced, after we'd discussed various options. 'B and C Company will secure airfield and push out foot patrols to dominate the area. Machine Gun Platoon and Mortars Platoon will set up positions around airfield. D Company 2 PARA will be heli'd across the Freetown Estuary, to secure the ground and block the rebels coming into Freetown.

'Now, we need to project a force into the interior to find and fix the rebels and provide an early warning system,' he continued. 'Let's send The Pathfinders in to do what they do best – being our eyes and ears up country.'

The entire Pathfinder Platoon had been flown in on a C130 pretty much alongside us, and they'd set up their own mini-HQ in a room above our own Ops Room.

'RSO, I need good comms with all parties,' the CO continued, 'and that includes the PF. In fact, see if you can get their ops room moved down to ours, so we can better co-ordinate. I also want naval gunfire support co-ordinated for the PF and for 1 PARA.'

'Right, sir.'

'Go find where HMS *Illustrious* is. Commandeer a helo, fly out to them, and brief them on my plan and make sure they can provide naval gunfire support to all parties. Make it happen.'

'Yes, sir.'

As I turned to leave, he stopped me. 'One more thing: I want you to be liaison officer to the SAS. I want you to make sure they fucking tell me if they have any significant info or if anything happens we need to know about. That's crucial. Oh, and you're also LO to The Pathfinders as well. I need this all to function as one, well-oiled machine and all reporting to me. Got it?'

'Got it.'

With British soldiers being held hostage in the deep jungles, the focus of the SAS right now would be on any hostage-rescue missions they might be called upon to execute. They had one Sabre Squadron, so several dozen blokes in-country, and a multiple and fast-evolving hostage crisis to deal with, plus there was also a detachment of SBS blokes in-country alongside them.

With the PF getting out on the ground, we'd thus have several forces of sneaky-beaky types moving through the jungle up country and we could easily have a blue-on-blue if it wasn't co-ordinated properly. I was dripping with sweat from the heat as I left the CO's briefing, but it was also due to everything I had to do now.

I went to speak with 00-Joe. 'Fuck me, I'm getting beasted. I've got to liaise with the SAS and the PF. I've got to fly in a helo to the Navy to get gunfire support sorted; plus I've got to sort all the comms with all the assets in-country.'

'Right – Starky! Speedy!' 00-Joe yelled. These two massive signaller blokes come running. 'Start sorting all comms with all forces on the ground, and what their call signs and frequencies are.' He turned to me. 'Boss, let us get on with the comms, while you go see PF, SAS and the Navy. We'll hook up when you're back and run through it all ...'

I headed out of the terminal and spotted a couple of Army 350cc trials bikes parked outside. They'd been airlifted in with the Military Transport (MT) Platoon, and they were earmarked for the OC's head-shed. A young 1 PARA bloke was standing guard over them.

'I need to use a bike,' I told him.

'Erm, you need to speak to the MT officer ...'

'No time,' I told him. 'Clear it with the CO.'

I jumped on the nearest bike, wearing no helmet and with my SA80 slung over my shoulder and set off down the runway. The SAS had a small camp on the eastern edge of the airport. I headed in that direction, the wind blasting like a hot hairdryer in my face. Technically, I should have put my PARA helmet on, but I didn't have the time or the desire to go fetch it from my Bergen.

It was a five-minute ride to the SAS camp, and it was the first time since being here that the sweat on me had actually dried. Pretty quickly, I'd realised that having half my kit still damp from the laundry back home didn't matter a toss out here. Whatever you wore, within minutes of putting it on was soaked in sweat.

There was another great thing about being on the bike. The roar of the slipstream meant no one could call me on my radio, for I'd never be able to hear it – and that meant the CO couldn't get hold of me to pile any more work on my shoulders.

I reached a couple of small wooden huts that the SAS lads had made their HQ. They were well tucked away from any prying eyes and surrounded by thick jungle. I headed for the one they'd made their ops room, and spoke to a couple of blokes inside.

'Hi guys, I'm Dave, from 1 PARA,' I told them. 'The CO's asked me to liaise with you, and to co-ordinate any naval gunfire support you guys might need.'

'Sure,' one of them replied. 'Let me figure out who we can make as our LO, and I'll send him across in a bit.'

'What intel have you blokes got from anywhere around about the airport?' I asked.

The guy shook his head. 'Fuck all. We've got a couple of patrols deep up country, but we're not in control of what's going on around here. Plus we've got a couple of guys at the British High Commission, guarding the Commissioner. That's it.'

My SAS-liaison visit done, I burned the entire length of the runway, caning it on the bike just for the hell of it. I stopped at the far end and did a quick walk around C Company's positions. The blokes were well dug-in by now, with trenches manned and patches of jungle cleared, so as to give them better arcs of fire, plus they'd already started to push out foot patrols into the jungle.

It was all good.

I headed back to the terminal and went to have a chat with the

PF, in their room above our own. In the British military everyone knows who the SAS and SBS are. Not so with The Pathfinders. My knowledge of them was limited to what I'd seen of them on exercises, plus seeing the odd PF guy around Aldershot Camp, plus my chats with Lenny, 1 PARA's Ops Officer.

The PF's UK base was a special, cordoned-off area that lay adjacent to the Brigade HQ. It had a screen of high fencing surrounding it. The PF wore no insignia or marks of rank, plus their longer hair and their age marked them out as being something special. They were generally older than your average PARA, and they were always away on ops. They certainly had the mystique.

The Pathfinders were known informally as 'the bastard son of the SAS', but they were quite distinct from both the SAS and their sister Special Forces unit, the SBS. I knew their motto was 'First In' and that their real speciality was doing HALO and HAHO insertions behind enemy lines.

Parachuting was the absolute high point of what we did in the Parachute Regiment, but HALO and HAHO were a whole different ball game. It was such highly-skilled and specialist stuff that only a very few of the world's absolute elite forces ever got trained and equipped to do it. In short, The Pathfinders were the zenith of what any PARA dreamed of in terms of airborne means of insertion.

I climbed the stairs to their ops room and knocked. A couple of faces glanced up at me. One I recognised instantly. It was Mark Jackson, the son of General Sir Mike Jackson. I'd first run into him when I was doing P Company. He was a tall, handsome, Steve McQueen look-alike. He had longer blond hair than the average, plus these piercing, enigmatic eyes above a warm smile.

We greeted each other, then Mark introduced the bloke sat beside him. 'Dave, this is Tricky. He's running PF signals. Tricky this is Dave, 1 PARA RSO.'

I explained to them that the CO wanted their ops room merged with his own, downstairs, so we could work more closely. I saw

Tricky's hard blue eyes grow even harder and there was a spark of anger there, too.

'No fucking way,' he growled. 'I've got antennae fucking set up everywhere. Moving all that – no way. I'd have to cut comms and re-route it all and we've got blokes going out on the ground, operating on their own forty ks north of here. It can't be done.'

Jacko smiled. 'No can do, mate. Can you screw the nut and square it away with the CO?'

I shrugged. 'Yeah, I guess so.'

'Plus can you see if you can get some Tacsats for us or some satellite phones?' Tricky asked. 'The radios we have are shit. I've got to keep changing frequencies every hour, and if our guys have a contact they might not be able to get comms back to us.'

I told Tricky I'd try, but satphones were about as rare as rocking horse shit right now. Everyone wanted one. I'd come here wanting a favour out of these blokes. In typical PF fashion they were instead trying to work a favour out of me.

That done, I managed to blag a flight out to HMS *Illustrious*. I spoke to the ship's captain, and we worked out he'd have to move his vessel nearer to the coastline to be able to give gunfire support from his main guns, and especially if he was to do so up country, for The Pathfinders. We worked out some call signs, in case we did have to dial up the big guns, and we were good.

From there I was airlifted across to Freetown itself, to sort out details of the NEO, which was being co-ordinated from the city's Mamma Yoko hotel, for want of a better alternative. I ran into a couple of Kiwis at the hotel, who turned out to be ex-Kiwi SAS. They were doing security and comms for the head of UN peacekeeping, an Indian general who they reckoned was fond of wearing make-up, or some such shit.

They had rakes of Gucci comms kit, and I managed to blag a couple of satphones on the quiet. I flew back to the airfield, and brought the satphones up to the Pathfinder lads. I saw Tricky's eyes light up at the sight of them. Satphones might be insecure comms but they were bulletproof. They never failed. And they were often the best tool to get the job done that needed to be done.

I handed them to Tricky. 'Got you a present, just like you asked.'

He grinned. 'Mate, that is a fucking result.'

'Yeah, well don't lose them or trash them. I've been lent them on the QT by some Kiwi blokes doing comms for the UN, and they'd like them back.'

As I left Tricky playing with his new toys, neither of us knew what a vital role they would play in the coming battle.

With most of the pieces of the operational jigsaw now in place, we got the NEO under way. Tristars began flying into the airport, to pull the expats out. The terminal filled up with crowds of civvies looking tired and terminally stressed, and clutching bulging suitcases and bundles tied up with rope and string.

Some were clearly in rag order. They were basically running from homes that had been looted and worse. They were scared and in shock, but we had little time to comfort them or care for them. Our job was to throw them onto the rear of the Tristars and get them gone. We began sending load after load of expats out that way, but surprisingly quickly the crowd began to dwindle.

The trouble was, now that the PARAs were in Sierra Leone the majority of the British expats didn't want to leave any more. With PARAs out on highly-visible patrols, Freetown had started to feel safe again, so why would they want to go? Why should they be forced to run away in the face of a bunch of murderous thugs and killers, now that we were here to protect them?

Behind the scenes the overall commander of Operation Palliser, Brigadier David Richards, had given his personal assurance to Sierra Leone's President Kabbah that no rebel force would be taking Freetown. He'd managed to win the backing of Tony Blair to put a stop to the rebels once and for all. After Kosovo, this was to become the second of what would be known as 'Blair's Wars'.

That night I was comatose on my conveyor belt bed, when I woke to a cacophony of shouting and screaming. I grabbed 00-Joe and the two of us raced outside, weapons at the ready. We practically stumbled over some of the so-called UN peacekeepers, this lot being Nigerians. They were here supposedly to 'help' with the NEO, but frankly we'd rather have done without them.

They were wearing the distinctive light blue UN berets and armbands, but right now they were kicking the living daylights out of some guy who was lying on the ground. It was that bloke who was doing all the screaming. Those who weren't giving him a kicking were smashing him around the head and shoulders with these long wooden batons that they carried.

The guy on the ground was this youngster, dressed in the ubiquitous shorts, flip-flops and T-shirt of the locals. He didn't look like a rebel to me. As they slammed their boots and their truncheons into him, he was screaming with agony, but the Nigerians were laughing and joking uproariously. It was like some scene from *A Clockwork Orange*.

And these guys were the fucking peacekeepers.

00-Joe and I waded right in. 'STOP! STOP! *What the fuck d'you think you're doing?*'

One of the Nigerian blokes turned and started yelling right back in our faces, his lips flecked with spittle and his eyes alight with what I could only read as *enjoyment*. I couldn't understand a word of what he was saying, but whatever it was the others started to laugh uproariously. I wasn't sure if they were laughing at the poor bloke curled up on the ground, or at 00-Joe and me.

I glanced down and realised that their victim had knife cuts all over him. They'd been slashing him too, as they beat and kicked him to death. If he didn't die from the beating, the wounds would likely go septic and finish him. The Nigerians outnumbered 00-Joe and me, but that didn't mean shit. 00-Joe alone could have floored the lot of them, and they could read that much in his eyes.

The beating ceased and they started to back away from their victim. A big part of me wanted to smash the fuck out of them, but right now our priority had to be the bloke on the ground. They walked away as if they knew they were in the wrong, but smug in the knowledge that as 'UN peacekeepers' we couldn't touch them.

I left 00-Joe with their victim and went to fetch one of our medics. The last I saw of the bloke was the 1 PARA medic tending to his wounds, so hopefully we had managed to save him.

I told our Ops Officer, Lenny about it, the next morning.

'Dave, mate, that shit goes on every day here . . .'

Lenny and I briefed the OC and we did get a formal complaint lodged with the UN. We knew it would have zero effect. The UN operation here was a total, unmitigated disaster. But at least we had tried. If one of us lot had been caught kicking a local's head in, we'd rightly have faced a Court Martial. But as for the 'UN peacekeepers' they were a law unto themselves, and a shocking number of them were bullies, cowards and worse.

It would take real fighting men with an unshakeable moral and physical courage to sort out the rebels in Sierra Leone – and unbeknown to us that was what was just about to happen.

By now The Pathfinders were well dug-in up country, at a village called Lungi Loi, some 30 kilometres north of the airport. They'd constructed a series of concealed defences, called ATTAPs, which basically consisted of a trench dug in the ground with a thick cover made of branches and leaves. From anything other than a few yards away, the Pathfinders would remain unseen by the enemy.

Machine guns had been set up with carefully worked-out arcs, so if the village was attacked they could put down a murderous rate of fire, plus they had mortar pits to put down supporting fire. The Pathfinders' forward HQ was situated right in the centre of the village, with ATTAPs radiating out from it. In short, from whatever direction they might be hit the Pathfinders were ready.

And they fully expected to get hit.

It was all but impossible for the rebels to by-pass Lungi Loi, en route to attack Freetown. The Sierra Leone capital sits on a narrow peninsula, the neck of which is even narrower. Lungi Loi was at the narrowest choke-point – hence the forty fighting men of the PF watched and waited for the enemy attack they knew was coming. They slept in their webbing and their boots and with their weapons. That way, they were always ready.

It was two days after the NEO when the radio traffic coming through the Ops Room came to a sudden end. The net had been cleared completely, for the rebels were even now advancing on the PF's positions. They were in their hundreds and, as was typical, not only had they done nothing to hide their presence, but they were actively advertising it with their weird, chilling monkey cries and other animal noises.

The first I knew of the coming battle was when I was shaken awake on my conveyor belt bed. It was one of the signallers warning me that a contact with the rebels was imminent. I was on my feet instantly and I hurried into the Ops Room. I was just getting on the radios to alert HMS *Illustrious* to have her guns ready, when Mark stuck his head around the door.

'Dave, you've heard? PF are in a contact.' The Ops Room fell silent as we waited for more. 'That's all I got. But it's kicking off right now.'

'Right, I'll get you air, plus there's *Illustrious* with her guns.'

Mark nodded. 'I'll let you know if we need 'em.'

I got the gunners on *Illustrious* on standby, then dialled up the Combat Air Patrols we had in the air right now. Harriers had been launched off the ships an hour or so earlier, so I got them to orbit over the Freetown Estuary, just in case the PF needed to call in air strikes. That done, there was bugger all else I could do but monitor the net and wait for any update from Mark.

As I sat there in the dawn hum of the Ops Room, I could just imagine the scene up country. The jungle would only just be coming to life. In the dawn light the Pathfinders would be invisible in their hidden positions. And just to the north they'd see the rebels, child soldiers and all, moving forward to attack. And there was a big part of me that hungered to be out there with the PF preparing to do battle.

It was a good couple of hours, and still Mark hadn't been down with any update. For all of that time the airwaves had remained strangely, eerily silent and I wondered what on earth had happened to the PF comms. As a result of the ominous silence, the tension in the Ops Room had been steadily mounting.

I could just imagine what had happened. The PF had faced a real problem over the past few days, for they suspected the rebels were disguising themselves as villagers so they could wander into Lungi Loi and infiltrate their positions. If that had happened maybe rebels disguised as villagers had risen up and swamped them, taking down their comms and cutting the PF lads to shreds.

Finally Mark's head popped around our door. 'Contact over,' he announced. 'PF: No casualties. Large numbers of enemy dead and injured. Will update you as soon as we have more details.'

Then he was gone.

The CO turned to me. 'Dave, get on that motorbike of yours and go let the SAS know.'

'Sir.'

I jumped on the trials bike and burned it onto the centre of the runway. I felt a huge surge of elation at what the PF had just achieved. It wasn't a 1 PARA firefight, this one. We'd basically played no role in it. But some 60 per cent of the PF are ex-PARAs, and we felt very close to that unit, as if it was a very close relation of the PARA family.

As I hammered down the tarmac the morning sun was beating down from a cloudless African sky. It was furnace hot already. I got to the SAS end of Camp, and found the same bloke I'd talked to before. He was in shorts and flip-flops and looked like he'd only just woken up.

'PF were in contact this morning at Lungi Loi,' I told him. 'They took out a serious number of rebels, no casualties themselves.'

He smiled. 'Nice.'

'Anything your end?' I asked him.

'No, mate. Nothing much to report.'

That was about it. As I rode away from the base I figured the SAS would only get to see any real action if a hostage-rescue mission got the 'go'. They got to do all the truly sneaky-beaky kind of stuff, but on balance I was drawn more to The Pathfinders. When it came to it, whether it was HALOing out of a C130 at 30,000 feet, or taking on the murderous rebels head-to-head in the African jungles, in the PF you seemed to get to do it all.

I reached the terminal and was parking up the motorbike when Mark emerged. He gazed into the sun, a look of relief mixed with deep satisfaction on his features. He'd been the Ops Officer for this one, so it must have been a total buzz to have seen it all go so swimmingly.

He turned to me. 'Dave, mate, thanks for the satphone. Come the moment the shit hit the fan, that's the only comms that was fucking working.'

One satphone had been sent up country, on a resupply run in a Chinook, so satphone had been able to speak directly to satphone as the bullets started to fly. That pretty much explained why the airwaves had been so unearthly silent during the battle. The PF had been using their own, private, civvie means of comms – or rather one that the UN had unwittingly supplied to them!

Apparently, the rebel fighters had been high as kites on drugs. They'd rushed the PF positions in human waves, and some had kept on coming even after they'd been hit several times. The Pathfinders had smashed them with withering barrages of machine gun fire, plus their dug-in mortars, and pretty much annihilated the lot of them.

The PF Platoon Sergeant was Stan Harris, a legend of a bloke in such circles. He'd shown exceptional bravery during the battle, not to mention brilliant leadership, keeping the machine-gunners and mortar teams firing even when it looked as if their position was about to be overrun.

From what Mark had told me, it sounded like some kind of an epic battle. He fixed me with this look. 'You ever thought of trying for it? The PF?'

I gave a sheepish kind of a smile. 'Maybe ... But only if you go easy on me during selection, as payback for those bloody satphones. Talking of which, where are they? I got to return them to the UN ...'

Mark laughed. 'Some hopes, mate ...'

We were out of Sierra Leone just a couple of days later. The media had jetted in en masse by now, and the whole thing was becoming something of a circus. In any case, an amphibious assault force of Royal Marines was scheduled to relieve 1 PARA, so that the British military could consolidate its position and keep taking the fight to the rebels.

Just before we did leave, there was some more good news. Major Andy Harrison, of the PARAs, my old mentor from Sandhurst, plus Phil Ashby, were rotated through the airport, en route to the UK. And in proper PARA Regiment tradition, they'd pretty much managed to escape from the rebel's clutches all of their own accord.

We'd evened up the score a little. More than a little, actually.

As we flew out of the country, the PARAs were once again making front-page headlines in the British newspapers. Not only that, once again it was 1 PARA leading the way. It was Kosovo Mark Two. Colonel Gibson had pulled it off once more. And in a sense that made Sierra Leone a bittersweet experience for me.

On the flight out I got to sit next to Gavin, the 2IC of the Pathfinders, plus Lenny. Gavin gave us a blow-by-blow account of the battle for Lungi Loi, and there were other PF blokes – Tricky included – throwing in comments from the sidelines. It was all first name terms and free and easy, and I loved it.

I guess Gavin and the rest of them could see that I did, too.

'Mate, you should join us,' Gavin said. 'If you pass selection, you'd love it. Tell the CO that's what you're doing.'

As RSO of 1 PARA my chances of getting into the kind of action they'd just been in were non-existent. I decided my time had come to move on from 1 PARA.

I was going to try for selection into The Pathfinders.

*

CHAPTER NINETEEN

B y now I'd been RSO 1 PARA for barely six months. It was supposed to be a two-year posting. I was going to have to ask the CO if I could leave after doing barely a quarter of my time. Moreover, I didn't just want him to let me go. I wanted him to allow me time off from my duties so I could train for PF selection.

After I'd recovered from the massive post Op Palliser piss-up, I went to see Colonel Gibson. 'Sir, I want to apply for PF selection.'

Colonel Gibson barely flinched. 'Okay, no problem. Go for it.'

That was it. Discussion done.

I couldn't understand why it had been so easy. Then I remembered: the Colonel was out of here in a few days' time, for a new CO was coming in. *That was why it had been so easy.*

Colonel Gibson's replacement was Colonel Mick Perry, who had commanded other elite units. He'd served in the First Gulf War, when the SAS had lost the Bravo Two Zero patrol. This guy would know his bloody onions. I had to put the same request to him, and it didn't go down quite so well.

I could see he was thinking – *Who the hell are you to ask this of me? Your appointment as RSO doesn't finish until the end of next year. I need my comms to be shit hot, so why on earth would I want you to leave?* He didn't say as much, but his silence spoke volumes. I tried explaining that the PF had asked me to try for the slot of 2IC of the unit, and that meant I had to go for this winter's selection.

'Okay, I'll allow you the five weeks to do selection,' he relented. 'But you get no time off to train.'

Well, at least he hadn't stopped me.

It was the summer of 2000, and finally I couldn't avoid doing the RSO training course any longer. I had to go for three months' 'training' at the Army College in Warminster in what I already knew. I was burning up with frustration, especially as it left me zero time or opportunity to do any training for selection.

By now 1 PARA had been moved to a new base at Dover. When I got back from Warminster I started running over the White Cliffs, and I persuaded Jack Quinn – the ex-SAS wheel-stealer – to help me train. But the White Cliffs of Dover were hardly Pen y Fan, and it was clear that I needed to get myself up to the Brecons and the Elan Valley proper.

I decided to start driving up there on my weekends, so I could train over the actual terrain where selection takes place. During Kosovo and Sierra Leone I'd spent zero money while I'd been overseas. I'd managed to save up eight grand, with which I bought myself an ageing metallic blue BMW 3 Series 2.8i. It was a fast and comfortable drive, and it was going to be my escape route into the Brecons.

Being based at Dover put an extra two hours on the journey, which was shit, but at least I now had a motor that was made for the drive. The other problem was my semi-unofficial status. In theory, anyone training for SAS or PF selection was supposed to check in with Sennybridge Camp. An officer from your parent unit would arrange for you to team up with other blokes doing selection, so you could file routes beforehand and go out in pairs.

In essence, your parent unit sponsored you to do selection. Yet I'd been given no time off to train and I could expect zero support. I alone from 1 PARA was trying for PF selection, and I was going to have to keep very much under the radar.

It was late autumn when I first drove up to the Brecons, so two months prior to January selection. The BMW proved great for getting up there, but horrendous for the night. I left Dover Barracks on a Friday at 5.00 p.m. sharp, and ragged it the entire way. But I didn't get to the Brecons until well after 10 o'clock, and now I had to find a place to sleep for the night.

I had a duvet from my room and some Army dog blankets from the stores. With the front seats reclined to the max, I figured I could just about curl up and get some kip. I'd keep my boots inside the car, in an effort to keep them dry. I'd got a bulk supply of Ginsters pasties, and they'd do me for breakfast, lunch and dinner if need be.

I found my way to the Beacons Reservoir, the start and finish point for the most horrendous of all PF selection trials – Endurance. I drove around a bit and found a lay-by with an overgrown track going up one side of it. I figured if I backed the BMW up that I'd be able to hide it in the undergrowth. I did just that, pulled some dead branches across and figured I was pretty much sorted.

The only way anyone would ever discover the car was if they walked up an unused track that went nowhere. I couldn't afford for anyone to see me, for if I got reported to the cops they would in turn report me to the military. Doing your training solo wouldn't go down too well. Blokes had died attempting selection, so it was fair enough really that they wanted any training to be done in company.

Trouble was, I didn't have any option but to go it alone.

The Beacons Reservoir is the start point for the 'Fan Dance' as they call it. You do The Dance several times on both SAS and PF selection. You begin near this isolated pub called the Storey Arms, you race up the sheer-sided monster of Pen y Fan, down the other side and start climbing again. It was what Jack Quinn had warned me about – the notorious 'VW Valley'.

I figured there was no better starting point for my training.

I kept waking up every hour that first night, freezing cold and with my jaw chattering away. I switched the motor on, got the heater blasting and played a bit of music – Hendrix, an ex-paratrooper – to cheer me up. I had the seat reclined so far back I couldn't use a piss bottle, so I had to slide out into the freezing cold for a wazz. If I needed a crap it'd be a hole in the woods for me.

I was up with first light, for it flooded in through the car windows bright and early. I'd brought a hexi stove with me and some leftover Army rations. I used that to make a brew to wash down a breakfast of pasties. Then I locked the car and set off into the hills. I tabbed for all of that day, and I didn't see a soul on the hills. By the time I got back to the reservoir I was soaked through, and I reckoned I was going a bit fucky-ducky in the head.

I couldn't afford to burn too much petrol, so I tabbed down to the pub to try for a bit of beer and warm food. I got to the Storey Arms and ordered myself a Guinness and a massive plate of chips. It had occurred to me that pulling a chick might be a good idea. It'd be a free bed and shower and far preferable to a second night in the car.

Then I took a look at that night's clientele in the Storey Arms. It looked as if most of those present had a brother and sister with them, or a mum and dad. I guessed it was the car for me, after all. The bizarre thing was that not a soul asked me who I was or what I might be doing there. I was clearly the only stranger in the entire place, but maybe they were used to big blokes turning up alone and in rag state, and with a crazed stare in their eyes.

The chips alone weren't enough after a day's tabbing over the Brecons, so I drove into the nearest village and grabbed a kebab. There was an outdoor pursuit shop that was still open, so I went in and bought myself a fresh pair of socks. They were called the '1000 Mile Sock'. They came with a guarantee that you could do a thousand miles in them and not get a blister. We'd see.

I got back to my lay-by, pulled the Beamer up the lane, dragged some branches across the track and settled down to sleep. I kept waking up the whole night with horrendous cramps. The exertion of the day, plus the cramped and freezing sleeping conditions, was proving a nightmare.

I was up with the crack of dawn, feeling tired and aching all over.

As I brewed up I consoled myself with the thought of those brand-new, dry, miracle socks. I pulled them on, slipped on my sodden boots – a night in the Beamer hadn't done much to dry them – and set off for The Fan once more.

I did ten miles that day over the hills, and sure enough I ended up with massive blisters. I limped back to the car as darkness fell, and a part of me was tempted to take the bloody things back to the shop and show them my feet. But for seven quid I couldn't be bothered. I was in bloody Mordor here and I wanted to get myself gone.

I had a five-hour drive back to Dover ahead of me, and I had to be at work at 0830 hours sharp. I set off for London on the M4 and stopped at the services at Reading to grab a burger. I knew I was exhausted and it was dangerous to be on the motorways like this. After I'd wolfed the burger I had forty minutes kip in the car. I got back to Dover well after midnight and snuck into Camp.

I trained hard in the Brecons every weekend, then headed for a final session in the Elan Valley. If anything, it was more Mordor than Mordor. For the first time ever I experienced the babies' heads, and I hated them. There was no easy way through, so I just had to resign myself to fighting my way over this ankle-twisting, nightmarish terrain.

When I got back to the BMW at the end of day one, I wrung the bog water out of my socks and it was red with blood. My ankles were swollen, and my toes had rubbed themselves raw while traversing the horrendous ground. Either I got my feet seriously hardened up, or there was no way I was going to survive the coming weeks of selection.

I'd got Jack Quinn to teach me the toe-strapping technique. You had to wrap each toe separately in zinc oxide tape, leaving the closing seal on top of the toe, where it was least likely to rub and come undone. I'd taped my toes that morning, but the trouble was I'd forgotten to use a pair of scissors to cut the tape. I'd ripped it in my hurry to get going, which had left a series of ragged ends. They'd rubbed free, and that had allowed the tape to come undone.

It was a hare and tortoise kind of a lesson. More haste, less speed.

The next morning I wrapped up properly, using neat cuts to seal the tape across the tops of each of my toes. Then I shouldered my Bergen and set off into the Valley. It was freezing, pissing with rain and miserable. I had a heavy pack, which was deliberate, for I wanted the same kind of weight that I'd have to carry on selection.

My Bergen was stuffed full of tins of baked beans – fine eaten cold – pasties of course, water, medical kit, plus a Gore-Tex bivvie bag. The bivvie bag was a vital piece of survival gear, and I'd never go anywhere without it on the hills. If you got injured or lost, you could crawl into it and keep dry in all and any weather conditions, and dry means warm. And that could save your life.

I tabbed for hours, racing across the hard tufts of bog grass to try to keep my pace at something like what I'd need on selection. I was hours into the tab and I guess I had mild exposure. You can wear all the Gore-Tex wet weather gear you like, but rain like they have in the Elan Valley still works its way into the seams and up the sleeves, and you'll still end up piss wet through, just as I was now.

I stopped to refill my water bottles from a stream. I chucked in the Steritabs and took a long pull. As I tried to get the chlorine taste out of my mouth, I decided to do a map check. I hadn't done one for a good hour, and the weather had really come in bad. I was surrounded by a thick blanket of mist and rain, and visibility was down to barely a few yards.

As I pored over the map, I began to realise that I didn't know where I was. All the navigation training I'd ever received had always hammered into me the one, vital lesson – *trust your compass*. An hour back I'd done a map and compass check. I'd decided the terrain didn't marry up to what the compass was telling me, so I'd set out on a route that I believed was right, and in defiance of my compass.

In short, I'd got myself completely lost. I'd thought I knew better than my compass. Some hopes. It was well past midday by now and I was glad I was on my own, for it meant that no one had seen me fuck up so badly. On the other hand, I was alone, I didn't know where I was, and I had to be back at Dover that night for work, or questions would start being asked.

I decided to do the only sensible thing: I struck off on a compass bearing due west – one that should eventually lead me to a stretch of road. Even in this weather I couldn't miss stumbling across a linear feature like a road. I set off practically running, for I knew I was up against it. As I stumbled across the babies' heads I was cursing to myself: 'You fucking, fucking dick!'

I dropped down the side of this massive mountain and it was starting to get dark. I had to lose altitude, before the night really came in. I figured I was a good two-thirds of the way down when I hit a sheer cliff face. I had no option but to contour around it, until I found a route that would get me down. I did just that and eventually I made the flat, and within minutes I hit the road.

It was a tiny, single-lane stretch of tarmac and it was utterly deserted. I turned south and began a forced tab. It was dusk now, and the fog had enshrouded everything in this ghostly cloak of grey. Eventually I hit a tiny crossroads, and thankfully one with a signpost. I read the names of the villages, and I couldn't believe how I had gone so badly wrong.

I was miles away from where I had thought I was. I was soaked through and chilled to the core, and my brain clearly wasn't functioning properly. I should have been able to keep track of where I was by counting my steps, and doing a simple time over distance calculation. Instead, I'd been charging about like a headless chicken, and even telling my own compass it was wrong.

I now had a good six-mile tab along the road, to get back to the car. I was exhausted, and this was going to be the forced march from hell. More to the point, if anyone did come along the road and see me, they'd know for sure what I was doing and why. And that could get me reported.

As luck would have it, I made it back to the car without being spotted. And somehow I made it back to Dover Barracks without falling asleep at the wheel, though I only got there in the early hours of the morning.

The experience taught me two things. One: never, ever defy your compass. Two: never, ever underestimate the effects of even mild exposure on the body, or the brain's ability to think clearly.

A few weeks later I would find myself on PF selection for real, and holed up in a frozen, snowbound scrape on an OP, cuddling up with Al as we tried to last the longest night of our lives.

Compared to the Elan Valley this was extreme exposure, and of the type that would near as hell kill us.

*

CHAPTER TWENTY

As dawn broke over the farmhouse where the PF hunter force was holed up, Smudge, Jez, Al and I gazed out of our grave-scrape of an OP, wondering how the hell we'd managed to last the night. The outside of Al's black woolly hat was a latticework of ice, his face beneath it ashen grey and doughy with the long night's chill.

Beneath us, our arse-sized slices of carry-mat were crackly and stiff with the frost. And beneath them, the floor of the scrape had been transformed into a sheet of lumpy ice dusted with a hard crust of snow. But at least with sunup the weather was letting up a little. Snow still drifted down in the odd, angry flurry, but it was no longer the full-on blizzard of the long night that had just gone.

We were pulled out of the OP later that day, and rode the four-tonners back to Camp taking full advantage of the steaming tea urn. We were dumped on the snowy expanse of the parade ground, and it was clear right away that something was wrong. Stan Harris – the PF Platoon Sergeant and the hero of the battle for Lungi Loi, in Siera Leone – was stood out front, and he practically had steam coming out of his ears.

He fixed Pete with a look like murder. 'Right, listen up. Sergeant Terry's fucking patrol decided it was okay to get a brew on 'cause they were cold and wet and feeling sorry for themselves. They also put their OP way too close to the enemy in a crap position. They compromised themselves. If you'd done that for real on ops you'd all have been captured, got the shit kicked out of you and tortured, pokers shoved up your arse and executed.

'You'd also just have blown the entire fucking plan for the assault force to come in on the back of you and strike those positions – so endangering good men's lives – and all because a Grenadier guardsman put an OP in a shit position and thought it okay to get a brew on. Fucking well done, Sergeant Terry.'

I could see Pete cringing under the verbal assault. 'The rest of your kit that you left behind when you ran away is in the wagon. You left your fucking notebooks, fucking radios, and fuck only knows what else to the enemy. You're on a warning; one more fucking strike and you're out.'

'Staff.' Poor Pete was looking red-faced and sheepish as fuck.

I was fucking glad not to have been on that patrol. Al and I might have come that close to dying, but at least Stan Harris hasn't got lock-on with us. Once we were dismissed I got the full story from Pete. They'd got spotted in their OP, the Pathfinder hunter force had come after them in strength, and they'd been forced to go on the run. They'd bugged out leaving a rake of kit behind, and they'd had to do a fighting withdrawal.

They'd been beasted by the hunter force across half of the Sennybridge Training Area. And when they were finally overrun, Pete got a double-beasting because he had his Gore-Tex trousers on. In spite of the weather, they were still a total no-no, being noisy and cumbersome and a dead giveaway to any enemy.

Still, Pete hadn't quite got himself binned, and now all we had ahead of us was the Final Exercise Week – a live, six-day exercise operating as a Pathfinder patrol and combining all skills learned. Final Exercise Week would include a long tab in, setting up an OP, a close target recce, being forced to go on the run from an 'enemy' force, getting captured and going 'in the bag'.

After going in the bag we'd be put through a SERE – survival, evasion, resistance to interrogation and escape – trial, in which we would have to last out forty-eight hours of a frighteningly realistic capture and interrogation by the 'enemy'. Or at least that was what should have happened.

As bad luck would have it, the day we finished OP Week the foot-and-mouth crisis hit the UK. When Lenny gathered us together to announce that all military training had been cancelled across the UK – and that included PF selection – because of 'foot-and-mouth', none of us even knew what that was. But that didn't alter the fact that for now at least PF selection was over.

Lenny had decided that all twelve of us who had survived thus far would have selection put on hold. When the foot-and-mouth crisis was over we'd face our Final Exercise Week and SERE, and still have to pass them as normal. This was a massive anticlimax, to put it mildly. In essence, none of us knew if we were in. Selection just fizzled out with no massive piss-up or anything.

It was late on the Friday when Lenny made his announcement. I said a brief farewell to the lads – Pete, Jez, Al, Mark, Smudge and the rest – and hit the road. I was exhausted, covered in sores and blisters and welts, unshaven and unwashed, and I had a five-hour drive to Dover ahead of me. But where else was I supposed to go? I wasn't in the PF yet, that was for sure.

As I headed down the M4 I was struck by a thought. What the fuck had happened to all the money the DS had fined us? I'd lost a good twenty quid or more. I guessed the PF were going to swallow the lot.

I knew how tired I was, so I stopped at just about every service area on the way. I piled down the carbs, and loaded up on Red Bull, and that's how I made it back to Dover Barracks, and returned to my life with 1 PARA.

That September 9/11 happened, and in an instant the world changed forever. I'd actually visited the Twin Towers, when I'd been in the States on a Sandhurst-sponsored competition, and I felt the attack against America very personally. We knew it had to be Al Qaeda behind it, and that meant that British soldiers would very likely be seeing action in Afghanistan.

I was still RSO 1 PARA, and if anything 9/11 fuelled my hunger to get into The Pathfinders. When the air strikes began over Afghanistan I knew that UKSF and The Pathfinders would be getting in on the ground. If I was in the PF I'd be part of this by now. As it was, 1 PARA were about to be sent on a six-week training package to Kenya, which wasn't exactly where I wanted to be.

Exercise Grand Prix involved doing a lot of parachute jumps into the remote Kenyan bush, and tabbing through the African desert and the heat. I was four weeks in when I got called into the CO's office, which right now was a length of canvas in the middle of the Kenyan bush.

'PF are deploying to Afghanistan,' he told me. 'The Brigade Commander has ordered that you be recalled immediately to the UK, so you can join them.'

'Yes, sir. Of course, sir.'

I got out of his tent and yelled out: 'YEEEESSS!'

As much fun as a training exercise like this was, and as much as I'd loved my time in 1 PARA, I was desperate to get into the PF and onto operations, hunting Al Qaeda for real. This was my chance.

I flew out of Kenya on a Herc. I got back to Dover, threw all my kit in my BMW, and drove up to Wattisham airbase, site of the new and purpose-built headquarters of The Pathfinders. I turned up at the gate dressed in civvies, and with my life piled in the back of my motor. Happily, I'd left my ironing board in Dover, for I wouldn't be needing that for a long while now.

I showed security my Army pass, got waved through and was taken to my billet. I dumped my kit, and made my way to Lenny's office. I found him in a conflab with his sergeant major, a bloke whom everyone knew affectionately as The White Rabbit. He had snow-blond hair and pale blue, almost albino eyes. He had a real intensity about him bordering on the insane, plus a towering reputation as an elite and edgy operator.

Lenny held out a hand to me. 'Good to see you, mate. Right,

we've got two PF patrols about to deploy to Afghan, and we've pulled you in early so you can work as a GPMG gunner on one of the patrols. It's so you can get experience of being on the ground with a patrol, before you take up your post as 2IC.'

'Bloody great,' I enthused.

'We may be in Afghan for some time. Gavin's commanding one patrol, and you'll be in the other, under a bloke called Gall. We're on twenty-four hours' notice to move. We may well go before Christmas, so get all your cards sent. If we're very lucky we might get Christmas Day at home, but not a lot more. That's about it.'

It was 20 December right now, so only four days to Christmas. It seemed like I'd made it just in the nick of time.

As a bit of light relief, Lenny shared a quick story about what had happened to him a few days back. One of the female admin officers had cycled over from the main part of the camp – Wattisham was chiefly an Apache attack helicopter base – to have a good moan. She'd complained bitterly to Lenny that none of his men ever seemed to salute her, or address her properly as 'Ma'am'.

'They don't even salute me,' he'd told her, 'so they sure as hell aren't saluting you.'

As with the SAS and the SBS, The Pathfinders embodied a relaxed, rankless culture, a meritocracy. It was one in which merit, regardless of rank, was what mattered. I couldn't have felt happier to be here. Of course, at some stage I'd have to do my SERE and all the other stuff, but right now the absolute priority was Afghanistan.

'Report to Gall, mate,' Lenny told me. 'You'll find him in the Interest Room.'

Gall turned out to be this giant of a bloke, one who hailed from the Household Cavalry. He had big, staring eyes, huge fists and great bushy sideburns that ran all the way down to his chin. He had longish black hair and was thirty-three years old to my twenty-three, so he had a decade of soldiering on me.

'Hello, Dave, this is the rest of the lads …' he told me, as he started to introduce me to the other blokes on the patrol.

We were in the PF's Interest Room, and I was somewhat in awe of the place. There was certainly nothing like it in the PARAs' Dover Barracks. There were scores of photos of PF blokes HALOing into exotic parts of the world, plus there was the 'Glory Wall' which included the photos of all those who had lost their lives on operations.

It was like a permanent, living memorial, with those who had perished pictured in their skydiving rig or on motorbikes, and each portrait with the inscription 'In memory of ...' and their name. Here in the PF, those who had given their lives certainly weren't ever going to be forgotten.

Alongside that were various inspirational quotes, and two struck me immediately. One was from a speech given by Theodore Roosevelt shortly after the end of his presidency, in 1910, and I read it in full.

It is not the critic who counts; not the man who points out how the strong man stumbles, or where the doer of deeds could have done them better. The credit belongs to the man who is actually in the arena, whose face is marred by dust and sweat and blood; who strives valiantly; who errs, who comes short again and again, because there is no effort without error and shortcoming; but who does actually strive to do the deeds; who knows great enthusiasms, the great devotions; who spends himself in a worthy cause; who at the best knows in the end the triumph of high achievement, and who, at the worst, if he fails, at least fails while daring greatly, so that his place shall never be with those cold and timid souls who neither know victory nor defeat.

Wow.

That quote sat beside a poem called 'Invictus'. The simple act of reading it set my hair on end.

Out of the night that covers me,
Black as the Pit from pole to pole
I thank whatever gods may be
For my unconquerable soul.

In the fell clutch of circumstance
I have not winced nor cried aloud.
Under the bludgeonings of chance
My head is bloody, but unbowed.

Beyond this place of wrath and tears
Looms but the horror of the shade,
And yet the menace of the years
Finds, and shall find me unafraid.

It matters not how strait the gate,
How charged with punishments the scroll,
I am the master of my fate,
I am the captain of my soul.

It was by some poet that I'd never heard of before, one William Ernest Henley. It struck me that if only I'd had that poem with me on selection, it was the kind of thing I could have read to give me strength when I was at my lowest ebb. I decided I'd commit it to memory, for it encapsulated everything that had drawn me to The Pathfinders.

All around me blokes were busy stuffing kit into Bergens, in preparation for Afghanistan. Gall introduced me to his second-in-command, a guy called Bob who was also Household Cavalry. In contrast to Gall, Bob was very smartly dressed, with short back and sides. I sensed immediately that Bob was very, very bright, and that he could easily have made officer in the Cavalry.

Instead, he was a lance corporal of horse (LCoH) and a Pathfinder. Bob was also a Supervisor Forward Air Controller (SupFAC), which meant that he was able to supervise several blokes in the task of calling in the warplanes, so as to orchestrate a massive air war. Together, Gall and Bob ran the vehicle mobility side of The Pathfinders, which was great, for I figured I was going to learn a lot from them in Afghan.

Gall's driver was H, a moustachioed farmer from Yorkshire who was as direct and blunt as they come. He was also a Tandem Master, which meant he was one of the few elite soldiers in the world qualified to freefall another human being from 30,000 feet into target. He could HALO in far behind enemy lines with a person, or a sensitive piece of kit strapped to his body.

The GPMG gunner on Gall's wagon was none other than Lennie, the black dude who used to sprint for England, and whom I'd commanded when on Kosovo ops with 1 PARA.

I was going to be on Bob's wagon, manning the general purpose machine gun (GPMG) mounted on a special pivot on the vehicle's rear. Ginge was the driver on our wagon. He hailed from the Royal Engineers, and he reminded me a lot of Sandy, my section commander in 1 PARA. He was a relentlessly upbeat, human dynamo of a bloke, and a laugh a minute with it.

The blokes seemed highly amused to get me dropped into their team. I was a PARA Reg captain and the pending 2IC of The Pathfinders – but right now, and for the duration of their Afghan ops, I was going to be serving as the butt-fuck rear-gunner on one of their vehicles.

The regular Army just wouldn't allow this – an officer being commanded by his men. I could see they intended to put me through the mixer, but this was entirely the right thing to do. I was here on probation. I hadn't completed any of their specialist training cadres, and I was off with them to Afghanistan after only just having joined the unit.

I was the lowest of the low, which was just as it should be.

H was getting the comms kit sorted for our patrol. 'Dave, first job: give me a hand packing this shit.'

'No problem.' I glanced over the piles of radio kit. 'You want me to grab a 5.4 metre mast and some spare antennae?'

A 5.4 metre mast was like a load of plastic scaffold poles that you slotted together. It allowed you to elevate your antenna wire, so you could project your VHF signal a lot further and achieve greater range.

H gave a snort. 'How the fuck would I know what a 5.4 metre mast is? I'm Mr Air, mate. I HALO people in. But great – you seem to know your shit. You can do comms. Tricky!' he shouted over. 'You got one of them 5.4 metre mast thingamajigs! Dave wants one for our patrol.'

Tricky glanced up from his own pile of gear. 'Dave, you can take one: but they're a piece of shit. You'll end up carrying it for no reason. If ever you get the time to erect one of those, you're fucked. I run the comms here, mate. It's different to being in Battalion. Good being proactive, but I know what I'm doing.'

That shut me up.

It was only my second night in the unit when it came time for the PF's annual Christmas piss-up. We hadn't yet got the order to deploy so it was going ahead as planned.

It was The White Rabbit who gave me the nod. 'Dave, Christmas function 1900 sharp, at the NAAFI.'

I told him I'd be there.

If I played by Welbeck or Sandhurst rules, a Christmas function called for formal mess dress. I figured this would be different, so maybe M&S chinos and a tweedy sports jacket. But then again maybe not. I went and asked Lenny whether that was the right kind of gear to wear.

He cracked up. 'Dave, you need dress down mate, or you'll get savaged.'

I settled for jeans and a blue denim shirt.

I got to the NAAFI and the music was thumping out big time. Inside, the lads were already downing the beers, and there were these civvie barmaids they'd hired for the evening who were all over the lads, trying to blag a PF boyfriend. I spotted Al, Jez and Pete, my brothers from selection, and we naturally formed a gaggle of new boys by the bar.

Pete looked typical Pete. He was dressed in a sharp collared shirt, ironed to perfection. He had managed to lower himself to wearing a pair of jeans, but they were absolutely ancient and they even had knife-edge creases in them. I guessed you could take the man out of the Guards, but not the Guards out of the man. But the amazing thing was he'd actually broken the mould on one level and grown a massive pair of sideburns.

I congratulated him on them. 'Nice whiskers, mate.'

'Thanks.'

'But what's with the jeans?'

'Only pair I've ever owned. They're called The Devil's Cloth in my regiment.'

'Mate, you look like shit ...'

'Mate, I am a pad. I don't have any fucking money. The wife and kids take it all.'

It was good to see Pete again – and all the other blokes from selection.

We'd been drinking for a while when this bizarre figure strode into the NAAFI. He was dressed in full Elvis rig, including chest-hair, gold medallion, sunglasses, platform shoes, wig and all. Underneath the white suit and matching flares I figured he looked somehow familiar. He made direct for the stage, and amidst a wild chorus of cheering he started to rotate his hips about and sing his first Elvis number of the evening.

Then I realised who it was: it was fucking Smudge.

The last time I'd seen him was when we were dying of exposure on OP Week. He'd failed to mention back then that he was an Elvis impersonator, and a pretty bloody good one by the sound of things.

I glanced around the room and I could see the Old and The Bold of the PF – The White Rabbit, H, even Tricky – laughing their heads off as they tried to sing along to the lyrics. Another figure appeared and joined Smudge on the stage. This time it was Ginge, the driver on our wagon. He too was dressed up in some wild kind of gear, and I could only conclude he was supposed to be a Johnny Cash look-alike.

As the two of them continued crooning into the microphone, the rest of the PF boys were calling out requests – all Elvis, or Neil Diamond or Johnny Cash numbers. With each new song, another of the blokes was called up onto the stage and did a spell yodelling into the microphone. It didn't seem to matter how crap they were at singing. No one seemed to care.

I wondered if this was some kind of bizarre Pathfinder initiation ritual. It sure was different from a night out in Cheeks Nightclub scrapping pikeys. I wondered if Pete, Al, Jez or me were going to get forced up onto the stage and made to perform. I knew how bad my singing was. I'd once been shown a family video on which someone had caught me singing, and it was truly abysmal.

I tried to shrink in height and somehow grow less conspicuous. I really did not want to get hustled up onto that stage. No doubt about it, this was weird. It certainly wasn't what I thought of as 'normal' squaddie behaviour. These guys were wild, crazy, cracked. They were an extreme bunch who only seemed to have the one setting, which was full throttle.

No one seemed to give a damn what anyone else thought of them either. It was all very different from anything I had experienced before. But it was not long after 9/11 and we were about to deploy, so I guessed this was the final blowing off of steam.

I awoke the next day with a peach of a hangover, but at least I had no memory of anyone forcing me to sing. Word went around that we were being allowed home for Christmas Day. I drove up to Lincolnshire, to my parents' pretty cottage in the village in which they now lived. It was great to see my mum and dad and my two sisters.

My parents were worried about me going to Afghanistan, and especially with a unit like The Pathfinders. It wasn't quite how they'd imagined it when they'd sent me off to Welbeck. Back then there had been little chance of me seeing any action, or of Britain going to war. Still, it was great to have Christmas at home with them all.

The call came early the next morning, Boxing Day.

It was Lenny. 'Get back to Camp. We're going today.'

*

CHAPTER TWENTY-ONE

I did the drive back at breakneck speed on icy roads, but at least they were deserted. What other lunatics were going to be out on Boxing Day? Every sane person was eating curried turkey and watching *Mary Poppins*. I got to Camp, helped throw the last of the gear into the 'Pinkies', as we call our desert-adapted Land Rovers, and we drove onto the waiting C130s.

It was that quick and simple. Within hours of getting Lenny's call we were airborne, en route to an elite forces base in the Middle East, our stepping-stone to Afghanistan. We were sixteen in all: two patrols of six blokes, in two pairs of Land Rovers, plus the HQ element with Lenny in charge.

Mark Jackson was also with us, though how he'd managed to bluff his way on was anyone's guess. Sadly, he'd been injured in a skydiving accident. He was hobbling around the PF lines waiting for a hip replacement, but all credit to him that he'd blagged a place on the Afghan team as Quartermaster.

After a long but uneventful flight we landed in Oman and made our way to the British base. It was here that Lenny gave us our first detailed briefing on the coming mission.

'As you know Kabul has fallen, but there is zero US or British presence in the Afghan capital right now. A British general has been earmarked to set up ISAF – the International Security and Assistance Force – to fill the security vacuum, but right now they've got zero intel. It's our job to go in and get it.

'The SAS and the SBS are with the Northern Alliance, calling in air strikes as they push the Taliban and Al Qaeda into the mountains,' he continued. 'As the country is landlocked the only way in for us is by air. So, we'll fly into Bagram Airbase, on the outskirts of Kabul, and we'll be first into the city. Our tasking is to establish an intel and security picture in Kabul from scratch.

'There are thought to be rival warlords and militias scattered around the city, but nobody really knows for sure. There have been decades of internecine fighting in the city, even prior to the arrival of the Taliban, so in short pretty much anyone could be in there right now. We need to build up some ground truth, and fast, so that the general knows what he's getting into.'

The mission was a peach and the kind of thing The Pathfinders lived and breathed for.

We flew onwards to Afghanistan and put down at Bagram Airbase, then formed up in our convoy of vehicles for the road move into Kabul. We'd have to stick to the roads, for off-road there were scores of minefields most of which weren't even marked. As we set off into the night there were snowcapped mountains to either side of us gleaming eerily in the moonlight, and it was bitterly cold. It was the Afghan winter, hence the freezing conditions.

As we pushed ahead towards Kabul I was scanning my arcs with the GPMG. Up ahead I could see Lennie in the rear of the lead wagon, doing the same with his 50-cal. The terrain we were pushing into might have been cleared of the Taliban, but right now neither the British nor the US forces had people on the ground here. Bagram Airbase was about as much as they held.

Our vehicles were painted a light shade of pink, hence the name 'Pinkies'. Ever since David Stirling's SAS had taken the fight to the German and Italian forces, during the North Africa campaign of the Second World War, pink has been the colour of choice for desert-adapted vehicles. Pale pink was found to be the colour that best blended in with the desert, though right now I was wondering whether we wouldn't have been better off with snow-adapted vehicles.

It was bitterly, bitterly cold, and by the time we'd reached the outskirts of Kabul my ears were frozen stiff. We headed for Wazir Akbar Khan, the so-called 'embassy district'. Right now the city was pitch dark, silent and deserted, and not a thing could be seen moving out there. We pulled to a halt at a Soviet-looking block of buildings, which turned out to be an abandoned schoolhouse.

This was now PF headquarters. We chucked all of our kit into this one, bare, concrete-floored room and erected some camp beds. Sheer luxury. Luckily, one of the PF blokes had had the foresight to bring them, knowing we had the vehicles to carry them and that we'd likely be here for some time.

Matt Bacon, my old M&S brother from Sandhurst, had been parachuted in from Army intelligence to act as our intel liaison. We linked up with him at the schoolhouse, and it was great to see him. If nothing else it brought back fond memories of a blonde stripper in the Sandhurst bar unleashing lashings of sprayable cream.

'All right, mate, fucking blast from the past!' Matt exclaimed, just as soon as we'd clapped eyes on each other. 'Glad you're finally with the PF.'

He proceeded to brief us on what he knew, which was just about bugger all. 'I'll be honest, we've got zero intel right now. There are some scrappy bits of info from MI6, but it's fuck all use, as per usual. Bunch of useless fucking spooks that they are. Need to send in the real boys, so you lot can figure out exactly what's going on here.'

That was about the entirety of Matt's intel briefing. That done, Lenny set about giving us our taskings. He'd carved up Kabul into two, equal halves. Gavin's patrol was given the south of the city, while we got the north, though none of us had a clue which might be the better of the two gigs. It was just after first light by now, so Lenny sent us out directly into the city.

My first impression of Kabul – now that we had some light to see by – was that this was like nowhere I had ever seen on earth. It made Sierra Leone look like a Butlin's holiday camp. Everywhere we went the city was shot to pieces. This wasn't shot to pieces in the normal Pristina or Freetown sense of the phrase: buildings weren't bullet-riddled. Instead, whole neighbourhoods had simply ceased to exist. They had been blasted into flattened wastelands, entire streets pounded into nothing but rubble and dust.

Kabul was shot to pieces in the sense of the London Blitz, which was just what it reminded me of now. I couldn't seem to see a single building that didn't have at least one RPG-round or cannon hole blown into it, not to mention the shrapnel scars. Many areas were deserted ghost towns, and in places stray dogs seemed to be all that were moving. At first I couldn't understand what they survived on. Then I saw a pack of them tearing apart a human corpse.

This then was a city where the dogs were left to eat the dead.

To reach this level of devastation and savagery rival forces must have been at war with each other for a very, very long time, and indeed they had. Prior to the Taliban seizing control, there had been as many as six warlords battling it out for the control of Kabul. And they had used all possible measures to do so – including Russian-made Grads (multiple rocket launchers) and heavy armour.

Prior to that, the Soviet Red Army had occupied Afghanistan, and it was the Red Army that the warlords – then united in name at least as the Mujahideen – had fought to drive out of the city. But as soon as they'd driven out the Soviets they had turned on each other. The battle proper for control of the city had begun, and most of the devastation had been caused by rival warlords blowing each other's forces, and the city, to smithereens.

I noticed the occasional stick-thin male in dirty robes scurrying here and there, but there were no women that I could see. It wasn't your average Afghan civvies that we were interested in, anyway. Our key focus of interest was the status of the warlords, the militias they controlled, and what kind of claim they had staked to what parts of the city. The only way to find out seemed to be to drive around the streets of Kabul until we found them, and to ask.

We came across a group of dodgy-looking blokes hanging around on a street corner, all armed with AK47s or worse. They looked as if they were guarding the building to their rear, which had the typical Afghan thick and high mud walls – ones which effectively stop you from being able to see inside, and provide a great defensive perimeter.

We knew of the Mujahideens' reputation as fighters, and that they had once driven out the Soviet Red Army, so we knew to respect these guys as warriors. The radio station, the TV and all of the newspapers were down, so the gunmen on the street were likely as clueless about us as we were about them.

We stopped to speak to that first group, though without any terps there was only so much we could say to each other.

'Russian?' one of the Muj asked. 'Ruski? Ruski?'

I guess it was pretty clear that we weren't Americans, driving around in our pink Land Rovers as we were. They had six white guys packed into jeeps turn up on their doorstep, and they presumed the Russians were back. It was a fair one, really.

The Muj bloke was speaking to Bob, the driver on our wagon. He did have very white skin and very clear blue eyes, and there was more than a hint of the Eastern European about him.

Bob shook his head. 'No, no, no, no, no. No Ruski.'

'Americani? Americani?' the Muj tried again.

'No, no, no. English. England. Great Britain.'

The Muj had a look on his face like he didn't have a clue what Bob was on about. As far as he was concerned if you were white and you drove around Afghanistan bristling with guns, you were either Russian or American. We clearly needed a terp, or we weren't going to get very far with the present tasking.

Everywhere we went in Kabul there were gunmen. All across the city the atmosphere was tense as hell and febrile. It was clear that things could go either way right now: either we got some forces in to stabilise the situation, or it would all kick off. Kabul was a chaotic, war-blasted ruin, so what the hell there was to fight for Lord only knew. But there was every chance of it going very, very noisy very soon.

Whenever we stopped and we did manage to get a snippet of sense out of someone, there were always conflicting claims as to who controlled what parts of the city. Some would insist their leader was in control of one neighbourhood, then we'd turn a corner and get a counter claim. But slowly, piece by piece we started to build up a picture regarding the different sectors of the city.

Occasionally, we were invited into a 'warlord's' home, though when we got there none of them seemed to be that well-armed, or even to have that many fighters under them. We were obliged to sit and eat with them – invariably curried goat and rice – and if they were seriously top-notch they'd pull out a couple of cans of Coke, which seemed to be a special gift reserved for foreign guests.

Each one would proceed to claim that all the destruction and death had been caused by a rival. The Pashtuns would claim that the Uzbeks were responsible. The Uzbeks would claim it was all the fault of the Pashtuns. It was clear they were going to try to manipulate the situation, in an attempt to settle old scores. It was also pretty obvious that these guys were small fry. We hadn't even touched upon the big guys, those with the power and clout to really matter.

After days living on British Army rations we finally cracked and bought some of the local naan-like bread. It proved gorgeous and that became a staple of our diet. But the fresh fruit and veg that was for sale on the occasional roadside stall that had sprung up was a complete no-no. It was grown in the gutters, and it would render you sick as a dog for days.

'Anyone for a nice shiny red apple?' Ginge would call out, as we drove past some fruit and veg growing in a shit-filled, roadside gutter.

'Get away! Get away! It's poison.'

We were a week in when Matt Bacon briefed us on a more

interesting kind of a proposition. 'Right, there's this one place we've really got lock-on with right now. There's this fucking huge fortress on the western side of the city. No one's been in there, or made contact with the bloke who controls whatever goes on in there, but he's got a lot of guys under him, that's for sure.

'We've got no recent satellite imagery or photos and even the old shit we do have doesn't tell us much. It just shows a mass of bombed-out shit: Russian tanks; vehicles; plus loads of weapons ... Oh, and loads of blokes running about with guns. So, no surprises – we want you lot to drive out there and make contact with whoever's in the fortress and say hello. Get eyes on the place and his blokes and report back to us. Something like that, anyway.'

By now we'd been allocated a terp. Ali was a frail, camp-looking Kabul University student, who came complete with a side-parting and a thin moustache. He spoke good English and ostensibly he was a happy, smiley chappy. But inside you could tell he was hurting. Like so many Afghans in Kabul he'd suffered years of stress, unhappiness and trauma. God only knew the things he had seen.

Up until now he'd seemed happy enough that he was allowed to shave again, with the Taliban gone. We were also paying him a whacking great wage by Afghan standards, and that helped. But as Matt explained our mission to go speak to the mystery warlord in his fortress, the colour had drained from Ali's face. I figured he knew something about our warlord, and it wasn't all good.

We mounted up the Pinkies, with Ali perched on the rear of Gall's wagon, and unarmed. He was looking decidedly unhappier by the minute. I leaned across from our vehicle to have a word. Predictably, he'd earned the nickname 'Mr Bean'.

'Mr Bean, what's the score with this place we're going to then?'

Ali shrugged. 'Big warlord lives there. Very big warlord.'

'You have prior experience of him?'

But Ali had clammed up. On the 'big warlord' front he just didn't seem to want to be drawn. Strictly speaking he was an interpreter, not an intelligence source, so there was only so far we could push him. All the same, it wasn't particularly encouraging.

As we set off towards the western side of the city Ali looked like he was crapping himself, and I could sense the tension in the air. Right now we were still the only 'coalition' troops in the city, so if it all went tits-up it wasn't as if we had a Quick Reaction Force (QRF) to call upon as back-up. There just wasn't anyone else here.

It crossed my mind that Al Qaeda and the Taliban didn't particularly want us in this country, or their capital city for that matter. In fact, for all we knew this fortress might be the hiding place of Mullah Omar – the Taliban's founder – himself. The one-eyed Mullah might be hiding right under our noses and we'd be none the wiser until us lot blundered in there.

We were two wagons, so six blokes, and one unarmed Afghan terp. From the little Matt had been able to tell us, we reckoned the warlord had between 50 and 60 fighters under him plus who knew what kind of weaponry. Nice.

The fortress hove into view. It consisted of four massive mud walls, each some 300 yards long. At each corner I could see the silhouettes of watchtowers, and the fighters manning them. As we pulled into the shadow of the fortress, I could see that the walls were topped with battlements, forming a line of jagged teeth on the skyline above us.

The place reminded me of my dad's *Lawrence of Arabia* movie. It looked to be as old as the hills. Yet somehow it had remained largely untouched by the decades of war that had wreaked such havoc across this city. It was ominous and unsettling. What kind of power could have kept it safe during all of that savage infighting?

We approached the entrance – a pair of massive wooden gates studded with iron. A thick railway sleeper was laid across them to keep them barred shut. Two blokes were stood guard before the gates. One had an AK47, the other an RPG. Each was dressed the same: traditional Afghan flat hats – pakuls – above big beards and wiry, war-bitten faces. They looked very much the real deal.

We pulled to a halt. 'Open fucking sesame ...' muttered Gall. He turned to our terp. 'Tell them we're British soldiers, and we're here from ISAF – not that ISAF will mean much ... Tell them we're here to speak to their boss, so can they let us in, please.'

Ali translated. All he got in response was a blank, empty look and a shrug of the shoulders. They clearly didn't have a clue what ISAF was, and indeed why should they?

'I don't like the look of this fucking place,' H muttered.

It was stating the obvious, but someone had to say it.

'Tell them we're from Fedex with an urgent delivery,' Ginge suggested.

But no one was particularly laughing, least of all the couple of bearded blokes barring the entrance way.

'Tell them we represent the American and British forces in Afghanistan,' Gall tried again. 'Tell them we're here to meet with and speak to their boss. Basically we're the biggest guys on the block with the biggest guns ...'

Ali translated and the gate guards looked distinctly unimpressed. They had a walkie-talkie type radio, and one of them spoke a few words into it. After a few moments a small door in the gate swung open and a figure emerged. The guards said a few words to him and he hurried inside. He looked to be some kind of a runner, and presumably he was taking a message to the big man.

For several long minutes we waited. The guards seemed unconcerned by our presence and very disciplined, not to mention self-confident. I had a horrible suspicion they knew something that we didn't, and if we had known it we probably wouldn't have come here. My finger was heavy on the safety catch of the GPMG, and I'd noticed Lennie slip his makeshift safety catch out of the 50-cal.

Unlike most modern machine guns the 50-cal has no safety, but the PF had got into the habit of improvising one. If you slipped an expended shell casing under the trigger mechanism, it would prevent the weapon from firing accidentally – say if you jolted across an unexpected patch of rough ground. Lennie had just removed his, and I could sense we had itchy trigger fingers all around.

Long before the gates finally opened I'd felt the hairs on the back of my neck going up horribly. They swung inwards with a hollow creaking, and a couple of Afghans on motorbikes were there to receive us like some kind of an outrider force. They pulled ahead as we nosed through, their AK47s bouncing about on their slings as they rode across the rough ground.

I glanced to either side of me. Immediately to our left was a large, concrete block building and it was there that the riders were taking us. Directly across from the gate was another watchtower, so that was at least five that I'd seen. We pulled to a halt at the concrete structure, which was built onto the outer wall of the fort and was decidedly bunker-like in appearance.

I reckoned there were maybe six watchtowers in all, and each was manned by two or three blokes. Most were armed with AK47s and RPGs, but there was at least one DShK positioned on one of the towers. The DShK is the Russian equivalent of our own 50-cal heavy machine gun. It can only fire on automatic, and it unleashes its big, armour-piercing rounds at the rate of 600 a minute.

Its 12.7 mm bullets can chew their way through walls and trees, and a direct hit from one of those would take your head clean off. It was a devastating weapon when used against aircraft, or lightly armoured vehicles, and it'd make mincemeat out of our soft-skinned Pinkies. One round of 12.7 mm tracer into the fuel tank of our wagon, and that'd be Bob, Ginge and me nicely done for.

Right before us there were twenty blokes lounging about around the concrete bunker. All were wearing traditional Afghan robes – so there was not the slightest sign of any military uniforms – and the air was awash with a thick haze of ganja smoke. No one was menacing us with their weapons just yet, so I kept the GPMG low, but still I really did not want to be there.

I'd counted forty Afghan fighters at least, and those were only the ones that I could see. There were bound to be more in the buildings. Gall got down from the lead Pinkie and called Mr Bean. I saw the terp half stumble, as his legs practically gave out under him. Gall was trying to keep it friendly, but the atmosphere was knife-edge tense and Mr Bean was clearly finding it all too much.

Three blokes came wandering over to our wagon. One was cradling an RPG in his arms. He came up to me and held it out as if he wanted to show it to me. I could tell from his pupils that he was high as a kite on whatever he'd been smoking.

I tried a smile. 'Yeah. RPG-7. Nice. Know it well.'

He leant the RPG launcher with the grenade attached against the side of the Pinkie. He pointed to my SA80, which was strapped to the vehicle beside me. He said a few words, and his face was all smiles. Pally-like. I could get the gist of it, even without understanding the words: *That's your weapon; this is mine; nice, eh?*

He lifted the RPG and removed the grenade, as if he was trying to show me how it worked. Then in a flash he'd reached inside and grabbed my SA80. I realised that he'd just disarmed the RPG and got hold of my assault rifle, which was bombed up with a full mag. Worse still, I'd have to swing the GPMG around ninety degrees and depress it to the max to be able to engage him.

It was then that he lifted my SA80 and pointed it at my head.

I knew my weapon was made ready with a round in the chamber. We'd never go out on ops any other way. It had a safety catch, which I knew was on. I doubted if he knew where it was, for it was in an odd place compared to an AK47 or an M16. Whether he could work it out depended on how experienced he was with weapons, but I had to presume that he knew his guns.

I saw the other Afghans perk up mightily at seeing this. There was a clatter of weaponry, as AK47s were raised and hefted generally in our direction.

The guy kept the SA80 pointed at my head and started to yell: 'YALLA! YALLA! YALLA! YALLA! YALLA!'

'Yalla' didn't particularly need much translating. It was clearly the Afghan equivalent of 'let's get it on'.

He kept yelling like a madman. He was violent and aggressive and his eyes were bulging in their sockets. I knew for sure this was a hostage-taking situation unfolding before us right now. He was trying to provoke me into showing fear and vulnerability, and to force me down from the wagon. He'd seized the initiative, and was very likely trying to show his boss that they could take us.

By now Gall had been surrounded by a jostling crowd of the Afghans, though he dwarfed them all. For a long moment everyone seemed to freeze, as we waited to see who would be first to flinch or pull the trigger.

And still the guy kept yelling in my face: 'YALLA! YALLA! YALLA!'

If I showed fear, he'd know he could win this. But either way, we were in a shit situation now. With Gall out of the wagon, it wasn't even as if we could floor the accelerators and try and drive and fight our way out of this one.

I glanced over at Ali, the terp. 'Tell him he can have the weapon. It's a piece of shit anyway. I'll have his RPG.'

As I said it I leaned over, grabbed the RPG launcher, unhooked the grenade from where he had tucked it into his belt and settled back into my seat. In one smooth movement I slid the grenade onto the launcher, and patted it happily.

'Much better ... Tell him to keep the SA80. It's a gift. British. Crap. No problem.'

I could see that the Afghan was feeling stupid now. I'd got his RPG, and he'd got my assault rifle. He was on the wrong end of the exchange. Then I saw his trigger finger move forward and flick off the safety. Inside my heart was thumping insanely, as the adrenaline spiked massively. I was staring down the barrel of a weapon pointed at my head by a doped-up Afghan, and it was my own gun.

I forced myself to hold the crazy bastard's stare. I steeled myself to show no fear. For a long second we stared each other out, as each tried to psyche out the other. Then I heard a voice shout something from the entranceway of the bunker. I didn't understand the words, but the voice had the ring of authority.

I saw the Afghan's gaze falter for an instant, and his grip relaxed slightly on the SA80. In that instant I levelled the RPG. Now things were evened up a little. I heard the authoritative voice yell out another few words of some kind. The Afghan vacillated for an instant, then dropped the muzzle of my assault rifle and tried a forced smile.

He held the weapon out to me, butt-forwards. The gesture was clear: *Here's your rifle. Can I have my RPG?* We exchanged weapons, but all the while I didn't take my eyes off the fucker. It had been that close to kicking off – which pretty much meant me getting a bullet in the head at point-blank range, or unleashing an RPG down his throat, depending on who got the drop on the other. Even with the weapons down, the atmosphere remained tense and volatile as hell.

SA80 and RPG lowered, Gall went forward to speak with the big man – the bloke who'd ordered his bloke to stand down. He certainly looked the part of the Afghan warlord. He was about as big as 00-Joe in terms of build, but it was mostly fat. His black beard fell halfway down his ample gut, and his creamy robe was wrapped around and around him in thick, self-important folds.

He looked as if he'd been involved in just about every battle there had ever been here in Kabul, and every other Afghan in that fortress was clearly shit-scared of him – including, of course, Ali our terp. He was obviously very surprised to see us lot pitch up at his castle, but he was trying not to show it.

He offered Gall some tea and via Ali's good offices they had a bit of a chinwag. The chat was over in ten minutes, through all of which time the guys on our side never once took their eyes off the guys on the other, or their hands off their weapons.

Then Gall was back in the lead wagon, we fired them up and got ourselves the fuck out of there. As we turned through the massive gates and pushed out onto the highway, Bob turned to me.

'That, mate, was a fucking close call. Well bloody done for keeping calm in there ...'

We headed back to the schoolhouse. We delivered a full report on what we'd seen and heard – including numbers of fighters in the fort and their weaponry. We illustrated this with sketch-maps of the place, identifying the key gun-emplacements and other fortifications. No one seemed to know whose side the warlord was on, but if it did come to full-on confrontation with the bloke, at least now we had the low-down on how best to take his fortress.

There was a strange sense of euphoria amongst the six of us that evening – well, seven, including Mr Bean. I felt as if I was on this massive high, as did several of the others. It was the sheer, unadulterated relief of still being alive. And it was a feeling that I was going to learn to know and love well, as further operations went down with The Pathfinders.

We'd been in Kabul for ten days when we got our orders to extract. By now every man and his dog was getting onto the ground in Kabul, which usually meant it was time for us to get ourselves gone. Norwegian and Swedish Special Forces had arrived, though oddly their governments seemed reluctant to let them go out on the streets. It was left up to 2 PARA, who had just been flown in to theatre, to get out there doing their distinctive foot patrols.

There were more Afghans on the streets now, including some women. It was clear that the situation had turned. For now at least, the various factions in Kabul had decided to opt for peace. We'd built up a good intel picture of who most of the key players were, including the Big Guy in his impregnable fortress – which in fact wasn't so impregnable now that we'd been across it.

Baz and I got called in to see Lenny, and we were told we were getting flown from Kabul pretty much direct to California. That was where the PF ran their High Altitude Parachute Course, and we were about to head off there to do our HALO and HAHO cadres.

'Dave, is your dental up to scratch?' Lenny asked me.

When skydiving from 30,000 feet the intense pressure and airspeeds can cause you problems with your teeth, especially if any were vaguely dodgy. I did have a wisdom tooth that had been causing me a few problems.

'Got a wisdom tooth that's been causing me a bit of gip,' I told Lenny.

'Best get 'em all pulled. Go see the Army dentist. There's bound to be one with the 2 PARA lot.'

And so it was that I had all my wisdom teeth ripped out in Kabul, prior to heading to sunny California to learn how to jump from the very roof of the world.

CHAPTER TWENTY-TWO

We mounted up the C130 Hercules as two patrols of six, laden down with our specialist HAHO gear. When doing a High Altitude High Opening jump such as we were tonight, we'd drift for dozens of kilometres under the vast expanse of our BT80 parachute system. For much of that time we'd be surrounded by a freezing mass of air, one that was all but bereft of oxygen.

To give this some context, we'd be jumping at an altitude higher than the peak of Everest. Mountaineers need specialised breathing equipment and extreme cold weather gear to survive at such extreme altitude. We needed the same to do a HAHO jump, but with the added burden of having to carry all our food, weaponry, water and ammo for the coming mission.

The BT80 is basically a massive oblong of silk, one that is perfectly designed to fly 90 kilos of bloke slung beneath it, plus 60 kilos of war-fighting gear. It's a durable yet delicate piece of kit, and in a HAHO jump it could keep us airborne for forty minutes or so. Each of us had a parachuting helmet clamped onto our heads, an oxygen mask strapped over our faces, an oxygen bottle fixed to our front, plus the BT80 para-pack and our Bergens strapped to our rear.

It is all but impossible to walk with such a massive amount of bulk and weight on your person, so we shuffled awkwardly up the C130's open ramp like a flock of zombie penguins. Our progress was made even more ponderous by our bulky Gore-Tex jackets, which were designed specifically for high-altitude jumps. They were made from an ultra-thick outer layer that was windproof and waterproof, with internal insulation to provide a good degree of warmth.

It was late February 2003 by now, and I'd been with the PF for just over a year. In the spring of 2002 I'd been made the 2IC of the unit, and right now we were preparing for what seemed inevitable – Iraq. We'd been warned off to deploy, and there was every chance we'd be going into Iraq by HALO or HAHO means – hence the last-minute rehearsals, so as to fine-tune our techniques for going to war.

As 2IC of the unit I got the best of both worlds. I got to have my say in the planning of ops, but I also got to go out with my patrol on the ground. Happy days. Jason was the second-in-command of my six-man patrol and he was also the most experienced parachutist. He was a squat, powerful, Popeye look-alike who'd knocked out most of his teeth playing rugby. He was invariably the last on a platoon run, but he was unbeatable when tabbing under a crushing load.

Right now Jase had the worst job of the lot of us. As a Tandem Master he was carrying another person on this HAHO jump. Jason's human cargo was a guy from the British Army's electronic warfare (EW) specialist unit – the LEWT. The Light Electronic Warfare Team is a small, bespoke unit within 14 Signals, and they specialise in locating and countering enemy electronic warfare capabilities.

With war in Iraq looming this had become a key priority, for the Iraqi military were known to have good EW capabilities. EW is aimed at intercepting and potentially blocking any comms capabilities of an adversary. If the Iraqis could do this to us, we'd be a tiny team of Pathfinders dropped behind enemy lines, and with no way to make comms back to headquarters.

Our LEWT bloke carried with him a magic box of tricks. It

included direction-finding kit, which allowed him to pick up enemy signals and locate exactly where they were coming from, plus jamming gear. It scanned the usable frequencies, picked up the enemy transmissions, pinpointed their position of origination, and recorded what the enemy was saying.

Phenomenal.

This was largely offensive EW as opposed to defensive. It would allow us to locate enemy positions with great accuracy and to read the enemy's intentions, and that in turn would help us steer around them as we made our way to the mission objective. What the LEWT bloke didn't have was the ability to parachute from 30,000 feet deep into enemy territory – hence that was why Jase had to fly him in.

Our LEWT attachment was a nice enough guy, but as you can imagine with a bloke who spent his time punching keys and twiddling dials, he was something of a geek. He was scrawny, ginger-haired and goggle-eyed, and there was something about his look that suggested he wasn't quite all there. But he was clearly a fantastic LEWT operator and abnormally intelligent with it.

His real name was Ken Carruthers, but we'd nicknamed him Ken Barlow, after the *Coronation Street* character of that name.

Someone had asked: 'Where's the Interesting Bloke?'

Someone else had said: 'Who?'

'Ken Barlow.'

And that was it, the name had stuck.

We'd gone through the long ritual of strapping on all our HAHO gear – and fixing most of the same onto him – and Ken had kept asking us all sorts of eager questions about what this did and what that was for. We'd have to nursemaid the bloke through any mission into Iraq, but not when it came to communications intercepts: he was the unchallenged master of that universe.

HAHO was a jump technique that had only recently been pioneered. The Army's Cougar personal radios had been adapted so we could wear an earpiece inside our jump helmets, so as to maintain comms between each other as we fell. They had around a two-kilometre range, which was more than enough to stay in touch while in the air, for you'd never space your jump stick that far apart.

We also carried a navigation board – a piece of metal around the size of a laptop fastened around our waists. It carried a compass, plus an SPGPRS – a GPS system that was encrypted so that it couldn't be jammed by the enemy. The night vision goggles (NVG) that flipped down from our helmets were another vital bit of kit, for a HAHO jump would almost always be done at night and under cover of darkness.

On the rear of the helmet we each had an infrared (IR) firefly, one that would flash when switched on. It was only visible via NVG, which meant that we could see each other as flashing IR strobes as we drifted through the darkness, but we'd be invisible to the enemy (that's unless he happened to be scanning the night sky with infrared-capable night vision kit, which was unlikely).

At 2100 hours the C130 got airborne and set a course over the North Sea. The aim of tonight's exercise was to jump from extreme high altitude and drift for dozens of kilometres across the water and into the UK, landing just to the south of Sculthorpe, in Norfolk. This meant we were going to fly under our chutes further than the distance across the English Channel, crossing a sovereign nation's border presumably without anyone noticing.

In the UK the further north you go the less air traffic there is, hence the choice of Sculthorpe for the landing. Sculthorpe Aerodrome generally proved to be a conveniently quiet and deserted place to put down, and this was where our elite units did much of their HAHO jump training. Tonight the designated impact point (IP) was a patch of open grass sandwiched between two runways.

There was no landing on water when doing a HAHO jump, or at least not for us. That kind of stuff was the domain of the Special Boat Service, and you'd actually do a low-level jump into the sea. The drill if we did ditch in the sea was to jettison all the heavy gear that would drown you. We'd lose the Bergen by pulling an emergency relief lever that cut it away completely, undo the chest straps and leg straps and get out of our parachute harness.

You'd normally have your Bergen lined with a black canoe bag – a tough, waterproof sealable sack more normally used by canoers to store kit on their boats. One of those used to line the pack served a double purpose: no matter how soaking wet your Bergen might be it kept your kit dry, and if you did go down in the sea it turned your pack into a flotation device. You'd hold onto your Bergen so as to keep afloat and wait to be rescued.

As the Hercules powered across the ocean it was black as pitch inside the aircraft. I could follow our progress on my SPGPRS, and plot it on the map, but once we'd jumped there would be no map-reading any more. Trust me, it just isn't possible to get a map out and read it while drifting under a parachute. Instead, we'd use the GPS to steer us into the DZ, with the compass as a back-up.

Trouble was, there were two blokes on tonight's jump who didn't have navigation boards, for there weren't enough to go around. We'd requested more, but the Army had failed to provide them. Normally, you all follow the stick-leader into the DZ, so it isn't critical for every bloke to have a nav board. But if we did get separated in the air those two blokes were going to have problems.

We'd been in the air a good hour by the time we got the signal to make ready. The Parachute Dispatchers (PDs) – RAF guys whose job it is simply to get blokes like us into their parachuting-gear and out of the aircraft – helped us to our feet, and guided us towards the rear ramp. We'd been breathing off the Herc's own oxygen tank during the flight, but now we had to do the quick switch to our own.

I reached the open ramp and bunched up close with the guys in my patrol. Jase would go first – with Ken Barlow strapped to his front – for he was stick-leader. Tricky was in my six-man patrol, and being a super-experienced HAHO/HALO guy he'd take up the rear, making sure every bloke had got out. I was sandwiched in the middle, with the rest of my patrol – Steve, Joe and Dez – to either side of me.

When doing vehicle ops, Steve was my driver and Tricky the rear-gunner on my vehicle. My place was in the passenger's – or vehicle commander's – seat, behind a bonnet-mounted GPMG. Steve was a laid-back, slick operator with dark, Italian good looks. He was the Pathfinder's Armourer, so he sure knew his guns. He was also a very funny bloke, and he never ever stopped talking about his real passion in life – women.

Jase commanded the other vehicle, with Dez as his driver. Dez was a Royal Electrical and Mechanical Engineers bloke and the Army was his life. He was covered in tattoos from all of the units he'd ever served with. He was also a bit of a cleanliness freak, which made him something of a misfit in the PF, for you couldn't afford too much soap and washing when undertaking the kind of ops we did. He was a decent bloke though, and a total wizard with the vehicles.

Joe, the last man in my patrol, was the youngest bloke in The Pathfinders. He looked it, too. He had a spiky-haired, boyish look to him, with these wide sea-green eyes. We weren't even sure if he'd done enough soldiering to qualify for the PF. You had to have served a minimum of three years to be able to go for selection, and most had served closer to six. Whatever, Joe had passed selection and that made him one of us.

The pilots were flying on 'black light' – so with the aircraft totally dark. The interior of the Herc's hold was a mass of shadows, as the wind from the open ramp roared around my ears. Above us there was a thick bank of cloud cover, which obscured any moon or stars. Below us there was only the cold expanse of the North Sea. It was utterly empty and devoid of any lights or the slightest sign of life.

I took a step closer towards the howling void. Nothing. Swirling darkness. There were only seconds to the 'go' now, and I had my eyes glued to the red bulbs glowing faintly to either side of the aircraft. Jason's squat form had the LEWT bloke held tight up against him, as he shuffled closer to the ramp. All I could see of them was a dim silhouette against the jump lights.

From one side of us the PD yelled: 'Tail off for equipment check!'

From the back of the line Tricky yelled 'SIX OKAY!' He whacked Joe on the back, just to make sure he'd got the message. The move and the shout rippled down the line – 'Five okay! Four okay! Three okay!' – until it reached Jason at the front. *Everyone in our stick was good to go.*

We shuffled tighter. Too much space as we jumped would result in too much separation in the sky, and we might lose each other. We stood on the very edge of the ramp, icy gusts buffeting and rocking us, and trying to rip us out of the aircraft.

The green light flashed on and the PD bloke stepped backwards: 'GO! GO! GO!'

Jason forced the LEWT guy forwards and suddenly they were gone. Further figures plummeted into the darkness. I jumped, hit the C130's slipstream and felt the powerful blast trying to flip and twist me around. An instant later the static line triggered my parachute, there was a crack like a ship's canvas filling with wind and the chute blossomed above me.

I counted in my head: one thousand, two thousand, three thousand … Craning my neck to check on the chute I grabbed the steering toggles which sit around shoulder height, and pulled them hard: One! Two! Three! I could feel the air pumping into the canopy, as it billowed and spread above me, the individual sections trapping the thin air and increasing the rigidity of the chute.

I glanced at my feet and further into the night. My eyes searched for Jase but I couldn't seem to see him anywhere, so I flicked down my NVG, switched to IR mode and scanned the night. Right below me there was the faintly flashing strobe of Jason's IR firefly marking his position. I pressed the light button on my SPGPRS. You can't read the GPS with the night vision goggles down, so I flicked them up a bit until I could see under them like a pair of reading glasses.

The GPS was displaying a clear dotted line stretching from where we were now at our release point to the impact point (IP) – the exact place where we intended to land. I could afford to leave the power running on the GPS, for at this altitude no one would be able to see us from the ground, and via the gizmo's faintly glowing screen I could easily track our progress into the IP.

As far as I knew no force had ever HAHOd into war. A year before Special Forces had done a HAHO jump into the Afghan mountains, to find a tactical landing zone (TLZ) for a Hercules. A TLZ was basically a flat bit of usable ground that a C130 or similar aircraft could put down on. This might well be a training mission, but we were very much preparing to do this for real – to covertly cross an enemy border and drop silently into war. It was all in deadly seriousness.

For the last year we'd been stretching the distances we could cover when gliding under a canopy, and tonight's HAHO was at the limit of what was possible. As the wind rustled by me I tried to keep one eye on Jase below me, and another on Dez, the bloke who was next above me in the stick. In that way, we'd keep the stick together beautifully and follow each other right to the IP.

I figured I was travelling at around 40 knots, which meant another 25 minutes and we'd be at the IP – and that meant another 25 minutes in these totally freezing conditions. I was wearing layer upon layer of cold weather gear below my Gore-Tex HAHO suit, so much so that I felt like the bloody Michelin Man. I even had two pairs of gloves on – a pair of thin, leather aircrewman's gloves under black, insulated Gore-Tex ones. But even so my hands were cramping up with the cold as I kept them on the toggles, minutely adjusting my line of flight to keep right on Jason and Ken Barlow's tail.

We drifted onwards, six blokes alone on the roof of the world. I glanced west, towards where I knew the British coast had to be, but all I could see was the cold and inky darkness. My chute was caught by a blast of wind and I felt tiny ice particles pinging into the exposed skin of my face, each like a tiny needle. At least when we did this in Iraq – *if* we did this in Iraq – it wouldn't be so mind-bendingly cold.

My NVG picked up the first, fiery pinprick of light, away to the west of us and glowing like a drop of molten gold. It had to mark the UK coastline. More lights emerged, blinking away amidst the darkness. I flipped up the NVG, so I could see them more clearly. Any strong light source tended to 'white-out' the NVG, so overpowering it with a blinding glare.

As we grew closer I could make out what looked like individual streets, each lined with the dinosaur-necked silhouettes of glowing street lamps. We were still very high and falling beneath a BT80 didn't actually feel like parachuting at all. It felt more like being in a highly-refined and specialist aerial vehicle.

In theory, we were completely undetectable by any nation's defence systems. Radar bounces off solid and substantial objects, like an aircraft's metal wings or its fuselage. That is how radar detects enemy warplanes far out to sea. With a stick of HAHO parachutists like us, the radar beams would simply bend around our forms and continue on into the night.

Thermal imaging kit would be next to useless. The best such equipment can only penetrate three or four kilometres, and as cold as we were now we'd be throwing off very little body heat, if any. In fact, with all the cold weather gear we were wearing there would be almost zero thermal signature to detect.

We were all but silent as we flew, so there was no risk of anyone hearing us. We were falling under black parachutes and dressed all in black, and with our faces 'blacked-up' with camo cream – so no one would be able to see us, either. HAHO was the ultimate in covert cross-border penetration techniques. Even James Bond hadn't done this kind of shit in the movies. Not yet, anyway.

We approached a thick band of cloud. There was more of it at this altitude, and it was banking up over the coastline. There was no way around it so Jason opted to fly right through. As we slipped into the fluffy white mass of water droplets I checked behind me for Dez. I couldn't see him any more, but by now the cloud vapour was thick all around me. I could feel it condensing on my skin and running down my face in little rivulets.

It reminded me of a recent exercise we'd been on. We'd been giving a bunch of regular troops a good slagging, just as they were giving it back to us. Tricky had put his hand in his pocket and pulled out a bit of balled-up tissue. He'd stared at it in surprise. 'Oh, what's this? Must be some leftover cloud from my last HAHO jump.' It was his way of giving shit to conventional forces, for when did anyone ever get to fly through cloud so you can reach out and grab some?

By the time I came through the far side of the cloud bank I was coated in tiny droplets from head to foot. *And Jesus, was I cold.* I figured we'd flown a good five kilometres in the cloud, but still I picked up Jason almost immediately and right to my front. But when I glanced behind me there was no sign of Dez, or any of the others in my stick.

I pressed 'send' on my radio and spoke into the mouthpiece. 'Dez, it's Dave: where are you?'

Nothing.

I repeated the call.

Still nothing.

We'd lost the rest of the stick and by now they had to be well out of radio range.

I heard Jason's voice come up over the air. 'Dave, we'll crack on for now, get to IP, and we'll re-org on the ground.'

Jase was right. There wasn't much you could do when you'd lost contact with the rest of your stick on a HAHO jump. If you went into a holding pattern, and started to circle about trying to look for them, you could easily crash into each other in the darkness. You'd also lose too much height and miss the IP.

Ten minutes later I saw Jase start spiralling vertically downwards towards the earth. When you land as one person you can run it off, so easing the impact with the ground. When landing as two in a tandem there's no way you can do that. Two blokes strapped together can't exactly run very far.

I heard Jase hit with an almighty whump, and he ended up being thrown forward onto the ground, the LEWT bloke with him. I hit the metal levers which release the Bergen. I felt it drop away, as the pulleys allowed it to fall some 25 metres below me. Like this the pack would hit first, so taking its own weight.

I heard it slam into the ground, then flared out my chute to slow me down. Seconds later my boots connected with the earth. Running forwards a few paces I let the expanse of silk come down and past me to the left, where it bundled itself into the ground. I unslung my assault rifle from my right shoulder and got a bullet up the spout. I was 30 metres from Jase and his LEWT buddy and I was good.

'Mate, ready,' I hissed in his direction.

I could hear them dusting themselves down after their heavy landing, then the clack-clack of guns being made ready. I moved in on their position, for Jase as stick-leader was the muster point for us all. We now had half of the patrol down on the IP.

But as for the rest of the blokes there was no sign of any of them. This wasn't quite what we'd intended. Two patrols had jumped, so twelve of us in all. It turned out that Steve and Tricky had landed several kilometres distant from the IP, for they had run out of altitude after losing us in the thick cloud. Others were scattered even further from the intended point of landing.

Smudge and Dean – both on the other patrol – had come down in just about the worst place possible. They had landed right in the middle of a village. They were the guys who had no SPGPRSs with them. When they'd hit the cloud and lost the bloke they were following they'd had to fly in on a compass bearing only, and take whatever landing zone they could – which turned out to be the village green.

It was a salutary lesson. If we'd been HAHOing in for real, we'd now have one patrol horribly fragmented and very likely on the run, because they'd have landed in an enemy village. Our patrol might well have linked up at an emergency rendezvous (ERV), a meeting point offset from the IP. But there were never any guarantees. HAHO was the ideal means of making a covert, cross-border entry into enemy territory if it went right.

But as tonight's exercise had proved the risks were legion.

*

CHAPTER TWENTY-THREE

The line of tracer squirted into the night sky, lacing a fiery trail across the darkness. It was clearly a signal: *Get ready – they're coming.*

There was nothing worse than driving down a road directly into an enemy ambush, and knowing you were massively outnumbered and outgunned. But that was exactly what we were about to do now, in our three-vehicle Pathfinder patrol. We were lights-off and dark, nine men speeding along a two-lane highway deep in Iraq, and we were about to get smashed.

Some eighteen hours earlier we'd been back near the Kuwaiti border, and we'd been given what for any Pathfinder was the mission of a lifetime. Three hundred kilometres ahead of the British lines lay Qalat Sikar Airfield, a small, run-down airbase deep inside Iraqi territory. Our mission was to get to the airfield, recce and mark it, and call in 1 PARA. They'd fly in on C130s or Chinooks, put down on the runway and in one fell swoop we'd have leapfrogged the Iraqi front line.

Seizing Qalat Sikar would enable British and American forces to by-pass the Iraqi positions and advance on Baghdad. It would be a game-changer in terms of executing the war. We'd been briefed that the surrounding territory at Qalat Sikar was 'relatively benign' – which meant largely free from hostile forces. We'd been briefed that the Iraqi military were generally ill-fed, ill-equipped and demoralised, and poised to surrender in their droves.

At first we'd presumed we were going to HAHO or HALO into Qalat Sikar. It was the ideal means of rapid insertion to seize an enemy airfield. But the British high command must have baulked at us doing a parachute-borne insertion. At the last moment we were ordered to undertake the mission by vehicle, driving our thin-skinned, unarmoured Pinkies the entire route overland.

So here we were, 40 kilometres short of the mission objective and surrounded by the enemy. And in truth, the level of Iraqi resistance had proven far from 'relatively benign'. We'd departed from the British front line and linked up with the US forces at Nasiriyah, a city that lies on the road to Baghdad (and to Qalat Sikar).

At Nasiriyah the US Marine Corps had stumbled into what would become known as 'the mother of all battles'. In taking the city, they'd had their forces ripped apart. They'd lost dozens of Marines killed in action, and suffered many more wounded. In the confusion of the street-to-street fighting, they'd taken 'friendly fire' from their own warplanes and been hit by Iraqi Fedayeen fighters disguised as civilians.

It had been murder in Nasiriyah – so much so that the US Marine Corps' commander had tried to stop us from going forward to achieve our mission.

'Guys, there's no fuckin' way you want to be going north any time soon,' he'd told us.

Like us, the Marine Corps commanders had been told to expect 'little or no resistance'. Instead, they'd stumbled into a ferocious and brutal shitfight that had lasted from dawn until dusk. Two-thirds of the Marine Corps' Charlie Company has been left injured or dead. Alpha and Bravo Companies had fared little better, losing many men and several armoured fighting vehicles.

The mighty US Marine Corps – the iron fist of America's airmobile forces – had been fought to a standstill. Trouble was, we couldn't afford the slightest delay. We'd been ordered to reach Qalat Sikar by 0400 hours, which had left us some twenty hours in which to achieve the mission. 0400 was the scheduled L-hour – landing hour – for 1 PARA, by which time we needed to have the airfield recce'd, cleared of enemy forces and ready to call them in.

So we'd pushed past the US front line and on into the gathering darkness, and that was how we'd ended up here – a few dozen klicks short of the airfield and with the enemy to all sides of us. In the interim we'd driven through three or four Iraqi positions, and passed several of their vehicles on the road. Largely we'd managed to sneak through undetected. The night was dark, the wagons were showing no lights and we were driving on NVG.

But at some stage we must have been rumbled. We'd just managed to evade a hunter force of some 200 Iraqi Fedayeen – a well-armed and mobile militia fiercely loyal to Saddam Hussein. They'd come after us driving fast and heavily armed Toyota pick-ups, forcing us to leave the road and head into the rough terrain. But by now we had enemy to our rear and to our front, and the road ahead to the airfield was closed to us – for it was blocked by the Fedayeen.

It was then that we'd faced the decision of a lifetime.

We knew we couldn't go north, for we'd actually seen the Fedayeen setting up their ambush positions ahead of us on the road. We couldn't go south, because we'd just driven through heavy concentrations of Iraqi forces that had been alerted to our presence. We figured there were some 2000 Iraqi troops in well dug-in defensive positions in that direction.

We couldn't go east or west, because the terrain to either side of us was swampy and impassible. As we'd sat in the darkness talking through our options, it became clear that every which way we were fucked. It was then that I'd suggested we push onwards *on foot*, and try to reach the mission objective that way. But Tricky, Jase and some of the other Old and Bold were adamant that we had to keep the vehicles: they were our mobility and our firepower.

Most likely they'd made the right call.

In the First Gulf War the Bravo Two Zero patrol had been forced to go on the run on foot. They were hounded by Iraqi hunter forces, and only one man managed to escape, the rest being captured or killed. Bravo Two Zero had proved to be a salutary lesson for British Special Forces, and one we were painfully aware of today. And so it was that we'd made the seemingly unthinkable decision to drive back the way we had come, in an effort to link up with the US forces.

Nine against 2000 was hardly promising odds. We were all but certain we were going to die. We'd requested air cover – so that we could use any British or US warplanes that might be available to smash the enemy we now knew were here, and open up a corridor of escape.

It was then that we were told there was no air cover available, and that we were 'on our own'. So certain were we that we were finished, we'd destroyed all our secret equipment and our cryptographic materials – those that allowed us to talk to headquarters in code.

And so we'd headed back to the main highway, turned south and prepared to fight to the last man and the last round. As we'd thundered along that dark road we'd driven into a series of savage ambushes and roadblocks. We were hit by everything the enemy had – from small arms to DShK heavy machine guns, from rocket-propelled grenades to four-barrelled anti-aircraft cannons.

Ours was the third vehicle in the convoy, with Jase taking the lead. He was chucking smoke grenades as we went, to try to hide us from the enemy guns. But even so we'd had RPG rounds skip over our bonnet and explode on the roadside, and I'd seen an RPG go right under the wagon to our front, passing between the front and rear wheels.

At times the volume of fire had been so intense I could feel the pressure waves thrown off by the bullets slamming over us. And all the time we were under fire our wagon and those in front of us had been taking hits. I'd seen the lead wagon smash its way through a roadblock where I'd been convinced the enemy had us. I'd seen Dez, the driver on that wagon, taking on the enemy one-handed with his Browning pistol.

Things had become so desperate that my driver, Steve, had one hand glued to the steering wheel and the other throwing grenades. He'd even managed to take out a roadside bunker that way. At one stage I'd come face to face with an RPG gunner, and blasted him with my GMPG at point-blank range, as he unleashed his grenade right over the very top of our heads.

By the time we limped back into Nasiriyah our Land Rovers were riddled with bullet holes. Several of us had taken rounds, though miraculously no one was badly injured. It was unbelievable that we had managed to fight our way out of there. At first the Marine Corps guys refused to believe where we had just come from and what we had done. They'd seen this massive firefight erupt on the night-dark horizon, only to learn it was the nine of us waging war.

Impossible.

But once we'd got to the Marine Corps' command post – shot-up, totally burned out with exhaustion, plus high on adrenaline and the buzz of making it out of there alive – I was able to pass across to the Marine Corps commander the details of the Iraqi positions that we'd found. In effect, we'd completed a 160-kilometre recce-by-fire. We'd drawn the Iraqi fire, so forcing them to reveal themselves.

I was able to pass across a series of six-figure grids, ones that Jase and I had worked out together. Come sunup, those positions – the key Iraqi defences north of Nasiriyah – were torn apart by US air strikes. That in turn meant that the US Marine Corps were no longer poised to advance against 2000 Iraqi fighters in superb defensive positions, ones that all of our electronic wizardry, satellite imagery and spy planes had failed to detect.

A nine-man British patrol had found them, and while that wasn't our mission objective, in doing so we had saved many American lives. Arguably, we'd also helped change the course of the war, by opening the way for the US advance on Baghdad. But by the time those US air strikes were going in, the nine of us were limping south on the main route leading back to our headquarters.

Several things became clear as a result of the Qalat Sikar mission.

One, the Iraqis were far from ready to surrender. In fact, they seemed more than ready to fight to the death to expel the 'infidel invaders' from their country. Two, if we were to keep operating behind enemy lines we'd need to do so in greater numbers, so as to give us any chance of pulling off our missions.

Shortly after the US forces ran into such resistance at Nasiriyah, British troops hit trouble on the road north-west of the Iraqi town of Ad Dayr, near Basra. A squadron of light tanks from the Household Cavalry had been pushing into the desert, when they stumbled into a mass of hidden Iraqi positions. Hundreds of Iraqi T55 main battle tanks were dug in hull-down in the sands, and skilfully camouflaged to make them all but invisible from the air.

As with the Americans at Nasiriyah, British forces had little idea the enemy were there, for air recces and satellite photos had failed to detect them. During the fierce gun-battle that erupted, the Household Cavalry lads had called in air strikes, but sadly the US warplanes had hit the wrong target. In a tragic blue-on-blue incident an A10 Tankbuster aircraft had repeatedly strafed the British Scimitar tanks, killing one British soldier and wounding three.

At that stage it was clear that we needed proper intel about what was on the ground out there. We needed a force to go in and find and fix the enemy, so warplanes could be called in to hit them. And that, of course, was a classic tasking for The Pathfinders.

A few months before deploying to Iraq Lenny had moved on from being OC Pathfinders. He hadn't wanted to go, but two years was about the maximum you were allowed to do in that post. Our replacement was called John McCall, a bloke I knew well from my 1 PARA days. John had been a fellow PARA officer, and I knew his ambition was to go right to the top of the British Army.

It was late afternoon when John called us in for a briefing. We were based at this abandoned Iraqi military compound to the west of Basra. We had the wagons parked up in this giant hangar, which must once have housed Iraqi trucks and armour. Our Pinkies still had the bullet and shrapnel holes in their thin aluminium sides, but we'd taped them up with green gaffer tape, as a makeshift repair job.

John called my patrol over, together with Geordie's. Geordie was a corporal in the PF who was small, wiry and hard as nails. He was a hugely-experienced operator, having been with the unit for years. He'd yet to see the kind of action that we had in Iraq, so his patrol was getting the lead on this mission. We each of us grabbed a brew and gathered in one corner of the echoing hangar.

'Right, situation,' John began. 'As you may have heard Iraqi resistance north of Basra is proving far more significant than anyone expected ...'

'Nasiriyah revisited,' I interjected.

'Indeed,' said John. 'There are Iraqi positions north of this location that have been actively shelling British forces and an American patrol. British forces can't push any further north until those positions are located and destroyed. Problem is no one knows exactly where they are. That's where you come in.

'As Dave's intimated, the level of resistance at Nasiriyah proved to be completely unexpected, so we will now operate in double patrol strength as much as possible. Geordie – your mission is to find those Iraqi positions in the vicinity of this area,' he pointed to the map, 'with Dave's patrol in support.

'I'll give you approx grid squares afterwards. There is air on-call this time. Air is requestable because American fighter planes are moving directly along the air corridor to your north. However, you need to be very aware of the danger of blue-on-blue, because, as I'm sure you all know, not far from where we are now a US pilot unloaded onto a Household Cavalry recce squadron.'

'Understood,' Geordie confirmed.

'Dave, as I said you're in support on this one. Geordie takes the lead. Your job is to move forward and provide fire support to him, to get him out of the shit, and also to act as a QRF if the situation become anything like Nasiriyah.'

'Got it.'

It made sense. I was glad not to be leading this one. Most of the blokes on my team were still recovering from the nightmare of Qalat Sikar, as was I. I'd position my patrol in overwatch of Geordie's, so ideally on some high ground and with him in range of our machine guns. That way, if he got engaged we could put down covering fire and help him extract.

Mark, the Platoon Signaller, stood up to give the call signs and radio frequencies for the mission.

'Your unit call sign is Maverick. Dave, as you're 2IC Pathfinders you're Maverick One ...'

We finished scribbling down all the details in our notepad, then John rounded off with this.

'Geordie, you'll need to get under way by 2000 hours. That leaves you two hours to plan, back-brief, get some food down you and get on the road. One more thing; on the way through you'll cross our front line, held by 3 PARA. Make sure you liaise with them so they know exactly what routes you'll take in and out of there.'

This was a crucial part of the plan. Crossing back over your own lines is potentially one of the most dangerous moments of any such mission. It was made all the more challenging here in that we had no direct means of making radio contact with 3 PARA, for they were on a different radio net to our own.

'Any questions?' John asked.

There were none.

We returned to the vehicles, and the first thing we did was take a good look at the maps. We were crouched over our battle-worn Pinkies and contemplating yet another tasking which appeared to be borderline insane. The only difference was that by now we knew just how fiercely the Iraqis were going to fight.

When you go through something like we had on the Qalat Sikar mission, it either tears you apart or bonds you closer together. My team felt incredibly tight right now, and I figured the rest of the patrols could sense this about us.

'Jase, tell Geordie to let us know what he wants of us.'

'Boss,' Jase confirmed.

He headed off to have words with Geordie. He was back a minute later. 'Geordie says best to get some scoff on, 'cause we'll be leaving in a bit.'

It was typical Geordie to be taking this all so coolly. He was busy as fuck as he ran around sorting out all his shit so that he could lead this one. But he was a fantastic soldier and he'd never let anything rattle him – not even a mission such as this.

We were being sent into a nightmare here – going up against a network of Iraqi armour and artillery positions, with infantry in support. There were scores of Iraqi T55 tanks perfectly camouflaged in the terrain out there. Each was a 40-tonne monster, boasting 20-centimetre-thick armour. Each had a 100 mm rifled cannon as the main weapon, and as secondaries they were fitted with either two 7.62 mm machine guns, or our old friend the DShK.

We were twelve men in four, thin-skinned Pinkies.

Only yesterday the Iraqi guns had pounded the PARA's front line positions, and they'd also hit a US Special Forces patrol that had been trying to sneak into their territory. And from the maps it was clear they'd chosen their place of hiding very, very well. We would be moving into terrain thick with bush, palm groves and reed beds, which would make for horrendous going.

Our mission was to get eyes on the enemy positions and radio in their co-ordinates. At that moment high command would make a decision whether to call in air strikes or an artillery bombardment from our own heavy guns. It was massively more effective to have men on the ground to call in such attacks. So, we'd have to remain in position to guide in whatever hits were coming.

'Mate, I'll plot some waypoints into my GPS, just in case we need them,' I told Jason. 'Take a look over the route and the terrain and see if you can scope out some fire-support positions for our patrol.'

'Got it.'

'I'll get the hot water on for a boil-in-the-bag,' Steve volunteered. 'Any preferences?'

There was a chorus of voices in reply. 'Anything but fucking Lancashire hotpot. It's minging.'

The six of us shared a quick brew and a scoff over the maps.

'Fucking nightmare terrain,' Jase grunted, through a mouthful of pasta. 'Of all the areas in Iraq, we have to keep fighting in the fucking wet ones. It's going to be impossible to drive cross-country 'cause it's so marshy and overgrown. We'll have to use the main road to get up there, and even when we cross the front line we'll have to stick to farm tracks, or we'll get bogged in, and sticking to the main tracks is a dead bloody giveaway.'

'It's not the Garden of fucking Eden, mate,' Tricky remarked, 'it's the Garden of Hell.'

H appeared. He was going in on this mission as part of Geordie's patrol. 'Anyone for a shiny red apple?'

It had been the catchphrase for our Kabul mission. It got everyone laughing.

We back-briefed John on the plan, and were cleared to go. At 2100 hours we moved off, four wagons probing ahead into the dark and muggy night. We were an hour or so into the mission and nosing our way through seemingly impenetrable terrain, when Geordie practically had a heart attack. He'd suddenly remembered the need to check in with 3 PARA, but we'd already crossed their front line.

The night was black as a witch's tit, with thick cloud scudding across the sky. It blanked out the heavens and made driving on black light and night vision all but impossible. NVGs work by boosting any available light – that thrown off by the moon and the stars. When there wasn't any, they barely worked at all. Somehow we must have snuck past the 3 PARA lads without them seeing us, or us detecting any sign of them.

We stopped for a hushed Chinese parliament – a heads-up amongst all the blokes. Because I had 3 PARA's front line positions waymarked into my GPS, I offered to lead the patrol back to them. That way we could make for their headquarters, warn them of our plans and head back out again. We did an about turn, and crawled our way along this narrow track with our wagon taking the lead.

We were challenged by a 3 PARA sentry who all but opened up on us. Luckily, at the last moment he recognised the silhouettes of the Land Rovers. He directed us towards 3 PARA's forward HQ and we set off in that direction. We took a right turn, and Steve pushed ahead cautiously as he tried to steer a path through the gloom.

And then we went over the edge of an unseen ravine and rolled the wagon.

I passed out with the impact. I came to sometime later with the weight of the wagon on top of me, and in total agony. The Pinkie had landed upside-down in some fetid Iraqi swamp. Being a tall bloke, I had the weight of the wagon driving my head further into the stinking mud, like a hammer pounding a nail. I was trapped, I had water up to my eyeballs, and I felt as if I'd snapped my neck in two.

Tricky crawled under and somehow got a hand to me. As the wagon had rolled everyone else had been thrown clear. I was alone and unable to move, and it was only Tricky digging out a breathing hole that was keeping me alive.

Tricky may have beasted me through selection, but we'd grown close over the year or so that I'd been with the PF. It meant everything to have him there and to hear his voice, and to know that my team was here and trying desperately to rescue me.

Whenever I tried to speak to Tricky the words came out as a choked, gurgling murmur. I could taste the blood and the swamp water that was bubbling up from my lungs. I kept drifting in and out of consciousness.

It sounds like a cliché, but my life started to flash before my eyes. All the happy moments – my dad's cowboy movies, ton-up in Grandpa's Capri, showjumping with my mum, the Sandhurst stripper girl – spooled before my eyes, like scenes from a movie.

This is what they say happens when you are about to die.

The lads were going spare trying to get me out from under the wagon, but there was no way on earth that the eleven of them could lift several tonnes of Land Rover, plus all the war-fighting equipment it was carrying. They tried using the high-lift jacks to lever the wagon upwards, but the base-plates of the jacks simply sank into the soft ground, uselessly.

As the swamp water started bubbling into my nose and mouth, I drifted out of consciousness completely.

Back at 3 PARA's HQ there was total chaos. The area where our wagon had ended up was well within range of the Iraqi guns. Twenty-four hours earlier an American convoy had been shelled and a wagon disabled in this very spot. A specialist truck with a winch and crane system had been called out from the Light Aid Detachment (LAD), part of the Royal Electrical Mechanical Engineers, so as to recover the stricken vehicle.

The LAD team consisted of four blokes, commanded by a Corporal Reuben Boswell. He'd taken his men forward, only for them to come under fierce Iraqi fire as they tried to lift the US vehicle. They'd suffered a good few near misses, as Iraqi shells slammed into the thick bush all around them, and eventually they'd been forced to abandon the task due to the weight of fire.

Corporal Boswell was now back at 3 PARA's forward HQ, watching events unfold. As word had reached 3 PARA that our vehicle had rolled, they'd prepared to send a company forward – so 100 blokes or more – to physically lift the vehicle. The 3 PARA medic – a Territorial Army bloke attached to the unit – had returned to their HQ, having been at the scene of our overturned vehicle. Unbeknown to me he'd slid in alongside Tricky to get a proper look at me, and to assess how I was doing. I was unconscious at the time, so I missed it all.

When he reached 3 PARA HQ, someone asked the medic: 'How long has he got?'

'Only a few minutes now,' he replied.

Upon hearing that Corporal Boswell volunteered to go forward with his Foden recovery truck to see if there was anything he could do. As far as he was concerned that only put his small team at risk, as opposed to an entire company of PARAs.

'It's up to you,' he was told. 'No one's ordering you to go. You'll be going up against live Iraqi artillery at a spot they've already hit, and where you almost got killed the last time.'

'He's only got minutes left,' Corporal Boswell replied. 'I'm fucking going in.'

*

CHAPTER TWENTY-FOUR

Corporal Boswell loaded up his wagon and came steaming forward. He was going as fast as he possibly could, but he had to keep lights-off or he'd make too easy a target of himself. He got the truck parked on the track above our Pinkie, but he quickly realised that because of the angle and the sheer weight of our wagon, it could pull his truck over the edge if he tried to winch it out.

In desperation, he decided to try something he'd never done before. Effectively, he was going to use planks of wood and jacks to get the side of his truck suspended partly over the edge of the ravine. Like that, he hoped he could winch our wagon vertically upwards a few inches, which would enable Tricky and the medic to drag me out from under it.

But in order to build his makeshift platform his men needed lights to see by. And that was akin to calling up the Iraqi forces and giving them the grid reference to hit with their artillery.

While he got his blokes building that precarious platform over the precipice, he ran down to take a closer look at what he was lifting. It was at that moment that I came to momentarily, and heard a voice yelling under the wagon: 'Dave! Dave! Are you all right?'

I wasn't able to speak. Words just came out as a spurting, garbled whisper. But in my head I was thinking: *Of course I'm not fucking all right!* It was only the anger that was keeping me alive now.

Corporal Boswell could see that I was 99 per cent gone. There were hands trying to scrabble under the wagon with cups to bale out the water, and dig me a breathing hole. But inch by agonising inch the Pinkie just kept settling lower into the sand and the mud.

He ran up to his truck and began yelling orders at his team. He knew now that unless they did a perfect vertical lift, the Pinkie would swing and basically they'd tear my head off. I had the weight of a Land Rover, plus all of our ammo and war-fighting kit lying on top of me. But if they didn't attempt the lift I was gone anyway.

The winch was started and it took up the slack. Corporal Boswell yelled out warnings that they were starting the lift. I heard the winch's high-pitched whine, as it took up the strain. With all the noise I couldn't believe the enemy hadn't spotted us and opened fire.

Up above me, Corporal Boswell saw his 27-tonne Foden recovery truck start to tip towards the ravine, under the weight of the upturned Pinkie. For an instant he feared he'd got his calculations wrong, and the truck was about to crash down the ravine, and add its crushing weight to that which was already forcing me head-first into the Iraqi swamp.

But finally, the upturned Pinkie rose a fraction of an inch. The winch creaked and groaned with every turn of its drum, and as the cable hauled the vehicle upwards somehow the recovery truck held firm. Hands reached in and dragged me out from under the Land Rover's crushing weight, and I felt myself lifted onto a stretcher.

I was carried up the slope and slid into the rear of a field ambulance. A mask went over my face. I felt the sweet release of gas and oxygen. The pain faded, as tubes and needles went into my hands and face.

With that, I drifted out of consciousness.

Geordie's mission went ahead regardless some hours later. He led the remaining men in and they pulled up in a place of hiding right amidst the Iraqi positions. They pushed ahead on foot, with Geordie on point, so as to do a close target recce (CTR). And it was as a foot patrol that they practically stumbled upon the Iraqi forward HQ, one that no one had even realised was there.

It was a sandbagged bunker position, complete with carefully-placed camouflage netting and sprouting scores of radio antennae. Geordie was so close to it that there was no way the Iraqis wouldn't see him. In the intense darkness the patrol had literally walked right into it. He raised his SA80 and opened fire on the Iraqi commander – only nothing happened. He'd got a 'dead man's click' – a stoppage.

Geordie was the biggest hater of the SA80. It was a totally shit piece of kit that was always jamming. He dropped his main weapon, pulled out his Browning pistol and shot the first guy dead. From behind him Baz opened up, putting down a fierce barrage of fire with his Minimi light machine gun. Having hammered the Iraqi command post the patrol managed to withdraw.

That done, they called down a series of air strikes and obliterated a number of key Iraqi positions. But by that time I was back in the UK, in Taunton Hospital.

I'd been casevac'd out of Iraq rated VSI – very seriously injured. For most of the journey home I was out of my head on painkillers and drugs. I came to in Taunton Hospital with my neck in a brace and a tube in my mouth, and constrained in some kind of a plaster straitjacket. I was in an isolation ward, so at least I had a room to myself. I was still high on the morphine to kill the pain.

The consultant came to see me. I asked if he might come closer so I might speak. He got his ear right up close to my mouth.

'It's okay, I've got medical insurance,' I whispered. 'Keep me in here for seven nights and I get a hundred quid a night.'

He didn't seem to appreciate the humour. That was the difference between his world and mine. In my world, the more dangerous or dire a situation the blacker the humour. It was like Cloughy's joke when we'd seen the corpse with the horribly swollen head, in the basement of Pristina University: *Same size head as Powell, that's all.*

I was wheeled through to an open ward. The average age of the patients in there was seventy-five, maybe older. It was clear that this was where they put those who were going to die. Maybe this was the consultant's way of getting back at me for my joke about the medical insurance. If it was, it wasn't very funny.

Some forty-eight hours earlier I had been deep in Iraq, on my second mission behind enemy lines. I'd been half crushed to death, and I'd survived only by a miracle – plus the sheer bloody-minded bravery of Corporal Boswell and his team. Now I was here, sandwiched between the half-dead and the dying.

I glanced down at myself and I was still covered in sand and shit from the Iraqi swamp. I looked to my left, and there was an old lady being helped to take a crap. It was simply fantastic the way the British government looked after its wounded warriors.

A pretty nurse came to see if I needed anything. My response was to start to cry. She held me and told me it was all going to be all right.

I knew what I needed right now: I needed my mother. She wouldn't take this kind of shit. She'd sort the bloody hospital out, no messing. I was the second-in-command of one of the most elite units in the British military, one that was at war in Iraq, but right now I was dependent on my mother to come to this hospital and rescue me.

Come she did. She sat by my bed and talked to me in a calm and dignified way. She told me she was getting me out of there and away from this place where people were sent to die. My mother did the necessary. She got me back into a private room, and two days later she got me released from the hospital into her care.

I was half-carried into my mum's car with blankets draped around me, and with medics on either side of me helping me walk, and with my arm in a sling system. As we drove away from that hospital I asked her how many days I'd been there. She told me six.

Shit. No insurance pay day.

The prognosis wasn't particularly good. I had eight broken ribs on my right side. I had a chest-drain siphoning off the blood and the Iraqi swamp water that had filled my lungs. I could see the bag of red and yellow liquid lying next to me on the seat. I also had an 'AC' joint disruption to my left shoulder.

But the main problem was my 'brachial plexus' – in other words, severe nerve damage to my right arm. There was every chance my right arm would never recover. It might well hang withered and lifeless, flopping by the side of my body for the rest of my days.

I was placed on the Army's 'Y-list' – the list of those not yet discharged from the military, but too sick or lame to serve. I remained in my parents' wonderful care until June of that year, and gradually I did recover. But my arm remained thin and emaciated and would only lift a little from the elbow, if at all. My right hand felt cold and almost dead to the touch.

I saw various nerve specialists. I was told that at best the nerve damage might repair itself by a millimetre per day, and there were no guarantees my arm would ever be fully fit. But as far as I was concerned I had to get physically fit again, for only then could I get back into The Pathfinders.

And nothing else mattered.

I got referred to Headley Court, the military rehab centre in Leatherhead. I shared a room with two other Army blokes. One had a bad back and the other had suffered a motorcycle accident and both had got their 'injuries' in the UK. Johnson Beharry was also there – a bloke who'd suffered serious head injuries in Iraq, and won the VC for saving a load of his blokes from all but certain death.

I related to him and the other genuine war-wounded. But a few of the blokes were bluffers and slackers – the lame and the lazy who should never have been in the Army in the first place. They were there to wangle a medical discharge from the military, and as far as I was concerned a good few of those with the 'bad backs' had spines made of rubber.

I had lost a massive amount of weight since getting injured, and the doctors at Headley put me on prescription protein drinks. The therapists were superb and they told me what I already suspected:

even if the arm didn't recover fully in itself, if I smashed in enough exercise and weights I could maybe build up the muscle around it to compensate for the nerve damage.

So that was what I set out to do.

At first it was impossibly frustrating. I had to try lifting a tiny weight with my right arm, over and over and over. I kept snapping and going wild. 'WHY WON'T YOU FUCKING WORK?' I started doing aerobics and throwing my arms out to the sides – but only the one arm responded.

I started taking the minibus down to the local swimming baths, to try the arm in the water. On the way kids would stare at us as we passed like we were freaks or something. The blokes would start slobbering and gibbering at them out of the window, to play up to it. I had to laugh.

But there was a girl at Headley Court who had exactly the same kind of injury as me, and her arm was not improving. That was my greatest fear.

By now The Pathfinders were back from Iraq. There was no 2IC at the unit, for they were waiting for my return. In my absence Jason had taken over my patrol, and The White Rabbit was basically acting as 2IC.

By October 2003 I did make it back to my unit, and I took up my place again as 2IC. I had recovered partial movement in my right arm, but it was still weak. I was far from being fully fit or ready to deploy, but at least I was back with The Pathfinders.

I began training in earnest, hitting the gym with Tricky, Pete and some of the other stalwarts. I did weights and body core training, plus I started accompanying the lads on their tabs. I trained on my own in the gym at night. I couldn't lift the weights properly, but I kept pounding in the fitness and building the muscle.

We went to South Africa, to test that country out as a new training ground for HALO and HAHO jumping. I even managed to get a couple of jumps in. It felt great to be flying again. But even so, I knew my days with the PF were numbered now.

As an officer you're only ever allowed to serve for two years in any one post. The Army believes in moving officers around, so they get to experience all aspects of the military machine. By now I'd been with the PF for two-and-a-half years. For several months I'd been off with my injuries, but even so I knew I'd soon be forced to move on. I'd gladly have soldiered with them forever, of course.

I considered my options. I could leave the Army, which was not what I wanted. I could go back to the Parachute Regiment, which would mean saluting senior officers, ironing my kit, officer's parties and formal mess dress. That really did not appeal. There was the option of going back to the PARAs and then trying for the job of OC Pathfinders. But in truth I didn't want that.

As OC Pathfinders you never got to go out on ops. You were in the rear with the gear, planning and co-ordinating missions. In spite of my injuries I felt I had more battles in me – more Pristinas, Kabuls and Qalat Sikars. Most who leave the PF try for the SAS or the SBS. I'd been on countless training missions alongside those units, and we'd spent some time together on ops in Iraq and elsewhere.

That was the only thing that made any sense to me now – to try for the SAS. That way, at least I'd get two more years of the kind of soldiering I yearned for. The only real issue for me was my injuries.

In February 2004 I started to train for SAS selection in earnest. By now I was stronger on the bench press than just about any other bloke in the PF. I'd built up these massive upper body and shoulder muscles, but still my right arm looked as if it had a massive lump on top of the shoulder joint.

In fact, the joint had been crushed and as a result it hung lower than it should. At the time Johnny Wilkinson was carrying the same injury, and his role as the England rugby captain seemed permanently in jeopardy because of it. I asked my specialist whose injury was worse, mine or Johnny Wilkinson's.

'Yours is far worse,' he told me.

There seemed to be conflicting opinions as to whether I should have surgery or not, but if I was to go for SAS selection there was no way that I could. It would take months, if not years to recover fully from that kind of an operation. I decided to build up the training still further, and to carry the injury through selection.

I was accepted for an early summer 2004 selection. I had three months left in which to prepare. Baz and Dean, the PF lad with whom I'd done PF selection, were also going to try for the SAS. The three of us spent days tabbing in the Brecons. I felt good. I wasn't as quick over the hills as I had been during my PF selection days. I was a lot bigger and bulked out with muscle. But I felt good.

I was still only twenty-five years old, yet I was carrying a lot of injuries and I guessed I'd put my body through the mill by now. But I was just that little bit older and wiser, and more content to pace myself over the hills. I reckoned I had better overall endurance. I was more of a tortoise, whereas before I'd been a bit of a hare.

And so it was that in early summer I loaded up my trusty BMW and drove up to Sennybridge Camp once more. As I drove through those familiar gates it felt like PF selection all over again, only now it was the start of a beautiful English summer and I faced several months of being beasted through the hills.

Of course, you never knew how or when you might get injured, or whether you would quite hit the times required to achieve a pass. But if it wasn't for my Iraq injuries, I'd have been feeling more confident now than I had at the start of PF selection. I'd put in months of intensive training, far more than I'd ever done then. I'd given myself every chance.

I reported to the accommodation block. Just as before, I'd got here super early and I made a beeline directly for that lower bunk furthest from the door. I dropped down the dog blanket curtain and placed my piss bottle by my bedside: I'd learned during PF selection that you needed one of those. I got my two sets of boots out, together with my zinc oxide tape, and began wrapping up my toes.

Next in were a couple of Kiwi SAS blokes. Although they were already in the Kiwi SAS, they still had to pass UK SAS selection to get into Hereford. They looked tough, wiry and indestructible. I warmed to them immediately. Toes taped up, I laced on my boots and headed for the cookhouse. First up was the eight-miler, and I needed to pile on the carbs for the energy.

At the cookhouse one of the SAS DS handed around some forms. I was given one and told I had to sign it before I went any further with selection. It was a non-disclosure agreement. By signing it I would be bound for life never to speak or write about any of my experiences undertaking SAS selection or in the unit – that's if I made it in.

For a couple of decades now everyone has been made to sign one of these documents, prior to starting selection. I'd known this was coming and without even bothering to read it I duly scribbled my name. Then I joined the queue with the other hopefuls so I could load up on the carbs – burgers fried hard as shit, as usual.

The scoff was crap as always, but at least it was fuel for the journey ahead.

*

ENDNOTE

The full story of the Qalat Sikar mission is told in my first book, *Pathfinder*.

GLOSSARY

Belt kit *pouches a soldier wears on a belt to carry his ammunition, survival equipment, etc.*

Blue Force Tracker *military term for a GPS-enabled system that provides military commanders and forces with location information about friendly (and despite its name, also about hostile) military forces*

Browning *browning 9 mm pistol*

C130 *Hercules aircraft used by many armies for troop, vehicle and logistic transportation. Also used to transport and dispatch parachutists*

CR *combat recovery*

CSAR *combat search and rescue*

CTR *close target reconnaissance*

DPM *disruptive pattern material – commonly used name for camouflage pattern*

ERV *emergency rendezvous*

EPs *emergency procedures*

HAHO *high altitude high opening*

HALO *high altitude low opening*

HAPLSS *high altitude parachutist life support system*

HLS *helicopter landing site*

IA *immediate action*

Intel *intelligence*

IP   *impact point (at which a parachutist lands)*

LUP   *lying up point*

M16   *US-made assault rifle once used by the SAS and Pathfinders*

NAI   *named area of interest*

NBC   *nuclear, biological, chemical (warfare)*

NVG   *night vision goggles*

OPSEC   *operational security*

Op Massive   *soldiers slang for undergoing an intense training regime whereby they bulk up in muscle*

PARA   *term for a Parachute Regiment Battalion of about 650 soldiers or an individual Parachute Regiment member*

PJHQ   *permanent joint headquarters – UK headquarters which commands military operations*

Roger   *military speak for 'understood'*

SA80   *standard issue British Army rifle*

Sched   *scheduled time for a patrol to send a radio update*

SCUD   *tactical ballistic missiles developed by the Soviet Union during the Cold War and exported widely to other countries, including Iraq*

SH   *support helicopter – usually refers to Chinook CH-47 but can include Pumas, Wessex, Lynx etc.*

Sitrep   *situation report*

SOP   *standard operating procedure*

Snap Ambush   *hastily made ambush to observe any enemy who can then be fired upon*

Spook   *slang term for MI6 officer*

TAB   *tactical advance to battle – a very fast forced march and run done by most army units but especially by PARAs and Special Forces*

Webbing   *another name for belt kit*

PICTURE CREDITS

The author and publisher are grateful to the following for permission to reproduce photographs:

Andy Chittock (pictures 14, 15, 17, 18, 28, 29, 32 and 33)
Kevin Capon © MoD/Crown Copyright (picture 7)
© Ron Haviv/VII/Corbis (picture 10)
Edit by Getty Images (picture 36)
Tomas Munita/AP/Press Association Images (picture 37)